Skirts that Swept the Desert Floor

One Hundred Biographical Profiles of Nevada Women in History

VOLUME ONE

EDITED BY M.A. DUVAL

STEPHENS PRESS • LAS VEGAS, NEVADA

Editor: M. A. Duval
Project Coordinators: Mary Gafford, Joan M. LeMere,
and Nancy Sansone
Designer: Sue Campbell

ISBN 10: 1-932173-62-5
ISBN 13: 9781-932173-62-8

CIP Data Available

STEPHENS PRESS, LLC
A Stephens Media Group Company

P.O. Box 1600
Las Vegas, NV 89125-1600

www.stephenspress.com

Printed in Hong Kong

Dedicated to the pioneer women of Nevada, who were the community builders of our state, with a special thank you to Bernice Abreo Fischer.

Contents

Preface

These biographical profiles are a product of the Nevada Women's History Project (NWHP), a statewide educational and nonprofit delegate agency of the Nevada Women's Fund. The mission of the NWHP is to provide visibility and support for the gathering and dissemination of information about the roles and contributions of Nevada women of every class and ethnic background.

The NWHP's inclusion standards are broad, taking in early pioneers and businesswomen, as well as entertainers and national figures who chose to make Nevada their home. The purpose of this book is to recognize the accomplishments and contributions of Nevada women regardless of their race or standing in the world of their time and to acknowledge and recognize the influence that each of these women had on our state.

The Nevada Women's History Project would like to recognize the following people for their work:

Technical assistance and review: Jean Baker, Dorothy Bokkelman, Marion Bollinger, Joan Braun, Doris Drummond, Rose Irwin, Mitsi Johnson, Pat McNutt, Anne Reck, Jean Spiller, and all of the writers who volunteered their time.

Source material for the biographies comes mostly from oral and written histories, and interviews with friends, neighbors, and relatives of the subjects. The NWHP is grateful to the Nevada Library Association, the Special Collections at the University of Nevada at Las Vegas, the Nevada State Library and Archives, and the Nevada Historical Society for their assistance in locating additional materials for this publication.

The Nevada Women's History Project distributes this book free of charge to public and private school libraries on the secondary level and to public libraries throughout the state of Nevada.

The NWHP website (www.unr.edu/wrc/nwhp) has a full database of biographical and general information about the history of women in Nevada.

Eva Adams

Eva Adams was a Nevada native who became one of the few woman directors of the U.S. Mint. Born in the now-vanished Churchill County mining camp of Wonder, Eva Adams had a full life before her career in Washington, DC, including stop offs in Reno, Las Vegas, and Columbia University.

Eva was born in Churchill County because her father worked at setting up mining camps for his boss, George Wingfield. Eva's family moved often, since her father's job depended on following the work to where it was. Education in the one-room schoolhouses of the various camps meant that Eva was able to learn at her own pace; when she entered high school in Reno she was far ahead of her class. She graduated at age 14.

Eva won a scholarship to Vassar, but she thought that the New York campus was too far away, so she attended the University of Nevada at Reno. The highlight of that experience, according to Eva, was becoming a member of the Kappa Alpha Theta sorority. She credited that association with giving her confidence and pride.

By the time she was 19, Eva was teaching at Las Vegas High School. Many of her students

1910—1991
TEACHER, DIRECTOR OF
THE U.S. MINT

were railroad employees—boys who had worked before they entered high school—so Eva was faced with a challenging classroom population. It was during this period in her life that Eva became frustrated with a makeshift city library that had no record of its holdings and persuaded the region's Girl Scouts to create the library's first card catalog.

Eva attended Columbia University for graduate school, then returned to UNR to teach in the English department. One day, she received a call from Nevada Senator Pat McCarran. She and McCarran had met when they were both among a group of motorists waiting out a snowstorm in a Goldfield, Nevada hotel. McCarran hired her to work in his Washington office, and she soon became his office director.

Under Eva's direction, McCarran's office gained a reputation as the most efficient in the entire Senate. Eva was even asked to teach a class on running a Senate office! She was surprised to see among her students several senators and their staffs. Senator Margaret Chase Smith never missed a meeting, and Eva was stunned at the lack of organizational knowledge of the senators and their employees.

During McCarran's tenure as a Nevada senator, Eva Adams completed law school. She passed the bar exam in both Washington, DC, and Nevada.

Senator McCarran died in 1954, but Eva stayed on in her job, managing the offices for his successors, Ernest Brown and Alan Bible. However, in 1961, Eva experienced a major career change. President John Kennedy invited Eva to lunch in the Senate cafeteria, where he asked her to run the United States Mint.

Her boss, Senator Alan Bible, had suggested her as a candidate. He felt that it would make sense to have a director who understood something about precious metals and who was from a state that produced them. Secretly, he and Eva did not get along well, but she was so competent and so well known for her organizational skills that he felt should find her another job where she could use these abilities.

Eva needed all the skill she possessed to get the mint running efficiently. The employees were accustomed to doing their jobs in their own unique ways. There was total disorganization, and, to make matters worse, nobody had ordered new presses to deal with an impending coin shortage caused by the increasing popularity and variety of coin-operated vending machines. The lack of coin presses was a major problem, since the mint was the only organization using them, therefore they had to be individually created—a process that took months.

Eva and her crew searched through government buildings for substitutes. Machines for making rifle bullet jackets were retooled as coin presses. Even the old presses from the Carson City mint, long considered obsolete, were put back into use.

And just as Eva was embroiled in her coin-press panic, Congress ordered that silver be taken out of U.S. coins because the price of the silver used to make each coin was more than the coin's face value. When silver coins went out of circulation, they became prized by collectors, which further exacerbated the coin shortage. The lack of equipment to press coins and the dwindling coin supply made Eva's job a challenging one, to say the least.

Eva Adams resigned her job at the U.S. Mint during the Nixon administration and retired to Reno. She died in 1991 at 80 years of age. Eva remained a Nevadan at heart despite her long tenure inside the Beltway. One giveaway: Even though she was assured that coins made of non-silver common metals would work in coin-operated machines, the director of the U.S. Mint chose the ultimate test of success. On a trip to Nevada, Eva brought along some new coin blanks so that she could test them out in slot machines!

—*Fran Haraway*

Mary Jane Oxborrow Ashworth

Mary Jane Oxborrow came into the world on September 7, 1885, in St. George, Utah. She was the eighth of eleven children born to Mary Leitch, who had emigrated from England at age 11, and Joseph Oxborrow, also from England and one of the original "Dixie Pioneers" who had plowed some of the first furrows in St. George.

In January 1894, Mary Jane and her older brother Ted went to their Aunt Sophie's house to deliver a New Year's dinner. Sophie needed firewood and asked Ted to cut some bark that had been stripped from cedar trees. While Mary Jane was holding the bark on the chopping block as Ted chopped it, her hand slipped, and Ted accidentally severed the first three fingers of her right hand. Ted rushed to get their mother, who was a nurse to local physician Dr. Clift. The ministrations of Mrs. Oxborrow and Dr. Clift, plus a poultice of angleworm oil, brought about Mary Jane's recovery.

The next year, when Mary Jane and Ted were building a swingboard, Ted's saw slipped, and Mary Jane cut the knuckle of her left hand. Her concerned mother cried, "Oh, no! What has Ted done to you now?"

1885–1968
PIONEER

Mary Jane's father died when she was ten years old, and her mother supported the family by her nursing skills while Mary Jane, usually called Molly, cared for her younger sister, Vera. The summer she was 12, she did a local couple's laundry for first 50 cents, then 75 cents a week. From these wages she bought some material from which her sister Lizzie, a seamstress, made dresses. Molly was very proud of those dresses.

A popular local entertainment was the house party, during which housewives readied their homes for the coming winter. All the guests helped to take up the carpet and remove the underlying straw padding. Before the new straw was put down, Old Joe Worthlin would play the violin while everyone danced. At one of these parties, Molly met Earl Ashworth, her future husband.

Molly was 14 when her family moved to Lund, Nevada. Her brothers built a small frame house for their mother. The house also served as the town's Sunday meeting place and the social hall for weekly dances. Molly's brothers slept in the large unfinished front rooms, and Molly shared the back with her sister Vera.

In the winter of 1902, Molly went back to St. George to learn dressmaking skills from her sister Lizzie. When she returned to Lund, she began sewing for the area's other pioneers.

By this time, Earl Ashworth was one of Molly's steady suitors. Earl was the nephew of Tom Judd, a "Dixie" settler like Mary's father. When his uncle returned to St. George, Earl stayed in Lund to be near Molly. Mary Leicht Oxborrow was very fond of Earl, and on December 20, 1905, Molly took her mother's advice and married Earl. The ceremony was performed by a justice of the peace with the whole town of Lund invited to the reception at the Oxborrow home. The party lasted all night, and the guests stayed for breakfast.

The following spring, the Ashworths moved to Copper Flat, Nevada, where Earl and Molly's brother Ted hauled cordwood into the local mine to make the steam necessary to bring the cages up and down the mineshaft. She cooked for the miners until August, when she and Earl moved to Ely, where they lived in a tent for 11 months before returning to Lund.

Two months before the birth of Molly's first child, her sister Vera became ill and four days later died from what was probably polio or meningitis. Vera and Molly were very close, and the tragedy may have contributed to Molly's son being stillborn.

The Ashworths had moved into a four-room house across the street from Molly's mother, and Molly took great pride in her home. She also enjoyed helping her mother weave carpet on her loom.

In April of 1909, Molly had another stillborn child—this time a girl—but the following April, a healthy boy, Don Earl, was born to the couple. Five other children soon followed. All were born in Lund except Keith, the youngest.

In 1919, Earl and Ted leased a farm. They were in the process of buying it when a depression hit, and they were unable to sell their grain. To make matters worse, Ted was in an accident that resulted in the amputation of his leg.

In order to provide for his family, Earl, in 1923, went to Kimberly, Nevada, and got a job as a blacksmith. When school was out, Molly and the children joined him for what they thought was to be a summer stay. They spent the next 27 years there. In Kimberly, Molly was involved in church activities while Earl advanced steadily in jobs, finally becoming repair foreman in the shop where he worked. The Ashworths also bought property in Ely, only ten miles from Kimberly. The Ashworth children went to high school in Ely.

After almost three decades in Ely, the Ashworths moved to Las Vegas to be near children and grandchildren. In his retirement, Earl enjoyed helping his children with carpentry projects.

In 1955, Molly and Earl celebrated their 50th wedding anniversary. Two years later, Earl, a longtime asthma sufferer, contracted bronchial pneumonia and died on July 15, 1957. Mary Jane passed away in Las Vegas on January 9, 1968

—*Fran Haraway*

Edna C. Baker

E dna C. Baker—the first woman elected to a statewide office in Nevada—was born Edna Nevada Catlin in Carson City, Nevada, in 1878. She attended schools in Carson City and graduated from the University of Nevada in 1895. This began what was to be a lifelong commitment to elementary, secondary, and higher education. By 1899, Edna was teaching in Wells in Elko County but quit working in 1900 to marry Fred W. Baker, an engineer with the Southern Pacific Railroad.

The Bakers lived in Winnemucca for several years but moved in 1909 to Sparks, where Edna quickly became active in the local community. In March, 1916, the Women's Civic League of Sparks chose Edna to run for the four-year seat on the Sparks Board of School Trustees. Her opponent was James O'Brien, who was already a board member.

The campaign was a lively one, but on April 3, 1916, the *Sparks Tribune* reported that Edna Baker had beaten James O'Brien handily. At the first meeting of the new board, Edna was elected chair.

In September of 1916, Nevada's Republican convention named Edna Baker, without op-

position, to the candidacy for the open two-year seat on the Board of Regents of the University of Nevada. The *Sparks Tribune* noted that the Republicans "naturally turned to the lady from Sparks who by previous experience and successful candidacies has proven that she was entirely competent to fill the position as well as being a great vote getter." This latter skill was very important because until 1958, regents were elected on the statewide level. So, Edna needed to gather votes from all over Nevada.

In the 1916 regent's election, nine candidates were vying for only three seats. Throughout the campaign, Edna was linked with two Republicans who were running for two four-year terms—J. F. Abel of Elko and Benjamin F. Curier of Winnemucca. The *Nevada State Journal*, in its declaration that the open seats should go to these three candidates because they had pledged to reform the university, stated, "They have come out squarely for efficient management of the university, for the elimination of politics from university affairs, and for the widest publicity in all matters affecting the people's educational institution."

1878—1957
POLITICIAN

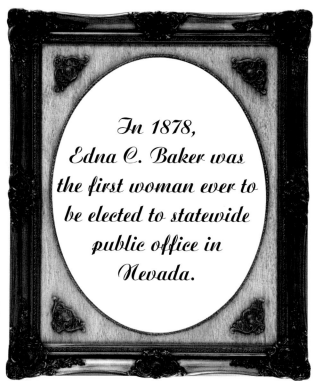

In 1878, Edna C. Baker was the first woman ever to be elected to statewide public office in Nevada.

No concern was ever expressed about a woman filling this office. In fact, the *Journal*, one of Reno's daily newspapers, regarded a female candidate as an asset, stating, "She will bring to the position native ability in management, combined with a warm sympathy with boys and girls at the university and an intuitive power to get at the heart of things and to make wise decisions."

The *Journal* also published editorials and advertisements appealing directly to women voters to support Edna Baker. The newspaper declared that, "A woman's influence in educational matters is always good."

Edna Baker defeated her opponents, well-known Democrat I. H. Kent of Fallon and Socialist candidate J. F. McQuestian, with an impressive 44 percent of the vote, and on November 7, 1916, she changed Nevada history by becoming the first woman elected to a state office. She carried 11 of the state's 16 counties (some by substantial margins) but, oddly lost in two of the three Sparks precincts. Her co-candidates also won their seats, but their margins of victory were not as wide as hers.

Although she was a state officer, Edna was not required to surrender her seat on the Sparks school board. She continued as chair of that body until early 1920. That accomplishment makes Edna Baker the first, and perhaps only, woman in Nevada to hold two elective offices at one time.

Edna's term as university regent expired in 1918. In July of that year, she announced that she would not seek reelection, explaining that she did not have the time necessary to devote to the office. The *Reno Evening Gazette* did not provide much comment on her term, other than noting that she had been one of the regents who had called for the resignation of university president A. W. Hendrick. Edna did not run for office again.

The Baker family moved to Palo Alto, California, in 1950 after Fred retired from the railroad. On July 12, 1957, Edna Baker died in Palo Alto at the age of 81 after a long illness. Her obituary in Carson City's *Nevada Appeal* recalled that she had been "…long active in Nevada political circles and women's service organizations." For 32 years after her election, there was always a woman on the University of Nevada Board of Regents.

Edna C. Baker was truly one of Nevada's education pioneers. Her political success at both the city and state levels showed other Nevada women that running for elected office was within the ability of every citizen.

—*Fran Haraway*

Ruth Ball

Ruth Alameda Owen Ball exemplifies the drive and sense of purpose that led the pioneering settlers of Henderson, Nevada, to turn a desolate, scorched wasteland located in the Mojave Desert into one of the fastest growing cities in the country. Ruth arrived in the fledgling township of Henderson in the early 1940s, at the age of 54, and quickly made friends with people from all walks of life, becoming a driving force for many of the area's church, community, social, and business activities.

During World War II, many citizens, including Ruth and Walter Ball, rallied behind the United States government's emergency war effort. Walter, an engineer, left Ruth in California to work at Basic Magnesium in Henderson. Magnesium was a critical element in the production of aircraft and munitions, and Basic was one of the nation's top magnesium-processing plants.

For a while, Walter bunked in the dorm-like quarters of nearby Anderson's Camp, but demountable houses, 1,000 in all, were quickly erected for plant workers and their families. Ruth joined Walter in the new community where there were only dirt streets without even trees or grass. The war town was designed with winding streets and dead ends to confuse an invading enemy. Judy Hampton, wife of the town's third mayor, explained that the houses had flat

1889–1974
PLANT WORKER,
COMMUNITY ACTIVIST

roofs and no fences attached to avoid detection from the air.

The houses were to be taken apart after the war but, being so well built, some still stand today. The Balls lived at 27 Nevada Way, and, as time went on, it became the scene of Ruth's famous ice-cream socials. Resident Corrine Gerrish Lynch recalled these as "big events...big affairs. Most everybody in town would go to the ice-cream socials. It was a good time to visit with friends."

WWII continued, and Ruth took a job at Basic Magnesium. Tina Smith, Ruth's daughter, explained that her mother "read technical instruments that controlled the quantity and quality of the product" and recorded the findings. During the early days of the city, Ruth's skills as a social arbiter were recognized, and she became the only woman appointed to the Colorado River Commission's citizen committee. According to Ruth's son in law, former Nevada state Senator Hal Smith, "It was a committee established after the war to negotiate with the Federal War Assets Administration the deposition of the huge plant and facilities."

When the war ended, Ruth joined the staff at Basic High School and served as its registrar. Betty Reason, daughter of the first woman mayor, remembered Ruth as "...being an inspiration for so many of my life experiences. She was always there for the kids, the younger generation." Ruth supported getting scholarships for students and instrumental in seeing the Youth Center built. In 1964, Henderson's Recreation Board recognized Ruth for her 20 years of outstanding service.

Her influence also extended into the business community, where Ruth became a charter member of the area's Business and Professional Women (BPW) organization, a national organization for working women. In addition to her professional and civic profile, Ruth Ball was fondly remembered by members of the Community Church, the P.E.O. organization, and her sorority sisters from Beta Sigma Phi. At the Community Church, Ruth was active with the Lydia Circle for women, on the Board of Deacons, and as an historian and recording secretary for Sunday school. She was also the church's pianist and organist, and played for a large number of weddings and funerals.

Ruth Ball was probably most comfortable with her sisters from P.E.O. and Beta Sigma Phi. Both were founded at a time when most women did not have an opportunity to attend college. These organizations provided women of all ages and backgrounds with a channel for having lifelong learning experiences and developing friendships. Ruth assumed leadership roles in both groups.

Ruth always acted like a lady and never appeared in public without a hat, gloves, dress, and

stockings. Older than most members, Ruth served as the Cultural Director of Beta Sigma Phi, and went on to become president of their chapter.

Longtime Henderson resident and P.E.O. member Dorothy Swackhamer recalled the wonderful P.E.O. programs Ruth designed and presented. "Ruth knew a lot about the history of Nevada and the women in Nevada." Swackhamer also appreciated learning about the finer things in life from Ruth because, "Everybody needs a little polish, and Ruth instilled in us the way a lady should be."

Ruth lived in a time when not many social services were available through government-sponsored programs. Members of Ruth's organizations reached out to meet many community needs. They sold peanuts, fireworks, brooms, and had ice-cream socials to carry on their charitable activities. It was Ruth's ice-cream socials that many residents still remember.

In Henderson, Ruth Owen Ball is remembered as petite, soft spoken, kind, and loving—someone who made you feel good about yourself. She was a musician and recipient of many awards, including the VFW's Outstanding Citizen award. Above all, Ruth Ball is remembered as being a lady through and through. When she passed away at the age of 85 in 1974, she had left her signature on the city of Henderson, a city she helped to build.

—*Joan McSweeney*

Clara Isabelle Smith Beatty

In 1912, Clara Isabelle Smith was in her second year of studies at the University of Nevada when Charlotte Anita Whitney, president of the California College Equal Suffrage League, paid a visit to Reno. Approximately 25 women—students and staff—attended the assembly, and after Whitney spoke, Anne H. Martin, president of the Nevada Equal Suffrage League, told of her own work on behalf of women's suffrage throughout the state. Those who attended the gathering were so impressed by these two women that they decided immediately to organize the College Equal Suffrage Club of the University of Nevada. Clara Isabelle Smith, strong and outspoken, was unanimously elected president. She set out immediately to make suffrage a more prominent issue in Nevada.

The only previous attempt at forming such an organization had been attempted by female faculty members in 1910. The Sagebrush Suffragette Club was started by Mrs. Clarence H. Mackay of the University Women's Faculty Club. Only two women joined—possibly because their husbands supported the cause—and it was generally understood that most women would not affiliate with a club of this nature. "So the people of this state are saved, at least for a time, from the latest of fads, 'votes for women,'" announced the September 12, 1910 issue of the University of Nevada *Sagebrush*.

The objective of the College Equal Suffrage Club was to study the question of votes for women in Nevada and other states. Clara Isabelle Smith displayed perseverance and leadership skills in organizing university women and in persuading university men to support women's voting rights. Her efforts were rewarded when the club's first event gave its members a great deal of positive publicity.

How the Vote Was Won was a one-act skit performed by the suffrage club members and "two daring college youth" at the opening of the new Reno High School auditorium in 1913. The plot concerned the way the women of Brixton, England, secured equal franchise. Funds raised from the fifty-cent admission fee increased the club's treasury but fell short of the amount of money needed to send a delegate to the national Suffrage Convention.

Before 1914, the College Equal Suffrage Club was regarded as a non-threatening entity. Meetings were held monthly, and one meeting

ABOUT 1890– 1967
WOMEN'S SUFFRAGE
WORKER, MUSEUM
DIRECTOR

each semester was open to the entire student body as well as the Reno community. The 1914 *Artemisia* described these meetings as gatherings where "...interesting papers tracing the growth and present movement of suffrage are presented, and tempting refreshments are served, thus indicating that the trend of suffrage is not entirely away from women's natural element."

In March of 1914, Clara stepped out of her "natural element" and challenged teachers throughout the state to let students who were old enough write an essay on the topic of suffrage. She asked that an afternoon be set aside for readings and requested that parents be invited to attend. Five-dollar prizes were to be awarded for the five best essays sent to Clara. The club would then pick the two best to be published in one of the local newspapers. Clara sent out 302 letters—one to every teacher in the state. She included packets of information from suffrage headquarters in Reno.

Tonopah school trustees were opposed to exposing students to such a "political matter" and refused to let the contest run in their district. Clara's correspondence and the reply from the trustees were printed in the *Tonopah Bonanza* of March 18, 1914.

The *Reno Evening Gazette*, which had a Republican slant and an anti-suffrage bias, predictably ran the headline "PROTECT THE SCHOOLS," and the accompanying article criticized Clara's contest, saying, in part, "...it [Clara's letter] asks them... to convert public schools into a campaign auxiliary for the furtherance of a socio-political doctrine or policy, to which a very large proportion, if not a majority, of the parents and the citizenship of the state, is honestly, conscientiously and openly opposed, and which other thousands regard as experimental at best."

Clara Isabelle Smith wasn't the type of woman who let anti-suffrage sentiment hold her back. Her rebuttal was printed one week later in the April 7 issue of the University of Nevada *Sagebrush*: "The trustees of one of the schools misunderstood the spirit in which these letters had been sent and forbade any essay to be written in the school. A newspaper took the matter up and accused us of having a political motive in mind. This mistaken plea was taken up by a Reno paper, and now we are overwhelmed by criticism.... The criticism absolutely unjust and uncalled for, because we are not a political organization, as any education person should know, and we have no idea of putting politics in the state schools."

Clara Isabelle Smith graduated that April and married Jessie O. Beatty in September. She played a significant role in the Nevada women's suffrage movements at both university and community levels and later in her life became the director of the Nevada Historical Society.

—*Fran Haraway*

Clara Bow Bell

Clara Bow Bell is most notably remembered as Clara Bow, the "It" girl, a personification of the emancipated flapper of 1920s Hollywood. However, to the state of Nevada, Clara Bow meant a great deal more than that. In addition to her movie career, she was also the wife of well-known Nevada rancher, store owner, and politician Rex Bell, Sr., who became lieutenant governor of Nevada and was a candidate for state governor. Clara Bow was also the mother of respected Las Vegans Rex Bell, Jr., and George Bell.

Clara Bow was born in Brooklyn, New York, on July 29, 1905. Her childhood was one of poverty and unhappiness. Clara's father was a waiter and handyman and was quite often unemployed. Her mother was chronically ill and clinically depressed; she died in a mental institution when Clara was just a teenager. Clara was in love with the movies and snuck off to the picture show any chance she got. In 1921 she entered and won a "Fame and Fortune" beauty contest sponsored by three movie magazines. Her first small part was in a movie called *Beyond the Rainbow*. In 1923 Clara signed a contract with Preferred Pictures

1905—1965
ACTRESS

in Hollywood and moved to California. She was usually cast as a flapper, a sexually emancipated young woman of the 1920s, and because of her success in this role became known as the "It" girl, a title symbolizing sex appeal and freedom. However, Clara did play other roles, some critically acclaimed, including the part of a World War I ambulance driver in *Wings* and an illegitimate half-breed and prostitute in *Call her Savage*. Many critics thought that Clara was a talented actress and believed that the title of "It" girl hindered her professional growth. Moreover, the pressures of Hollywood and its lifestyle began to affect her physical and mental health. Clara was ready to leave that world.

In December 1931, Clara married Rex Bell, a western cowboy movie actor and former star athlete at Hollywood High School, and moved to a ranch just south of Las Vegas, between Searchlight and Nipton. Clara and Rex build a beautiful 12-room Spanish-style home and settled down. Their first son, Rex Anthony, was born in 1934, and a second son, George Robert, followed in 1938. Clara Bow Bell tried to provide for her boys a life of affluence, security, and happiness—a life entirely different from her own childhood.

In an article in *The Nevadan* from October 6, 1974, Rex, Jr., claimed that life at the ranch in the early years was very good. There were horses for the young boys to ride, a swimming pool, lots of land to roam and explore, and a bighorn sheep named Billy and a deer named Jenny.

In the same article, Rex, Jr., said that Clara Bow Bell was a good mother. He said that occasionally the family went out together on their horses across the desert and into the hills. Clara was a good rider and a "pretty good shot with a rifle." The one thing that did upset her about life on the ranch and about which she complained loudly was the desert critters, such as tarantulas, scorpions, ants, and, of course, the lizards and snakes.

Rex Bell, Sr., became interested in community and political matters and began to travel a great deal. Clara didn't care to travel with him and was quite often left alone. Hollywood friends such as Betty Grable visited her occasionally, but she still missed Rex and resented his absences.

Clara began having problems with ill health and insomnia, which contributed to a dependency on barbiturates. After a stay at the Mayo Clinic, she was given a clean bill of health with a suggestion that her problems might be psychological. Although Clara's mother and two aunts had died in mental institutions, Clara refused to accept this prognosis.

In 1945, the Bells moved to Las Vegas, where Rex Senior could be at home more often and the boys could attend school. In Las Vegas, Rex opened up Rex Bell's Western Clothing Store. The Las Vegas move helped Clara's problems only for a short time. Her mother's legacy of depression and mental illness may have been too much to overcome.

She was not longer able to perform in her role of wife and mother. In 1950, the decision was made that, while Rex would remain in Las Vegas to run the clothing store and continue in politics, their two sons would attend military school in Los Angeles, and Clara, attended by a nurse/companion, would move to Los Angeles to be close to her primary doctor.

Clara's reclusiveness changed her lifestyle. For the rest of her life, her days were spent swimming, painting, and reading. She kept up with current events and was prolific letter writer to celebrities and politicians. Christmas was her favorite holiday. She was very generous with gifts to her family and friends, and enjoyed having her family with her on that special day. However, the rest of her life was spent in seclusion in Los Angeles. Her first public appearance in fifteen years was at Rex's memorial service in 1962.

Clara Bow Bell, the beautiful and famous "It" girl who gave up her Hollywood career to move to the Nevada desert to become a wife and mother, died at her Los Angeles home on September 26, 1965, at the age of sixty.

—*Carol A. Turner*

19

Laura Webb Bell

Laura Webb Bell, the first and only post-mistress of Boulder City, Nevada, was born in Los Angeles, California, in 1901. After attending California public schools, Laura graduated Phi Beta Kappa from Stanford University in 1926 with a degree in social science and journalism.

Shortly after graduation, Laura accepted a job with the *Humboldt Star*, a newspaper published five days a week in Winnemucca, Nevada. Her work included all aspects of newspaper production—writing news articles, editorials and headlines, and doing page layouts.

Three months after her arrival in Nevada, Laura married Vernon John Bell, known to everyone as "Dutch," and regarded by many as the town's most eligible bachelor. The civil ceremony was attended by Vernon's father, Johnny Bell, owner of the Buckskin mine and an important figure in northern Nevada politics.

The newlyweds first moved to the Bell home on Winnemucca Boulevard—a dwelling they shared with Johnny Bell and his eldest son, Forrest. A year after their marriage, however, the young couple headed for Buckskin Mountain,

1901—1998
POSTMISTRESS,
JOURNALIST

where Vernon had a lease and planned to mine for gold. For the trek up the mountain, they loaded their 15-year-old Ford with suitcases, canned goods, a new saddle (a gift from Laura's father-in-law), and, of course, some dynamite for mining. The saddle, Laura found out later, was purchased from a buckaroo who needed quick cash to make a getaway after shooting a man named Hoodlum Jack in a barroom brawl.

After stopping in the crumbling and possibly misnamed desert town of Paradise for glasses of the local moonshine, they—radiator steaming—continued on to their home, a building described by Laura as looking like "two houses that had slid into each other." They arrived just as the car engine coughed its last cough.

Laura's first night at Buckskin was enlivened by an uninvited and definitely unappreciated visitor. Laura woke up to find a porcupine strolling up her backbone. The window, which was very close to the ground, was no longer left open after that night.

Laura set up housekeeping in her new quarters, which featured an out-house and a coal bin. In addition to cooking and cleaning, she was required to host visitors interested in the mining operation. Laura quickly learned to read the dust trails on the road that indicated someone was coming. She brought out the field glasses to determine whether her soon-to-be guests were arriving by car or horse. Laura heeded her husband's belief that "If a guest stays less than three days, we will always wonder what we did to offend him."

Laura heeded her husband's belief that, "If a guest stays less than three days, we will always wonder what we did to offend him."

market. In her memoir, *Buckskin*, Laura says, "…for me and my husband, that was a golden month, that September of 1929. We had each other. We had our health. We had money invested in the booming stock market, with enough left in the bank to enjoy a winter of pleasure." Then, of course, came the Crash. Still, they insisted that the mine was their ticket to riches.

Their home was not well insulated, so in the winter of 1928–29, Laura came down from the mountain and stayed once again at the Bell homestead in Winnemucca. There she lived with her father-in-law and his sister, known as Aunt Nellie. She became a stringer for the Humboldt County morning paper, sending in news of mining, ranching, and various local events.

One of her best information sources was the local hospital, and it was there that she met two of her favorite Nevadans—Jean, a local madam who lent her services as a nurse when they were needed, and Adam Adrian, a veteran of the Indian wars. Both provided material for Laura's human-interest stories.

The Bells had three children: Dorothy (born December 2, 1932, in San Diego), Judith (born December 22, 1940, in Winnemucca), and Norman (born August 24, 1943, in Henderson).

In 1929 the Bells, on the advice of friends, invested some cash from the sale of ore from the Buckskin Mine in the rapidly expanding stock

The attack on Pearl Harbor ended life on Buckskin Mountain, and the family moved to Reno, where Laura continued her newspaper work. Then Dutch's job took them to Babbit—south of Reno—and to southern Nevada, where they settled in Boulder City. Laura worked there as a stringer for various Las Vegas newspapers and as a reporter even solved the mystery of a man's disappearance. She noticed buzzards circling in the desert and phoned in her story. The man's body was found where she indicated.

In 1959, Laura became the Boulder City postmistress, a position she held until 1973.

Dutch died in 1967, and, after completing her time as postmistress, Laura moved to Santa Cruz, California. In 1983, she married Dutch's brother, Norman Bell, a fellow reporter who had just completed a 30-year career with the Associated Press.

Laura Webb Bell died in 1998. She is buried in Boulder City, Nevada, beside husband Dutch, her partner in their adventurous life on Buckskin Mountain.

—*Fran Haraway*

Minnie Nichols Blair

innie Blair was born in Folsom, California, on September 9, 1886. She had a strong pioneer heritage: Her maternal grandparents came to the west coast around Cape Horn, while her father's parents had crossed the plains to settle in California. They thought the trip was too dangerous for their six-year-old son (Minnie's father), so they sent him on a ship with a baggage tag around his neck explaining he was to be sent via the Isthmus of Panama to California by Wells Fargo Express.

Minnie spent her childhood years in Folsom and Sacramento. After the death of her mother, she moved to Placerville to live with a married sister. It was there that she met and married Ernest Blair, an express messenger for Wells Fargo. Their wedding ceremony was held at 5:30 a.m. on December 26, 1908, so that they could catch the train to Goldfield, Nevada. Minnie and Ernest lived in the boomtown of Goldfield from 1908 until 1918. Ernest became a teller with the

1886–1972
COMMUNITY ACTIVIST,
FARMER

bank, and Minnie was a homemaker. She gave birth to their first child, a daughter, in 1910. A son, Seward James, was born in 1912.

From 1918 until 1924, the Blairs lived in Tonopah. There, Minnie became a community leader responsible for getting community support to buy playground equipment for the Tonopah School. She also kept the only tree in Tonopah, a Russian Olive, alive with leftover dishwater. Her second son, Ernest Blair, Jr., was born in Tonopah in 1922. When the gold slump of the 1920s came, Minnie worked to provide relief through charities to old prospectors. She was one of the first to be on the Red Cross roll call.

In 1924, Ernest was transferred to Wingfield's Churchill County Bank in Fallon, and it was there that Minnie would spend the rest of her life. She bought a ranch sight unseen on the outskirts of town because it had water rights and she knew that she could have a garden. She remained busy with her family and community. Minnie was known as a

friend to the local Indians and helped to collect donations to buy a generator for the Rattlesnake Hill Colony. One of her early projects, raising turkeys for Thanksgiving dinner, turned into a thriving business; eventually, Minnie was shipping her birds to 38 states and to Canada and Mexico. At the same time, Minnie supervised a truck garden and 800 laying chickens. During this time, she provided jobs for local people that sustained them through the Depression. With her market dwindling, Minnie finally quit the turkey business in 1947.

After tasting a spudnut (a doughnut) brought home from the grocery store one day, Minnie decided to open a restaurant. She was not able to purchase property downtown, so she decided to open the shop on her ranch. Despite speculation that she would not be successful, her Spudnut Shop opened on August 27, 1947. With her delicious pies and fresh coffee, the business flourished. Her daughter Helen took over management in 1953, the same year that Ernest died.

Minnie was a cooperative and enthusiastic memoirist for the Oral History Project of the Center for Western North American Studies. Her memoirs are in the special collections at the University of Nevada–Reno and contain her reminiscences about her early days in California as well as accounts of the social, economic, and political affairs of Goldfield and Tonopah, and descriptions of ranch work and other activities in Fallon.

Minnie Blair was known as a loyal friend and community leader who opened her heart and home to those who lived around her. In 1967, she was given the Distinguished Nevadan award by the University of Nevada. In 1977, the Minnie P. Blair Middle School was dedicated to her. Minnie died on August 26, 1973. She lived her life with courage and inventiveness, and serves as an example to women who want to live their lives in support of themselves, their families, and their communities.

—*Sally Wilkins*

Kittie Bonner

Kittie Wells was born on January 3, 1901, in Chiloquin, Oregon. As a young girl, Kittie came to Nevada in a covered wagon with her aunt and uncle, Mr. and Mrs. Bill Spencer. The family settled in the Dixie Valley area. There, Kittie met George Bonner, a foreman on the Williams ranch at Can Alpine. Kittie and George were married in 1926. Soon after their marriage, Governor Balzer selected George to establish a fish hatchery at Smith Creek, and in September 1929, the Bonners and their year-old son Richard moved to the Valley. The hatchery was 42 miles from the nearest town. When they first arrived at the hatchery site, construction of the hatchery was the first priority. Housing for Kittie, George, Richard, and the eleven-man crew hired to help in the hatchery was a distant second. Everyone lived in tents, and Kittie cooked for the whole crew. Fortunately, they had plenty of good fresh water.

The family enjoyed life at the fish hatchery and things were running smoothly until Christmas week of 1931, when a blizzard set in.

1901—1985
COMMUNITY ACTIVIST,
LAW ENFORCEMENT
OFFICER

It was just the beginning of a bitter winter. When the weather finally cleared, the snow was six feet on the level and up to sixteen feet in drifts. They couldn't even get as far as the nearest ranch, five miles away.

Kittie thought they had plenty of food supplies, but they were not prepared for the length of the hard winter. George had brought supplies from Austin just before Christmas and also brought back a trapper named Manuel. In January, a wild mare, a mule colt, and a gelding showed up at the ranch and were fed what hay and grain the Bonners had on hand. During a lull in the storm, Manuel rode the gelding to Reese Valley to get help for the Bonners, but no one listened to his appeal. Instead, he was pressed into a road clearing crew. Twenty days later Manuel was finally able to return to Smith Valley with supplies. The snow seemed to continue forever.

Manuel made it out again on a pair of homemade skis, taking with him a letter Kittie had written to a radio station telling of their desperate situation. At this point they were down to just a few beans. A Southern California station picked up the story, and it was through this broadcast that the Lander County Commissioners finally heard of the family's predicament.

The hatchery was closed in 1942, and the family moved back to Austin. They lived in an adobe house George inherited from his mother. Soon Kittie turned the adobe into a boarding house that served a family-style dinner for just 50 cents a person. The mines had reopened to produce minerals critical to the war effort, but the cafes had all closed. Once again, Kittie came to the rescue.

The Bonners lived in the old family adobe house for the remainder of their lives. After George's death in 1964, Kittie became quite a collector and the recipient of almost everything people in the town didn't want. One item was the town barber chair, which the executor of the barber's estate said was "too good to throw away." That is how Kittie became the town barber! She couldn't charge for haircuts because she wasn't a licensed barber, but she had a plate on a table near the door for donations.

Kittie was the only aid to the volunteer ambulance service, as well as a deputy sheriff, and until her death she held a badge as honorary constable. Kittie was always there to help those in need. She was the chairman of the Austin Chapter of the American Red Cross and was a longtime member and Past Worthy Matron of the Order of the Eastern Star. She was a talented poet and painter, and worked as a correspondent for the Fallon newspaper for 30 years. She was a great cook, providing a hot meal for anyone in need. The people of Austin remembered her for the birthday cakes she used to bake and for the way that she always brought a bit of cottage cheese to friends and neighbors.

Kittie once appeared on the television show "To Tell the Truth." The panel had to choose which of the three women questioned was the real sheriff of Austin, Nevada. In May of 1977, Kittie Bonner became the first recipient of the Distinguished Nevadan Award. At the UNR commencement exercises that year, Mrs. Bonner was presented with the award and was commended for her "…significant achievements contributing to the advancement of our State and Nation, and for exceptional service to the well-being of humanity." The Austin newspaper editor published a letter from a fan who said "if everyone were like Kittie Bonner, this would be the most beautiful world in which to live."

Kittie Wells Bonner died on January 27, 1985, in a Fallon hospital and was buried in Austin. She was survived by her son Richard, four granddaughters, one grandson, and fourteen great grandchildren.

—*Jean Spiller*

Alison Bowers

Alison "Eilley" Oram was born on September 6, 1826, in the Royal Burgh of Forfar, Scotland. At the age of 15 she married 19-year-old Stephen Hunter Fishcross, of Clackmannan, Scotland.

After six years of marriage, Stephen converted to the new religion of the Church of Jesus Christ of Later Day Saints, and in January 1849 the Hunters moved to America and the new Mormon city in the Great Salt Lake Valley. The Hunters traveled by ship from England to New Orleans, eventually joining a wagon train in Council Bluff, Iowa, before walking the rest of the way to Salt Lake City. Not long after arriving, the couple divorced for unknown reasons.

In 1853, Eilley married another Mormon from Scotland, Alexander Cowan. In the fall of 1855, Alexander was called on a mission to a small town on the westernmost edge of Utah Territory, known today as Genoa, Nevada. Even though it was uncommon for a wife to go with her husband, Eilley chose to go with Alexander and his recently orphaned 12-year-old nephew, Robert Henderson.

1826—1903
MINER, ENTREPRENEUR

Alexander and Eilley stayed in the small settlement over the winter. The following spring, Orson Hyde, the town's Mormon leader, decided to move the Mormons to Washoe Valley. The Cowans were among the first to arrive in the Valley and were able to purchase 320 acres of good farming land complete with a small house and corral.

A little over a year later, the U.S. government was having problems with the Mormon Church, which brought about the possibility of war between the church and the United States. Brigham Young called back all the Mormons from the small communities, so in the fall of 1857, Alexander agreed to return to Salt Lake City. Eilley and Robert chose to stay behind.

After the problems with the government and Utah were over, Alexander returned to Eilley for a short time but then chose to go back to Salt Lake City alone.

Eilley and her nephew moved to a small mining camp named Johntown (below Silver City) and built a small boarding house there. They quickly moved on to the new town of Gold Hill when gold was discovered

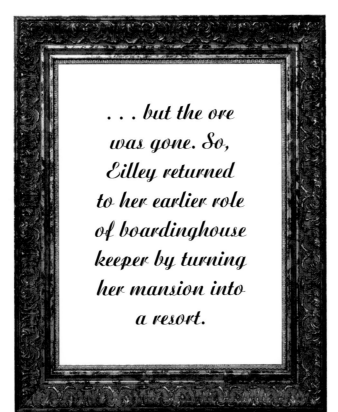

. . . but the ore was gone. So, Eilley returned to her earlier role of boardinghouse keeper by turning her mansion into a resort.

there in 1859 and built a new boarding house. Eilley took advantage of the situation by claiming several plots of mining land. One claim lay next to that of Lemuel Sanford (Sandy) Bower. Eilley and Sandy joined their claims and soon their lives when they married. Gold Hill and Virginia City were both exciting and flourishing mining towns producing the most concentrated amount of silver in the United States, and the Bowers were among the first millionaires of the Comstock Lode. Over the next two years, Eilley gave birth to two children who both died as infants.

The Bowers began the construction of a mansion in Washoe Valley on the land Eilley had acquired from Alexander in their divorce settlement. While the mansion was under construction, Eilley and Sandy went on a grand European tour. They returned home to Nevada with a baby girl named Margaret Persia, whom they adopted during their trip.

Even though the Civil War was continuing to rage, the Bowers enjoyed their riches. In October 1864, President Lincoln officially declared Nevada a state, but soon after, the mines of Nevada began to play out. The Bowers were losing money. Sandy moved back to Gold Hill to save their mine but died of silicosis in 1868 before he could. Eilley took over the business matters of the mine with the help of George Waters, but

the ore was gone. So, Eilley returned to her earlier role of boardinghouse keeper by turning her mansion into a resort.

In 1873, a new silver strike created a second boom for the Comstock Lode. With increased employment and money, the Bowers Mansion became the place to party. The Miners Union, Knights of Pythias, the Pioneers, and many other organizations sponsored large picnics there but this, unfortunately, did not help Eilley's financial situation.

In 1876, she finally lost the mansion at a public auction and was forced to move to a small house in Franktown. Eilley was so broke that she became a wandering fortune teller, using a crystal ball that she had kept from a more prosperous time. She continued this life until she suddenly disappeared from Nevada.

Eilley ended her days in Oakland, California, on October 27, 1903, in the King's Daughters Home. The new owner of Bowers Mansion had her ashes returned to Nevada and buried behind the house. In 1946, her mansion was purchased by Washoe County with the help of the Reno Women's Civic Club and public donations. It is now part of a county park.

—*Nancy Sansone*

Mildred Bray

Mildred Bray, dedicated educator and native Nevadan, was born in Reno (some accounts say Dayton) on May 14, 1892, to parents who were both involved in education. Her father, John Edwards Bray, was the principal of Reno High School at the time of her birth, and his students had participated in the event by suggesting names in a sort of contest—Mildred's name was pulled from a hat. Her maternal grandparents came to Nevada Territory by covered wagon in 1861, and her mother, Minnie Leslie, was born en route.

Mildred's mother was a teacher, and her father followed his career in teaching and school administration by being elected to the office of State Superintendent of Instruction. He served from 1909 to 1919 in a position that would one day also be held by his daughter. Mildred once wrote that during a period of 75 years, there was not once in which some member of her family was not involved in education.

Mildred never married, although she did occasionally enjoy the company of male friends. She loved children and felt badly that she hadn't had her own family. Mildred led a very busy life and one cannot imagine that it could have been less than full. She belonged to many organizations and was an avid reader.

1892–1975
EDUCATOR,
COMMUNITY ACTIVIST

Upon completion of her education in Reno public schools and her graduation from college, Mildred became a teacher. She taught at the Esmeralda County High School at Goldfield, which was then a bustling mining camp, at Minden Elementary Schools, and at Sparks Elementary School.

She varied her pursuits with travel all over the state and developed a lifelong interest in politics. She was employed for a year at the *Nevada State Journal*, worked in the state comptroller's office, and was a secretary for a private law firm in Reno in the early years. She was secretary in the Attorney General's office under the administrations of M.A. Diskin and Gary Mashburn.

From the time she worked as a secretary for the department, Mildred's abilities were recognized, and she was elected to the post of State Superintendent of Schools in 1938 after being appointed to fill out the term of the recently deceased Chauncy Smith. Mildred was State Superintendent from 1938–1950.

She was the only woman to hold the position until Mary Peterson was appointed in 1995 and the only person in Nevada history to be elected to three successive terms as State Superintendent. She held the position during World War II, an especially problematic and chal-

lenging time, and she saw the state's schools through the difficult transition period following the war.

She originated the Basic State Aid to Education plan (still in use in 1997), which secured state aid for rural schools and county aid for district high schools. In addition, during her years as Superintendent, the school code was revised, a minimum salary law for teachers was established, the public school teacher's retirement system was integrated with the state employees' pension system, statewide workshops were created, a curriculum development program was inaugurated, and a state committee was established for the evaluation and revision of high school curriculum. Nevada was the first state to have a statewide curriculum development program and served as a test case for the entire nation.

Following her retirement from the Nevada Department of Education in 1950, she became personal secretary to Governor Grant Sawyer. She called herself a "night person" and often dictated letters at three or four a.m. to be typed the following morning.

In addition, Mildred was affiliated with Delta Kappa Gamma Sorority and was a member of the Carson City Mineral Society and of both the Business and Professional Women's Club and the League of Women Voters. She was a charter member of the Desert Gardeners Garden Club. Mildred attended St. Peter's Episcopal Church, located just two blocks from her home.

Mildred was honored in 1969 for her dedication to the field of education. An elementary school in Carson City (the "blue school") was renamed for her. She was recipient of the Distinguished Nevadan citation from the University of Nevada Board of Regents for the indelible mark she made in her field.

She was also honored in 1973 by the Nevada State Society of Washington, DC. A plaque, with the names of all 20 women so honored, was on display in the J.W. Calhoun Changing Gallery at the Nevada State Museum in Carson City for many years. It was titled "The Feminine Frontier."

Mildred was such an avid Democrat that she would call her pet Boston bull terrier "Mike" (for O'Callaghan, Nevada governor) when he was good and "Dick" (for former President Richard Nixon) when he was bad. She was remembered as quite a "character" by Joan Houghton, who visited her when she was elderly, and Ellen Couch, a retired teacher and sorority sister of Mildred's, who taught during Mildred's tenure as superintendent.

Mildred Bray died in Carson City in the fall of 1975. Those who knew her considered her to be a unique person who cared very much about the school children around the state. She was a model for the women of her time, working tirelessly in her efforts to improve the school system for teachers and students alike.

—*Sally Wilkins from a research paper by Christine Gridley*

Ida Browder

In 1889, Ida Browder was born into an aristocratic family in Pressburg, Austria-Hungary. When she was a young woman, she immigrated to the United States, where she met and married Marbus Dean Browder, a civil engineer, Alexandria, Virginia. The Browders moved to Salt Lake City, and their children, Richard Marbus and Ida Katherine, were born there. Marbus Browder, who had served with the army engineers in WWI, died while the family was living in Sacramento, California.

Ida was a widow with two children to support—not an easy task during the Great Depression—so she moved to one of the few places in America where there were jobs to be had and work to be done: Boulder City, Nevada, site of the Black Canyon Project and the building of the Hoover Dam.

Ida Browder was one of the first people to have an independent business in Boulder City, a town otherwise completely under government control. In 1931 she built the Browder Building and opened Browder's Café, the first private restaurant in town.

While the Browder Building was under construction, Ida and the children lived in a tent on the property. The tent had been used by her son for scouting activities and boasted a wooden floor, walls made of board, and a small stove. When the building was complete, Ida sold the tent and moved her little family moved into an apartment in the building.

Late in 1931, Ida opened her restaurant, which featured "home cooking and individual table service." The latter convenience was important, because the only other place to eat was the Anderson Brothers Mess Hall, a cafeteria for workers building the Hoover Dam.

In those days Boulder City did not have a bank, so Ida came to the rescue. Dam workers who didn't want to be tempted to waste their pay would give it to her, and she would hide it under a mattress in her apartment.

Boulder City pioneer Erma Godbey recalled that when Ida was involved in the construction of the Browder Building, some locals decided to have a dance in the newly built recreation hall across the street. Ida invited them all over for coffee and cake at midnight. It had rained heavily that evening, and many men had to carry their wives and sweethearts across the street, where Ida was waiting

1889–1961
Restaurateur, Educator

Dam workers who didn't want to be tempted to waste their pay would give it to her, and she would hide it under a mattress in her apartment.

with hot coffee and dessert.

Ida Browder also helped to provide Boulder City with a social framework. On December 30, 1931, the first PTA was formed at a meeting in her restaurant, and, in 1936, the VFW Auxiliary was organized in her dining room. In between, she helped start the American Legion Auxiliary, the Girl Scouts, the Chamber of Commerce, and the March of Dimes. She headed the latter's county unit for four years. She was also the first woman on the Boulder City Board of School Trustees, and she helped obtain discarded Library of Congress volumes to start the Boulder City Library.

In April of 1932, the *Las Vegas Age* announced that Ida was enlarging her restaurant. In addition to "two twelve-foot counters and three root beer barrels," the menu was updated with citrus fruit, buttermilk, and orange drink, as well as limburger and salami sandwiches. In 1937 she sold her lunch-room but retained ownership of the building.

June of 1932 brought sadness to Ida and her family. Her son Richard died of spinal meningitis at age 13 in Salt Lake City, where he had been in a hospital for some time.

In 1933, Ida married A.E. Ireland in Yuma, Arizona. Mr. Ireland was a businessman with interests in the St. George, Utah, area.

Ida tried marriage again in 1937, this time with Thomas Hancock, once a foreman of the Southern Sierra Power Company. Hancock was involved in building the original power lines to the Hoover Dam site in Black Canyon. The newlyweds lived in Ida's apartment in the Browder Building.

After divorcing Thomas Hancock, Ida Browder moved away from Boulder City for several years, first to Salt Lake City and then to Sherman Oaks, California, where she became involved in senior citizens' activities and where she met Leonard A. Mountfort. The two married and returned to Boulder City, where Mountfort died in 1960. Still working for the town, Ida, with the blessing of the recreation association, organized a senior citizens' group locally.

In 1960, when Boulder City became an independent town, Ida Browder was presented with the first deed for a privately owned lot. She finally owned the land on which she had erected the Browder Building.

Ida died at her home on 5th Street on January 11, 1961. She was found by a long-time friend, Elton Garrett, who wrote an affectionate obituary for a woman he obviously admired, a woman he credited with greatly influencing the political, cultural, and social life of Boulder City, Nevada, the town that Hoover Dam built.

—*Fran Haraway*

Julia Bulette

The legend of Julia Bulette has grown beyond any recognizable reality and is certainly more interesting and agreeable than mere facts anyway. In Julia's life, journalists found the basis for a wonderful story and took great artistic license in adding to the glamour, benevolence, and humanity of it. Novelists discovered accounts of her in old newspapers and recognized the many possibilities inherent in her life's tale.

Julia's legend was born years after her murder and was perpetuated in the many books and articles about the "ladies of easy virtue" who frequented western mining camps. In the legend, Julia is portrayed as a dark-eyed Creole beauty, whose popularity among the rough miners during the earliest days of the Comstock Lode bonanza gave her the sudden wealth to build the first grand and lavish house in Virginia City. Amidst dreary shacks and rooming houses, this house, at No. 4 D Street, called "Julia's Palace," was the center of community social life for the miners. There, visitors were expected to behave as gentlemen while being surrounded by expensive French wines, fancy cooking, and imported fashions. As the madam of this enterprise, Julia hired refined,

1832–1867
PROSTITUTE

attractive girls from San Francisco. She drove a fancy carriage, had cut flowers brought by stage from California each day to decorate her palace, and adorned herself in diamonds, rubies, sable furs, and elegant gowns. Legend also has it that the Comstock miners came to her defense in one of the Paiute Indian battles that spread throughout the area. Julia was a flamboyant public show adored by the miners wherever she was seen.

However, her greatest pleasure came from being an honorary member of the Virginia City Fire Company, whose firemen elected her queen of the Fourth of July parade. She donated money to buy fire equipment on a regular basis and often rode to the scene of the fire on the engine. When hundreds of miners became ill due to Virginia City's arsenic-laced water or because of influenza and cholera epidemics, Julia turned her mansion into a hospital and helped to nurse the patients back to health. She raised funds for President Lincoln's Sanitary Commission (precursor to the American Red Cross) by speaking at the hilarious auction for Gridley's famous sack of flour. The auction, started in Austin and traveled the country, eventually raising $275,000 to help

wounded and sick Civil War soldiers.

By 1863, Virginia City was the largest city west of Chicago, and according to legend, Julia's business was second to none that side of Denver. But as the town grew in size and wealth, it also grew more conservative and respectable, and Julia saw her status change. She no longer sat with the rowdy miners at the town's theater but in a box out of public view. Although she was no longer the center of attention, Julia would not be driven into obscurity. Even in death she went out with great flair. One night in 1867, Julia answered a knock on her door. The next morning, she was found dead by the Chinaman who was hired to build her morning fire. Her jewelry, furs, and expensive gowns were gone. The mines and mills shut down as thousands formed the procession for her funeral. Every adult male in the area mourned, as the proper women of the town hid behind closed windows and doors. The mystery of her controversial murder was evidently solved three months later, when a Gold Hill resident reported that she had bought a dress formerly belonging to Julia from a John Millian. Millian was summarily tried, convicted, and hanged, as the total populace gathered at the gallows.

That is the legend. In reality, Julia was a native of England, not a Creole beauty. She was not defended and protected by the local miners at the time of battles with the Paiute Indians, since she did not arrive in Virginia City until 1863, well after the event. She was not the only unattached female on the Comstock in its earliest years. Julia did not own a magnificent house called "Julia's Palace" but lived in one of the small, hastily constructed frame houses (sometimes called a "crib") in the red-light district. She took her meals with another prostitute who lived next door. She had no French maid, nor was she a "madam." She lived and worked alone and did not have a beautiful carriage with a team of horses. Although no doubt a kind woman, Julia probably did not turn her small house into a hospital and nurse sick miners through illnesses and epidemics. Her unpaid liquor bills show no French wines but rather the usual miners' fare of whiskey and brandy. She was never wealthy, as the sale of her total estate was only $875, of which $791 was owed to creditors and $201 owed in legal fees. She died in debt.

But this part of Julia's legend is true: She was greatly loved by the miners of Virginia City and did provide them with refinements and kindness unknown in western camps. Any diversion from the hellishly brutal conditions of working 1,200 to 2,500 feet below the earth in temperatures of 100 degrees or more would be a heaven-sent luxury to these rough hard-rock miners, mockers, and timber men.

—Doris Drummond

Florence Lee Jones Cahlan

Florence Lee Jones Cahlan was born on June 30, 1910, in Long Land, Missouri. Her early life was spent traveling with her family to various places around the world, the last being Sumatra, Dutch West Indies, where her father was employed by the Dutch Shell Oil Company. Florence was home-schooled by her mother but returned to the Unites States for high school in Lebanon, Missouri, graduating in 1929. She then continued her education and graduated from the University of Missouri with a bachelor's degree in journalism.

When her family moved to Las Vegas, Nevada, Florence joined them. After being interviewed by Mrs. Garside herself, Florence was hired by the *Las Vegas Evening Review-Journal* (later known as the *Las Vegas Review-Journal*) as a cub reporter to cover local political and community events. While working at the newspaper, Florence met Johan Cahlan, and they were married in Kanab, Utah, on August 25, 1940.

Florence's first retirement from the *Review-Journal* was in 1953. For the next few years, she worked at writing the history of Las Vegas and the families who settled the area. She was co-editor with her husband of a two-volume book, *Water: A History of Las Vegas*. Florence also wrote the entire Anniversary Edition of the *Review-Journal* in 1955 and edited the book *Las Vegas as it Began, As It Grew*, by Stanley Paher. Paher even dedicated the book to her.

When she returned to the *Review-Journal* in 1963, Florence wrote the society column, "Socially Speaking." Due to illness, she retired for the second time in 1983. The Las Vegas community greatly missed her reports on the lives and events of families in the city.

Florence always entered into community and political activities with gusto and was a member of numerous organizations: the Junior League of Las Vegas, Las Vegas Jay Cees, Nevada Historical Society, Nevada State Museum, Southern Nevada Historical Society, PEO, American Red Cross, National Foundation for Infantile Paralysis, and United Fund.

Florence's activities encompassed the establishment of the city library, the establishment of the first ski facilities at Kyle Canyon, and the committee to restore the Old Mormon Fort.

1910—1985
JOURNALIST

Politics was one of her primary interests. Her affiliation was with the Democratic Party. As she said in 1973, "Until four years ago, I had not missed a precinct meeting since I came to Las Vegas in 1933, and most of the time I had the precinct meeting at my home." She was usually chosen as a delegate to the Clark County Democratic Convention and

always supported capable candidates. In one instance she persuaded Helen Cannon, a well-known Las Vegan, to seek office.

During the time of the building of Boulder Dam, Florence wrote stories on the progress of the construction for the *Review-Journal* as well as for the *Los Angeles Times* and Associated Press. As a reporter, she was allowed to climb and go to areas where no other women went. She reported on the dedication of the dam by President Roosevelt in 1935. Florence also interviewed many political figures of the time and covered many of their speeches.

In 1935, after the completion of the Boulder Dam, many Las Vegans were concerned about the city's future, so the Helldorado celebration was organized to attract outside visitors and new residents. As Florence said, "By 1935, the first Helldorado was staged in Las Vegas by the Elks Lodge. Because I once had watched a rodeo on a vacation in Colorado, I received the assignment of covering the rodeo events. I sat in the stands with the judges and announcers, attended the payoffs in the evening at the Apache Hotel, knew

the names of the best bucking broncs and Brahma bulls, and had a wonderful time."

At one time she was asked if gambling was an important recreational activity for her or her family. Her reply was "NOT AT ALL."

The Cahlans lived in Las Vegas during the time of the early above-ground atomic tests. The *Review-Journal* was a gathering place for all the correspondents of the world. Florence never went to the actual site but was always informed of the steps that were taken. She and her husband viewed the tests out on West Charleston Boulevard, where at that time there were no houses or lights. As she said, "We would watch the first glow of dawn behind Sunrise Mountain...Then in the immense quiet of the desert morning, we would feel the vibration of the detonation, and watch the beautifully magnificent and horrendous white mushroom cloud arise over the Nevada test-site area. It was unforgettable."

Florence received many awards for meritorious service. She was honored by most of the organizations she attended, and worked diligently for her city and state. She showed great compassion and love for family, for her friends, and for mankind. Florence was always there for all who needed advice, understanding, and comfort.

Florence Lee Jones Cahlan died on August 25, 1985, and her presence was greatly missed by her family, her friends, and the many readers of the *Review-Journal.*

—*Betty Middleton*

Florence Humphrey Church

When Mrs. Phoebe Humphrey gave birth to Florence in 1869, she could not have foreseen the impact her daughter would have in the advancement of women's rights.

Not much is known about Florence's early life beyond the fact that she attended the University of Michigan, an unusual accomplishment for a woman at that time. She abandoned her studies in her junior year to serve as the secretary for the YWCA in Bay City but resumed them a little later in Munich, Germany, where she met her future husband, Dr. James Edward Church. Florence and James toured Europe by bicycle, taking many photos and collecting art objects and paintings to help James in his lectures. They were married on July 2, 1894, and moved to Reno, Nevada, where she, her husband, and their two sons, Willis Humphrey and William Morris, lived for the rest of her life.

They traveled much of Northern Nevada by horseback and had a retreat on the shores of Lake Tahoe, now known as the Bliss Estate near Tahoe City. The Churches were known for their hospitality to students, and they always enjoyed music, dancing, and the great outdoors.

While traveling with her husband in Germany, Florence learned of the hardships of women's lives and wrote this in a letter to her husband's parents: "I never had any desire to be a nun, but if lived in Germany I would rather have that work than the slavery most of the women live in here. Women are good for work and raising children, but there is little companionship." These strong words portend her future interest and influence in the women's rights movement.

Florence also continued her academic studies at the University of Reno and completed her B.A. in 1902. She later received her master's degree from Reno University in 1914. Her master's thesis was entitled "William Morris's Treatment of the Northern Sagas."

Florence was active in the First Baptist Church and helped to start the Women's Sewing Circle, which in 1896 became known as the Ladies Missionary Society. As secretary of the organization in 1897, Florence helped make and sell aprons, bonnets, and cookies to raise money for the less fortunate Indians.

1869—1922
SUFFRAGETTE

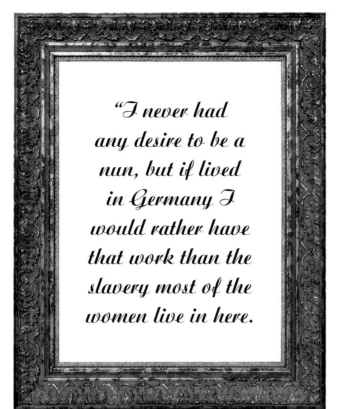

"I never had any desire to be a nun, but if lived in Germany I would rather have that work than the slavery most of the women live in here.

In 1920, the Ratification Committee called upon Mrs. Church to join them in the development of a plan to call a special session of the Legislature to ratify the 19th Amendment, which allowed women the right to vote. Florence's excellent letter-writing skills were utilized to contact legislators and ask their stand on the ratification issue and whether or not they would be willing to come to Carson City, at their own expense, for a special session. The 19th Amendment was successfully ratified on February 7, 1920. The measure was also passed by the state senate and signed by the governor, before being sent to the U.S. Congress.

During Florence's tenure as president of the Nevada Federation of Women's Clubs, several issues of national importance were addressed. The May 1921 issue of *Nevada Federation News* suggested that each club should participate in promoting the Fourth of July as Citizenship Day. It was suggested also that Nevada laws regarding women's and childrens' concerns be addressed. The Nevada Federation of Women's Clubs were encouraged to participate actively in efforts to have public or private kindergarten in their communities.

Florence enjoyed being a leader. She relished the job of organizing and motivating others to influence the future. She rallied people for political issues and helped to promote unity in the community through social gatherings. People were spread out in the early 1900s, but Florence made exceptional efforts to bring everyone in the area together to communicate one on one, a successful way to nurture education, peace, and charity.

Florence Church was low-key in her approach to active change in the culture and society of early 1900s, but her quiet conviction led others to believe in the causes she rallied behind. She won support both near and far with her firm belief in a better future. Through her writing and speaking, Florence encouraged others to promote women's and children's rights, foster peace, encourage education, and cultivate an appreciation for the arts.

Florence Humphrey Church died February 5, 1922, after suffering a stroke. Dr. James Church dedicated a traveling art collection, known as "The Florence Church Art Collection," to those who hunger for beauty in the western hills. The remains of both Florence and James Church are interred in a corner of the Church Fine Arts Building at the University of Nevada in Reno.

Florence was a leader in her day and is still considered a "Woman of Distinction"—a woman to be admired and imitated.

—Dale Meyer

Felice Cohn

elice Cohn was born to Pauline Sheyer Cohn and successful land-owner and merchant Morris Cohn on May 14, 1884, in Carson City, Nevada, where her grandfather, Rabbi Sheyer, led a synagogue. She, her brother, and her three sisters all attended school in Carson City.

At age 11, Felice was hired to teach first grade. She did not last long in that position, although it is recorded that between 1894 and 1903, she received three teaching certificates.

Felice attended the University of Nevada–Reno for a year before enrolling in Stanford, where it is believed she graduated in 1899 at the age of 15. It's recorded that she received a diploma from Nevada Business College in 1899 too!

In 1902 Felice was admitted to the bar through the United States Ninth District court, in Carson City, Nevada. At the time, the 18-year-old Felice was the youngest person to receive such a distinction.

1884–1961
LAWYER, POLITICIAN,
ADVOCATE FOR WOMEN
AND CHILDREN

Practicing law in both Goldfield and Carson City, Felice focused primarily on mining claims, other mining matters, and land issues. By 1906, she was made the first woman Assistant District Attorney. Her scope broadened in 1907 when she served as court reporter on the famous State Bank and Trust Company case. When the trial was over, Felice stayed on as court reporter while returning to her Carson City law practice.

Felice, in 1908, was admitted to the District Court of Appeals in San Francisco. She was employed by the U.S. Federal Government as Assistant Superintendent of Public Land Sales. This position caused her to travel throughout all western states.

The treatment of women in the business world led to Felice's strong efforts in support of women's suffrage. An early member of the suffrage movement, she led Nevada women through the 1913 passage of the Suffrage Act. A band of over 100 people joined her in 1916

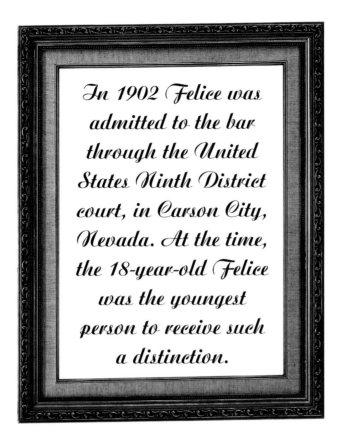

In 1902 Felice was admitted to the bar through the United States Ninth District court, in Carson City, Nevada. At the time, the 18-year-old Felice was the youngest person to receive such a distinction.

to lobby in Washington, DC, for the suffrage amendment.

Her accomplishments did not end there. Felice opened a law office in Reno in 1922. In March, 1926, she received the unsolicited honor of being appointed U.S. Referee in Bankruptcy for the District of Nevada. She served in this capacity for eight years (three terms).

In 1934, Felice refused to testify in the Owl Drug Store Company bankruptcy case and failed to be reappointed as U.S. Referee for Nevada. Appointed to take her place was Reno Attorney George Green, Jr. But Felice was then appointed national chairman of the Committee on Ethics of the National Association of Referees in Bankruptcy.

A founder of the Nevada Federation of Business and Professional Women's Clubs in 1936, Felice was also its first president. She actively participated in the Nevada Federation of Women's Clubs, National Association of Women Lawyers, American Women's Voluntary Services, and Reno's YWCA, as well as the Nevada and

California Associations. Felice successfully led the campaign to collect a $15,000 grant that led the Nevada Legislature to establish a permanent home for the Nevada Historical Society. And for many years, she was devoutly involved in the B'nai B'rth organization.

A strong force for the divorce rights of women and for encouraging other states to accept Nevada law on such issues, Felice made two un-successful bids for public office, in 1924 and 1927. Stoically accepting defeat, she was convinced that some time in the future women would gain equal rights with men.

The end of Felice Cohn's struggle for equality for women came with her death on May 24, 1961 in Reno, Nevada.

—*Mary Gafford*

Eliza Cook

Eliza Cook was born on February 5, 1856, in Salt Lake City, Utah. Her parents, John and Margaretta Cook, had emigrated from Birmingham, England, to join the Mormon settlement there.

When Eliza was a child, her mother left Salt Lake City with her and her younger sister Rebecca. They moved first to Soda Springs, Idaho, where Margaretta took in boarders. From there they moved to White Pine County, Nevada. In 1870, when Eliza was 14 years old, the family settled in Sheridan, Nevada, where Eliza's uncle John Cook already lived.

Margaretta and her two daughters all worked. Margaretta sewed and took in washing, while the girls worked for families in the Carson Valley. As there was no school in the valley, the girls often borrowed books from the families for whom they worked. Eliza "happened to read a little in a home doctor book and from that time on wanted to study medicine."

She got her chance during the winter of 1879–1880, when she was hired by Dr. H.W. Smith of Genoa to nurse his wife through a particularly bad case of puerperal fever. Smith noticed her interest in his medical books and her

1856–
DOCTOR,
COMMUNITY ACTIVIST

natural way with her patient, and suggested that she study medicine. When she said that she didn't know enough, he answered, "Oh yes, you do."

Eliza studied with Dr. Smith for six months and then entered Cooper Medical College (later the Stanford Medical School) in San Francisco. In her class of sixteen students, Eliza was one of five women. After she received her medical degree in 1884, she returned to Carson Valley to practice, making her home and office with her sister Rebecca and her brother-in-law, Hugh Park. She did not actually receive her Nevada medical license until April of 1899, since the state did not begin issuing them until that year.

After practicing medicine for several years and delivering babies everywhere from Genoa to Markleeville, Dr. Eliza Cook went back to school. She attended the Women's Medical School of Philadelphia during the 1890–1891 school year, then did graduate work the following summer at the Post-Graduate Medical College of New York.

Armed with both a medical degree and graduate schooling, Eliza opened an office in Reno in November of 1891. However, after about six months, she returned to practice in the Carson

40

Valley. As she said at the time, she had "never seen a place that suited her as well."

When she was just 14 years old, she had joined the Band of Hope, a temperance organization for youth. Later, she became a member of the Good Templars and was very active in the Women's Christian Temperance Union. Eliza attended the state WCTU convention in Carson City in 1892, and served that organization as state president from 1896 until 1901. She lectured in both Genoa and Reno on the "Need for Plain Living."

Eliza was a strong supporter of women's rights. As she wrote, "My first protest against the prevailing social order came when as a child between eleven and thirteen I read in the third chapter of Genesis: 'Thy desire shall be to thy husband and he shall rule over thee.' That man should rule over woman was to my mind unjust. I went to my mother with my protest and she told me the husband's rule was right only when it was a righteous rule. That silenced my tongue for a time but not my mental protest."

In 1894, Eliza wrote a letter to the *Reno Gazette* listing 11 reasons why she was in favor of women having equal voting rights with men. The letter was also printed in the *Genoa Courier*. In October of 1895, Eliza attended the meeting at McKissick's Opera House in Reno to form a Women's Suffrage Association in Nevada. At this meeting she was elected a vice-president, along with Hannah Clapp of Carson City. After her term was completed, Eliza became president of the Douglas County Equal Suffrage League. She continued to serve both organizations by circulating petitions, writing to legislators, and publishing letters in the newspapers.

Again, in her own words: "During all this time my protests against the injustices of our socio-economic system never ceased. I was a member of The Women's Suffrage Association and of The Women's Christian Temperance Union; circulated petitions for the former, talked on both subjects when opportunity offered and made myself very objectionable at times, I've no doubt."

In the spring of 1901, Eliza took a year's sabbatical from her medical and community responsibilities. She traveled abroad with a companion, visiting such places as the British Isles, Europe, Egypt, the Holy Land, Constantinople, and Greece. Upon her return, she spoke about the trip to many interested groups.

Eliza continued to practice medicine from the home of her sister and brother-in-law until she had a small house built for herself in Mottsville, where she moved her office in 1911. She retired from the medical profession in 1921, at the age of 65.

Dr. Eliza Cook died in her sleep on October 2, 1947, at the age of 91. On her bedside stand was a handwritten "Outline of My Life."

—*Cherry Lyon Jones*

Beda Brennecke Cornwall

Beda (Tabitha) Brennecke Cornwall was born on November 21, 1907, in Tulare, South Dakota, to Martha and Frederick William Brennecke, a German Evangelical Lutheran minister. She received her education at the University of Idaho, Southern Branch at Pocatello and at the University of Denver, majoring in education and social services. After that, Beda taught school for four years in Montrose, Colorado.

In 1932, Beda married Charles Norman Cornwall of Aspen, Colorado, a graduate of the University of Colorado Law School at Boulder. From 1935 to 1939, Beda worked under a federal appointment to do social work for the Farm Security Administration under President Franklin D. Roosevelt.

Beda and Charles had two children: a daughter, Gretchen, and a son, William Leo. In 1943, the Cornwalls moved to Las Vegas, where Charles became a well-known lawyer and served as City Attorney from 1944 to 1948.

During her first year in Las Vegas, Beda taught school at Dry Lake. She became very active in USO work during and after World War II

1907—1994
TEACHER

as well as in Travelers' Aide, Red Cross, and other social and civic endeavors. She served on the Las Vegas City Recreation Board and was appointed through that group and the City Commission to research what could be done to build an adequate library to serve the city's residents. Beda was instrumental in the formation of the Citizens' Library Association, composed of interested members of various local charitable and organizations.

Under Beda's leadership in 1948, the group launched an all-out drive to raise money for a library building. The city donated a building site at 4th and Mesquite in downtown Las Vegas, and the dedicated Citizens' Association raised $68,206 by public subscription and donations, representing over $3 per person in Las Vegas at the time. The new library was dedicated on June 1, 1952, and was at that time the largest and most modern library in the state of Nevada. Reba McKinster, who had come to Las Vegas in 1949 from Kentucky, served as the first City Librarian for nineteen years and worked closely with Beda to bring library needs to the public's attention.

In 1952 Beda was also chair of National Library Week and was honored by the American Library Association for her contributions to public library service. She continued as chair of the Citizen's Library Association Board, which functioned as the Library Board of Trustees for another 20 years until 1972, when the Las Vegas Public Library merged with the Clark County Library District.

Beda was president of the Service League (now Junior League) from 1950 to 1951. She also served as chair of the Clark County Social Agencies and of the Clark County Safety Council. The Shell Oil Company gave Beda an award for her outstanding contribution to public safety.

Also in 1952, Beda was named Mrs. Las Vegas by the American Legion for her work in the community, and she was recognized as one of the three Outstanding Women of the Year by the Soroptomists, a professional women's service club. The Hadassah Club of Jewish women also presented her an award of merit for outstanding service to the community.

Beda Cornwall was elected to the Las Vegas City School District Board of Trustees in 1954, serving until 1956, when school districts were consolidated to form the Clark County School District. In 1954, she was also campaign chair for the Community Chest.

Beda was one of the founders of the Home of the Good Shepherd Auxiliary, serving as their president from 1963 to 1965. She was a member of the Children's Service Guild, which provided assistance to abandoned and neglected children at Child Haven, run by the Clark County Juvenile Court Services. Beda was a member of the Founder's Club of the Clark County Boys' Club, whose library was named the Cornwall Library in honor of Beda and Norman Cornwall.

An avid gardener, Beda was a member of the American Rose Society and entered her flowers in several state competitions.

In 1978, the University of Nevada–Las Vegas library sponsored a special exhibit of artifacts, photographs, and papers that illustrated the history of public library creation in Las Vegas. It also held a large reception to thank those longtime library supporters; Beda Cornwall was a special honored guest at that event.

Beda remained an ardent library supporter and community worker until her death on June 13, 1994. Her son William was quoted in her obituary notice as saying, "She was a preacher's daughter. She felt good works were her responsibility."

—*Jean Ford*

Hilda M. Covey

Hilda Covey, daughter of Anna Seeley Dickinson and Lynn Dickinson, was born on a farm outside of Millerton, Pennsylvania, the oldest of three children. She graduated from the Elmira Academy in Elmira, New York, and later attended the Rochester Institute of Technology in Rochester, New York.

After being trained in the restaurant business by Howard Johnson's in New York City, Hilda opened one of the company's first restaurants in Rochester. The company at the time actually created and sold dozens of flavors of ice cream in their fine dining facilities. During the next ten years Hilda had much success heading a chain of restaurants in Sibley, Lindsay & Curr, a large New York department store. At this time, she was also the National Education Chairperson for the Stewards and Caterers Association.

In 1949, Hilda met and married New Yorker William H. Covey. They came to Las Vegas and opened an eatery called The Skillet downtown on Main Street. Bill ran the kitchen, and Hilda operated the front when she wasn't making the pies for which she became

1909–1982
RESTAURATEUR,
JOURNALIST

famous. Next, the couple purchased land from the Old Smoke Ranch and built the Coffeepot Ranch, a Las Vegas showpiece in its day. Hilda and Bill's Coffeepot on Garces and their Coffee Pot II were equally loved for good soups, pies, and a bottomless cup of coffee served with friendly banter and lots of tall tales.

The Coffeepot restaurants were extremely popular with architects and men in the construction trades, and, in 1953, Hilda, who worked up to twenty hours some days, saw the need for a specialized trade publication for the growing Las Vegas construction business.

In a back room at the Coffeepot, Hilda produced the first issues of *Construction Notebook*. A man named J.A. Tiberti was signed up as her first subscriber. *Construction Notebook* contained bid notices, a resource directory, and everything anyone needed to know about the local construction world, along with some charming cartoons and business-card-type ads.

Hilda and Bill were loved and respected in their community. They both became members of the 36th Ward of the Church of Jesus Christ

of Latter-Day Saints and were remarried at the Mormon Temple in St. George, Utah.

The Coveys were very involved in Las Vegas. Hilda served on the Board of Directors of Citizens for Private Enterprise and was on the board of St. Jude's Ranch and Nevada Economic Development Corporation. For twelve years, she served as Executive Secretary of the Las Vegas Chapter of the American Institute of Architects. And in 1978, she became the first woman president of the North Las Vegas Chamber of Commerce.

Hilda also wrote the witty "Sidewalk Superintendent" column in the *Las Vegas Sun* for many years.

Hilda was always in charge at her businesses and never hesitated to threaten obstreperous customers with what she called "a trip to the woodshed." A woman for all seasons and reasons, she is remembered for an amazing capacity for hard work, for prodigious numbers of Christmas fruitcakes and Relief Society pies, and for her infectious laugh and love of pranks. She could "dish

it out" and she could "take it." Once, after her return from a birthday dinner party, she found a gift from a well-known Las Vegas contractor, Vern Frehner: He had tethered a braying burro in her atrium, and she stayed up all night feeding it peanut butter sandwiches to keep it quiet!

Missed and mourned by family and friends, Hilda Dickenson Covey is at rest at Palm Cemetery on Main Street in Las Vegas.
—*Frankie Williams*

Martha Cragun Cox

Martha Cargun Cox, mother of eight children, was the founder and first teacher of several schools in the southern Nevada region. As an active Mormon, she gave her time as a Temple worker and was a genealogist, scriptorian, and counselor. In her later years, she wrote *Face Toward Zion*, a two-volume autobiography about her life as a pioneer. Martha was also a talented weaver.

Martha was the daughter of James and Elenor Lane Cragun. Her father was from Fayette, Indiana, and her mother was one of the Lanes from Virginia. Martha's parents joined the Mormon Church and made the trek across the United States as part of the Trail of Hope, the great Mormon overland migration to the West. They arrived in the Salt Lake Valley on October 22, 1849. Martha was born on March 3, 1852, in Salt Lake Country in a little adobe cabin that stood on the banks of Mill Creek. As a little girl she loved hearing stories about her family's adventures, and the stories became a source of inspiration and faith to her.

Martha loved to study but did not care for homemaking. Even before she was of school

1852–1932
TEACHER

age, she went to school as a visitor with her older brothers and sisters and learned the whole alphabet in one day. Her parents allowed her to attend school from that time on. Martha decided to become a schoolteacher in 1868, when she was just 16 years old. She never wavered in her choice of career.

Martha was 18 and preparing for her teaching certificate when she married Isaiah Cox, son of Jehu and Sarah Pyle Cox, in November of 1869. Despite her family's vehement objections, she prayed fervently and felt it was God's will that she enter into plural marriage. She felt the Lord's hand in this decision and that she must follow His directive. Martha knew Isaiah's other two wives, and she loved them and the Spirit of their home.

Martha had already been teaching in Utah when she was offered a position in the Muddy Valley area of Nevada. It was 1881, and she was notified that her examination would be held in Pioche, Nevada, on August 6. Martha had just buried her baby Amy, but she knew that she had to have this position, which paid the lucrative sum of $50 per month. One of the older boys of the family, David, 17 years old, drove her from St. George, Utah, to Pioche, Nevada, in a buckboard. It was a hard trip for her after the loss of her baby, and they arrived one day late for the examination. Dr. Alexander refused to allow her to take the test for teacher certification, but as she was leaving, a Mr. O'Dougherty said that if she could answer an oral interview, she would receive her certificate. She passed with flying colors and went home with her teaching certificate for Nevada, a new job, and a new future to look forward to on the Muddy. At the same time, her husband, "Mr. Cox" as she always referred to him, was called as first Bishop in the newly formed town of St. Joseph on the Muddy.

Once again, David took Martha on the four-day journey to the Muddy Valley School. It was late August, extremely still and hot, and one day the clouds grew dark and black and burst into a terrible rainstorm. So dreadful was the downpour that Martha recorded that "we experienced toads raining from the sky."

The day after her arrival, Martha went to the schoolhouse and found that it was not yet completed. Mr. McGuire, the leading trustee, greeted her and informed her that it would not be ready for three weeks. She told him that school need not wait a day. With such beautiful weather, she could begin class the next morning. The students would simply join her under the cottonwood trees by the side of the lovely stream. Desks and chairs were borrowed. Bonnets and hats were hung on trees, and her converted breadboard became a blackboard. On September 1, 1881, she registered nine pupils. Martha's duties extended beyond the classroom. She was also required to work in the fields and then help with the harvesting and canning. For this, she was given room and board in a small adobe cabin. Her days were extremely long and hard.

Martha's husband passed away in 1896 after fathering a total of 29 children. The next year, Martha Cox opened the first school in Mesquite, Nevada. The school at first was only a 16' x 16' tent with a dirt floor and no windows, no heat, and a few log benches to sit on. In 1901, after the school was well established, Martha went on to teach in the Mexican colonies until 1905, when she returned to teach at Beaver Dam and Cave Spring. She taught in Richfield and Gunlock, Utah. She took pride in teaching many Native American children. Martha's teaching career ended in the early 1920s, and the remainder of her life focused on family, scriptural studies, and Temple work.

In 1997 the Encampment Mall Monument at Dixie College in St. George, Utah included the name of Martha Cragun Cox among those honored.

—*Charlene Cox Cruze*

Clara Dunham Crowell

Clara Dunham Crowell was born on April 7, 1876, in Austin, Nevada. Her parents were Edward G. and Julia Guyla Dunham, Reese River pioneers. Clara obtained her education in Austin schools and then worked as a waitress at the Two Bit House restaurant, so named because dinner and dessert cost only 25 cents, or two bits. It was at the Two Bit House that Clara caught the eye of George Crowell. Crowell was a teamster for the six-horse stage running between Goldfield, Tonopah, Belmont, and Austin. George and Clara became friends and were married in 1898. They had two children, George Jr., who died in childhood, and Dolly Ruth. Crowell was highly regarded in the community and in 1916 was elected sheriff of Lander County. It was during her husband's tenure as sheriff that Clara learned the traits of a good law officer: when to anticipate trouble, how to shoot, how to remain calm, and how to take a stand against intruders. In spite of poor health due to bronchitis and heart problems, George was reelected as sheriff in 1918. But his health continued to decline, and upon the recommendation of his physician he went to Oakland, California, for further treatment. His condition did not improve, and he died on February 24, 1919, leaving Clara and their 11-year-old daughter without any means of support.

Deputy sheriff Thomas White had been in charge during Crowell's illness, and he and some other men applied to the county commissioners to fill the vacancy left by Crowell's death. However, these men graciously withdrew when the citizens of Lander County circulated a petition requesting that Clara be named the first woman sheriff in Nevada history. The commissioners agreed with the petitioners and named Clara to fill the remaining two years of her husband's term. Thus, in 1919, 42-year-old Clara Crowell became the law of Lander County.

The appointment was supposed to be in name only. Clara was to be a figurehead, and the deputy was to do the real work of sheriff. The salary was to help her raise her daughter. However, Clara was not satisfied with being a figurehead and decided to become a real sheriff by going to work every day and overseeing the duties of the office. There are reports of her arresting horse thieves, cattle rustlers, robbers, and assorted criminals. She went underground and disguised herself as

1876–1942
LAW ENFORCEMENT OFFICER, COMMUNITY ACTIVIST

an old Indian in order to apprehend the people selling liquor to Indians illegally. At a time when no respectable woman would be seen in a saloon, Clara is said to have broken up saloon brawls. She tracked and brought back a man accused of fraud by going into the mountains after him. She enforced the unpopular and largely ignored Prohibition Laws that outlawed the transport of bottled liquor.

Many Austin residents did not take kindly to the notion of a female sheriff, and accounts of her ability and effectiveness differ. Facts point out that Constable Jack Phillips handled the problems in Battle Mountain and northern Lander County, about ninety miles from Austin. Phelps did the brand inspections for horses being transported on the railroad, handled foreclosure sales of mining properties, and enforced laws regarding illegal liquor sales and auto traffic. But how much auto traffic was in Nevada in 1920? Clara's deputy, Thomas White, was also of great help in collecting license fees and livestock taxes. Adding to the dissatisfaction of some residents may be the fact that during her term, Clara had to take sev-

eral leaves of absence due to her mother's illnesses and her own health. Whatever the truth may be, the perception was that Clara Crowell and her deputies were among the toughest law enforcement officers in the West and that in Lander County the law would be respected.

At the end of Clara's two-year term as sheriff, she did not run for reelection. Because she also had nursing skills, Clara decided to become a nurse in the county hospital and worked in this position for 20 years, ending her career as administrator of the hospital. She retired in 1939.

Clara subsequently moved to Reno to live with her sister and died at the Washoe General Hospital on June 19, 1942. At her funeral in Austin, she was honored by the townspeople whom she and her husband had served with charity and kindness and was eulogized as the waitress who became Nevada's first woman sheriff.

—*Doris Drummond*

Dat-So-La-Lee

Dat-So-La-Lee was a Washoe Indian woman who was born, probably in 1829, near the place that became the mining town of Sheridan in Carson Valley. She was also known by her given name of Dabuda. Her father's name was DA DA uongala, and her mother's name is unknown. Dat-So-La-Lee lived in and around Carson City, Carson Valley, and Lake Tahoe all of her life.

Sometime around 1899 Dabuda became known as Dat-So-La-Lee. Just how she got the nickname is a subject of some debate. No official records of her first two marriages survive. Information provided by Dr. S.L. Lee indicates that Dabuda was first married into the family of "Lame Tom," who was called Assu and who possibly died of consumption. Other records indicated that she later married a man named Jim. Apparently, no children from any of Dabuda's marriages survived to adulthood.

In her earlier years, Dabuda washed clothes and cooked for the miners and their wives. In 1871, she went to the mining town of Monitor in Alpine County, California, and worked for the Harris Cohn fam-

ily. It was in 1895 that she began to make baskets for a living.

In 1888, Dat-So-La-Lee married Charlie Keyser, her third husband, who was part Washoe and took his name from the family that owned the Keyser and Elrod Ranch in Nevada's Carson Valley. It was at this time that Dabuda took the name Louisa Keyser. Charlie was 24 years younger than Dabuda and an expert arrow craftsman.

Dabuda came to Abe Cohn's attention in 1895 when he bought four willow-covered whiskey flasks she had made. He later became her sponsor, business manager, and press agent. By 1899 her baskets were being carefully recorded, in a ledger separate from the family's business ledger, by Amy and Abe Cohn, who recognized how skillfully they were made.

Dat-So-La-Lee and Charlie led a comfortable life with Abe and Amy Cohn. From 1895 until Charlie's death in 1928, all of their expenses were taken care of by the Cohns. They traveled to Lake Tahoe every summer, where Cohn had provided another home for them near Tahoe Tavern. Dabuda also traveled extensively with the Cohns to arts and crafts exhibits. In return for their patronage, the Cohns

ABOUT 1829—1925
BASKET WEAVER

received Dat-So-La-Lee's baskets. Her only vice, or so it is rumored, was gambling. She liked the games the Indians played with wood or bone dice hidden in the hands or under baskets and the new games of chance the white men brought to Nevada. Sometimes she gambled for two days and nights straight through.

Dat-So-La-Lee is probably best known for her degikup or "day-gee-coop" baskets. This type of basket begins with a small, circular base, extends up and out to a maximum circumference, then becomes smaller until the opening at the top is roughly the same diameter as the base. She wove baskets for Cohn's Emporium for nearly thirty years, until her death in 1925. Some reports put the number of baskets that she wove for Cohn at over 300; others put the total as low as 120.

Recognizing the difficulty of selling Indian baskets for anything approaching their true value, the Cohns manufactured many myths about Dat-So-La-Lee's past in order to enhance the baskets' value. One story stated that Dabuda was the daughter of a Washoe chief and had inherited the right to weave the sacred mortuary "day-gee-coop." The story goes on to state that after the Paiutes defeated the Washoe in war, the Washoe were prohibited from weaving these baskets, and the Chief and Dabuda burned the ceremonial baskets rather than allow them to fall into

Paiute hands. It is now generally accepted that Dabuda's designs were inspired by other weavers, probably Pomo and Miwok Indians.

Though she never attended school, Dat-So-La-Lee lived during a time that saw an enormous amount of change for her people. Since she was illiterate, she used her hand print, which was copyrighted, to certify bills of sale. The receipts included the hand print, a description of the basket, stitches to the inch, and design and time involved in its construction.

Esther Summerfield, writing for the Nevada State Historical Society, said of Dabuda:

Myriads of stars shine over the graves of our ancestors. Dat-So-La-Lee had seen some 96 winters, mostly in the Carson Valley, when death came. Last of the famed Washoe basket-weavers, her unexpressed dreams and her love of beauty were woven into her masterpieces. Her baskets were unsurpassed for their artistic conception and symbolical significance. She gathered all known materials, with the aid of her husband. This work was tedious and required careful attention. Her materials were cured, seasoned, and tied up ahead for the next year's work. She was among the last of those Washoe weavers. Her beautifully woven baskets will live on to remind us of the history and unique tribal artistry of her people.

—Sally Wilkins from an unpublished research paper by Kim Von Aspern, revision: Dixie Westergard, 2005.

Nellie Mighels Davis

Nellie Verrill was prepared to leave her birthplace of Crestwood, Maine, to enter Vassar when her mother died, leaving Nellie to care for her younger brothers and sisters. When she was 16, she met 29-year-old Henry Rust Mighels. Henry went away to the Civil War, was wounded, and then moved to Carson City, Nevada. Even though he had proposed to Nellie the year that they met, it wasn't until she was 20 years old that Nellie traveled from Maine to San Francisco to marry Henry. Nellie traveled across the Isthmus of Panama on narrow gauge railroad and by steamer to San Francisco, where she was met by her fiancé. After their wedding, the couple returned to Carson City, where Henry had become a successful newspaperman. As owner and editor of the *Carson City Morning Appeal*, Henry hired Nellie as his associate editor. Within a couple of years, they had also built the home where their five children would be born.

Nellie was the first woman to cover the Nevada legislature, in 1877 and 1879. Henry had taught her how to report by taking her to church

1844–1945
JOURNALIST

and having her write down the sermons. The sermons were then reported in the *Appeal*, much to the delight of churchgoers and ministers. Nellie learned to set type, write stories, and integrate herself into her husband's affairs, political as well as journalistic.

When Henry became very ill in 1878, Nellie took on a larger role at the *Appeal*, helping him with his editorial work and editing telegraphic items and exchanges. Nellie was 35 when she became a widow and sole proprietor of the Carson paper. She went on publishing the *Appeal* and soon hired Samuel Post Davis as editor. They were married on July 3, 1880. While Sam took over the operation of the paper, Nellie continued as business manager and reporter in addition to her duties running the ranch they had bought and raising their growing family.

In 1897, Nellie was the first woman to report a prize fight, when her husband was out of town and she took his place as reporter at the Corbett-Fitzsimmons fight held in Carson City. She was paid $50 for the story by a Chicago newspaper. Not only was Nellie the only woman reporter there, she was one

of only a few women—most of the other were prostitutes—in the entire audience. She used her maiden name on her fight story to avoid "disgracing" herself and her friends by her acknowledgment of being present at the fight.

In 1899, during the Spanish-American War, Nellie organized the Red Cross in Nevada and became the group's first state president. She also became involved in the Leisure Hour Club of Carson City in the early 1900s; she became its president for the first time in 1906. Instrumental in the building of a clubhouse for the Leisure Hour Club, Nellie was affectionately dubbed "The Mother of the Leisure Hour Club House." The cornerstone was laid in 1913 after seven years of planning. Nellie's two daughters and her granddaughter-in-law were all eventually president of the club as well. Her family members supported the club for over 50 years.

In 1908, Nellie was elected president of the State Federation, which was instrumental in helping to pass a state legislative bill giving mothers rights equal to fathers in the care and custody of a child, as well as another bill establishing a home for delinquent children at Elko. The Federation raised $100 towards the General Fund Endowment and approximately $1,000 for a loan fund to assist girls with their education.

An interesting sidelight was the fight over whether the Leisure Hour Club would be allowed to join the State Federation; the Federation didn't allow clubs with male members, and the Leisure Hour Club's membership included men. A compromise was struck; the Leisure Hour Club would be allowed to join, but the men would have no vote in Federation activities.

Nellie was left a widow again in 1919 when Sam Davis passed away. She continued her interest in Carson City and the political welfare of the state. At the age of ninety, she said, "Why do I feel young at ninety? Goodness knows. Because I am interested in everything that's going on. I have no recipe for youth. I eat whatever I like and plenty of it. I have never used cosmetics. When I was a girl, we did not use rouge or lipstick. Nice girls didn't."

Nellie Davis celebrated her 100th birthday months before her death on June 24, 1945.

—Sally Wilkins, from an unpublished report by Susan J. Ballew; corrections and additional information given by Sylvia Crowell Stoddard to Kay Sanders, fall 1998. Edited by Nancy Sansone.

Clarabelle Hanley Decker

Clarabelle Decker was the fourth of seven children born to David and Nellie Eloise Stotts Douglas in Bellevue, Colorado. Nellie Stotts had grown up in the genteel atmosphere of a southern plantation and was ostracized when she married David, a jockey. David and Nellie then moved west and lived in remote mining camps such as Oatman, Arizona, and Searchlight and Nelson, Nevada. Nellie instilled in her children a love of books and education and tried to compensate for the lack of cultural influences in their rugged surroundings.

According to an article published in the *Las Vegas Sun Magazine*, "Clarabelle took a headlong plunge into books early in life." This love of books never wavered throughout her life and her 50-year career in education.

Clarabelle began her formal education in Oatman, Arizona. As a high school sophomore, she entered the boarding school at Northern Arizona Normal (now Northern Arizona University) in Flagstaff, where she earned her teaching certification as well as her high school diploma.

Clarabelle attended the University of Arizona on a scholarship for one year and tutored blind students to help meet expenses.

1900—1984
TEACHER, LIBRARIAN,
COMMUNITY ACTIVIST

In 1920, Clarabelle married a classmate, Michael Hanley, who had just returned from serving in the Navy in World War I. They had one daughter.

While on a visit with her mother at the Techatticup Mine near Nelson, Clarabelle was pressed into service to fill in for a teacher who had left unexpectedly.

Clarabelle taught in Arizona and California, but, in 1930, she was hired to teach at the Fifth Street Grammar School in Las Vegas. Shortly after her arrival the school burned to the ground. Classes were held in all available spaces but mainly in tents. After the new building was completed, "Miss Hanley" taught English and home economics to grades six through eight. She soon became a member of the Las Vegas High School faculty, teaching English and world history. Her husband, Michael Hanley, a railroad accountant, died while Clarabelle was teaching in Las Vegas.

When she felt it was not necessary to attend summer school, Clarabelle worked as a cashier for the Nevada Power Company and as a clerk-typist for the Union Pacific Railroad and the Las Vegas Credit Bureau. But she continued to teach at Las Vegas High School, and, in addition to her

54

other duties, she joked that she was chosen to work in the library because the school administrators "grabbed anyone who seemed a little literate." After being chosen full-time librarian, she concentrated on earning an M.A. in library science, believing that "there's more to being a librarian than knowing books."

Many considered Clarabelle Hanley Decker to be the "Mother of Clark County School Libraries." She was the first full-time school librarian in the county. She wrote numerous articles for professional journals including the *Wilson Library Bulletin* and the *Nevada Educational Bulletin*. She published a *Handbook and Course Study for Junior High School Libraries*. Decker's other works include two 1970 publications: a booklet, *Old Oatman, Arizona*, and a book of poetry, *A String of Lights*. Her pursuit of higher education continued her entire life, both in and out of the classroom. She loved to travel, and she played the mandolin and the ukulele, sang, and danced. Clarabelle took correspondence courses from many schools, including the University of California–Berkeley, the University of Hawaii, Columbia University, the University of Oklahoma, and BYU.

Clarabelle Hanley and longtime Flagstaff college friend Francis L. Decker were married in 1950. They made their home in Flagstaff, where she taught and was assistant librarian at Northern Arizona University. In 1954 Clarabelle was asked to return to Las Vegas to set up the library at the new Rancho High School. She became the school district's first library supervisor and helped organize libraries for new high schools, junior high schools, and elementary schools. In her spare time she taught at Nevada Southern University, now UNLV, driving home to Flagstaff on the weekends. During the summer she taught classes in Book Selection and Children's Literature at NAU.

Mrs. Decker retired from the Clark County School District in 1960. She returned to Flagstaff and taught graduate courses at Northern Arizona University until her retirement in 1976. Her teaching career extended almost fifty years.

Both Clarabelle and her husband shared an interest in history, particularly that of Nevada and Arizona. After her final retirement in 1976, the couple moved to Camp Verde, Arizona, but shortly after the death of her husband in 1977, Clarabelle moved back to Las Vegas. In 1980, her book, *Common Sense Grammar*, was published.

She considered it "one of her proudest moments" to have a school bear her name. The Clarabelle Decker Elementary School was dedicated on January 16, 1978. A plaque on the school reads: "A tribute—for other within these walls who fulfill the American Dream for a better tomorrow—a challenge to do as well as she!"

—*Jean F. Spiller*

Hazel Baker Denton

Hazel Baker Denton was born in Monroe, Utah, the tenth child of Utah pioneer parents, William George Baker and Nicoline Marie Bertelson-Baker.

Hazel grew up in Richfield, Utah, where she went to school until she was sixteen. Her mother opened a little millinery shop after her father died in 1902. Hazel and her sister always had the prettiest hats in the village.

In 1903, at age 16, Hazel was appointed assistant teacher for an over-crowded first grade. The experience of those two years as an assistant encouraged Hazel to later get her state certificate to teach in Utah.

Hazel's mother died in 1905, and she went to Ogden, Utah, to live with her brother Ralph and his family, and to finish high school with additional courses completed at the University of Utah.

Her certified teaching career began in Richfield in 1907 at $50 per month. During the year, Hazel and another young teacher began to have some grand ideas about spending their summer in Europe. They hoped to borrow money from the local bank to add to what they had saved. The bank made the loan, and Hazel and her friend were off to Europe. She had to teach four more years in Utah to pay the bank back.

In 1914, the family of Hazel's brother Nelson was living at a new "boom" mine, the Prince, over the mountains west of Pioche, Nevada. Hazel was offered the job of teaching at the one-room/all-grades school there for $85 a month.

Hazel was married at Caliente on December 28, 1916, to Floyd Howard Denton, a native of Nebraska. She continued teaching until the first of four children was born in October, 1917; her other children followed in 1919, 1923, and 1925.

In 1922, Hazel was elected a member of the Lincoln County Board of Education, and in 1928, she resumed teaching in Caliente with the un-

1887–1962
TEACHER

usual distinction of being both a teacher and the president of the board of education at that time.

When her husband's business suffered reverses in 1929 and the early 1930s, Hazel became interested in the public affairs of her town, county, and state, and took a correspondence course in creative writing. Her husband died in 1951, and Hazel retired from public teaching in 1952.

Hazel's interest in community can be traced back to her years of teaching at the Prince Mine, where she also conducted a night class for foreign miners to them learn English. She was president of the Caliente Home Makers Club in 1921–1922 and president of the Caliente Parent-Teachers Association in 1926–1928, adding the job of librarian of the Caliente PTA Library when it opened in 1928.

Hazel Denton was one of the few Nevada women profiled in a 1935 history by James A. Scrugham, *Nevada: A Narrative of the Conquest of a Frontier Land*.

With the Nevada Federation of Women's Clubs, Hazel served as state chairman of child welfare; state chairman of library extension; president of the First District, NFWC, for the term 1932–1934; and state president during 1944–1946. Hazel was also a charter member and first president of the Caliente Business and Professional Women's Club, organized in 1941, and president of the Lincoln County Classroom Teachers in 1948–1949 and treasurer of the Nevada State Classroom Teachers during the same years.

In 1952, Hazel Denton was elected as a Democrat to the Nevada Assembly and was re-elected in 1954. While in the Assembly, Denton introduced several bills and resolutions aimed at improving the status of free public libraries and state parks.

Hazel's journalistic and literary leanings began in 1937 with a regular column in the Caliente newspaper. Both poems and paragraphs from her years of writing were included in her book *Ironing Day*.

Hazel Denton died in Las Vegas, and Governor Grant Sawyer delivered the eulogy at her services in Caliente.

—*Jean Ford*

Mary Stoddard Doten

Mary Stoddard Doten, one of Nevada's pioneer educators, was born in Westville, Connecticut. Little is known of her childhood, other than the fact that she was a member of a well-to-do family and received an education that included the study of French and Latin. Her diary tells us that she worked as an assistant in a Carnden, New York, public school and that, as a result of a liaison with a man named Edward Sperry, she had a daughter named Millie.

Mary Stoddard's Nevada adventure began in December of 1870, when she arrived in Virginia City to live with her aunt, Lucy Batterman, whose husband George was the supervisor of the Gold and Curry mine. Mary taught school in Gold Hill from 1872 to 1874.

In 1872, Mary Stoddard met journalist Alf Doten, and they were married on July 24, 1873. The nuptials took place on a steamer in the middle of Lake Tahoe and were watched by 100 guests—some invited and some just curious onlookers who boated over to see what was going on.

In 1882, the Dotens moved to Austin, Nevada, where Mary took charge of the first grade in the public school. Shortly thereafter, she studied for and took the teachers' examination and received her first grade teaching certificate. By that time, the Dotens had four children— Bessie, born July 13, 1875; Sam, born December 14, 1876; Alf, Jr., born September 2, 1887; and Mary Godwin, born December 5, 1880. Mary also had a stillborn boy in August of 1883.

In December 1883, Mary applied to the Reno public school system. When she was offered a position, she packed up the children and headed for Reno. There, she became known as an outstanding and respected Nevada educator. She taught algebra, geometry, physics, French literature, and, her specialty, English literature. In July of 1884, she ran her own private summer school for a six-week term.

Mary's teaching career ran from 1884 to 1903 and included many years as assistant principal at Reno High School. In 1887, she was presented with a life diploma. She was also the first woman to serve on the Reno Public Schools Board of Examiners and was actively involved in the Nevada State Teachers' Institutes—an organization that became the Nevada State Educational Association in 1901.

1845–1914
TEACHER, WRITER,
SUFFRAGETTE

"If women are fit to train them [men,] they should also be fit to vote with them."
—Mary S. Doten

The Nevada's women's suffrage movement claimed much of Mary's time, and she once shared a public platform with Susan B. Anthony. She wrote a popular poem about those denied the vote entitled "Idiots, Lunatics, Paupers and Women."

When the editor of the *Reno Evening Gazette* asked her to express her opinion of women's suffrage, she replied, "If women are fit to train them [men], they should also be fit to vote with them."

Mary's other civic interests included being a charter member of the Nevada Historical Society, an active member of the Rebekah Lodge (which she joined in 1889), and a member and officer of the Twentieth Century Club—an organization founded at the turn of the century whose purpose was to look to the future and "promote culture, general welfare and promote and preserve historic, scientific knowledge and general education." This was the organization that started a public library because Reno did not have one.

Throughout this time, Mary had been emotionally and often physically separated from her husband, whose increasing alcoholism affected his writing career. In his diary, Alf mentions that Mary had applied to the University of Nevada Board of Regents for a teaching position but was not accepted because of her husband's drunkenness. Still, she gave him an allowance, which he supplemented with occasional writing assignments. Alfred Doten died alone in a Carson City boarding house in 1903.

In addition to her educational and civic commitments, Mary Stoddard Doten was a prolific writer. She authored several essays and short stories for the *Reno Evening Gazette* and was also a well-known poet and playwright.

1912 brought the recognition that Mary Doten deserved when the Mary S. Doten School (grades 1–8) opened in Reno. The mission-style building, located at West and 4th Streets, remained in use until 1974, when it was closed and torn down.

Mary Stoddard Doten died on March 12, 1914, and was buried in Hillside Cemetery. She was preceded in death by her daughter Bessie, who died in 1905 from typhoid fever and by her daughter Mary Godwin, who committed suicide in 1911. Mary is remembered for her impact on turn-of-the-century Nevada, particularly in the field of education. Speaking of her life-long commitment, she noted, "Education begins when your eyes first open to the sight of the earth, and ends only when all conscious life departs."

—Fran Haraway

Geneva Smith Douglas

Geneva Smith Douglas was born in Gloucester, Massachusetts, and received her graduate degree in physiology from Mount Holyoke in 1956. From 1956–1959 she worked as a Research Associate at the University of Rochester Atomic Energy Project, studying the metabolism of nuclear fission products. In 1959 she joined the U.S. Public Health Service as a radiation biologist for the Southwestern Radiological Health Laboratory (later renamed the Environmental Monitoring Systems Laboratory) in Las Vegas, Nevada. In her dual role as Public Affairs Director for the U.S. Public Health Service and Public Information Director for the U.S. Environmental Protection Agency, Geneva acted as a scientific liaison between the nuclear industry and local communities regarding the effects of the nuclear weapons testing program at the Nevada Test Site. In Geneva's eventual capacity as the Program Operations Manager of the Environmental Monitoring Systems Laboratory, she developed an offsite radiation monitoring program and spent much of her time speaking, advising, conducting tours, and writing informational brochures and fact sheets about nuclear testing and community safety.

Although Geneva retired from the Environmental Protection Agency in 1985, she continued to advise the scientific community on matters relating to nuclear safety. She participated in and evaluated full-scale field exercises of the Federal Radiological Emergency Response Plan in Florida (1984) and Illinois (1986) and the VENTREX exercises at the Nevada Test Site (1986–1987). She also acted as a technical liaison and EPA spokesperson following accidental releases of radioactivity from U.S. and Chinese nuclear weapons tests, and advised the emergency response crew during the krypton-venting phase of cleanup following the nuclear power plant accident at Three Mile Island. In addition, Geneva prepared and delivered Congressional testimony relating to nuclear testing, radiation exposure, and nuclear-waste repositories.

To add to her busy professional career, Geneva was active at all levels of Soroptomist International, one of the five largest women's service organizations in the world. She was a charter member of Soroptomist International

1932–1993
NUCLEAR PHYSICIST,
BIOLOGIST

of Greater Las Vegas and held most club offices, including two terms as club president. In 1980, she was elected to the office of regional governor of the Sierra Nevada Region, which consisted of about forty-five clubs in California and Nevada. Between 1982 and 1984, Geneva served as Environmental Advisor for Soroptomist International of the Americas, a federation of clubs in twenty countries. Geneva attended her first international convention in Istanbul in 1983 as a silent observer and was appointed member of the Long Range Planning Group for Soroptomist International. Between 1987 and 1991, she served as the International Programme Liaison and was responsible for coordinating international service programs in the areas of Economic and Social Development, Education, Environment, Health, Human Rights/Status of Women, and International Goodwill and Understanding. As International Program Liaison, she developed a database of club service activities relating to international programs, helped write and revise Soroptomists' statements and positions, and created a roster of Soroptomists with special expertise for consulting purposes.

In 1986, Governor Richard Bryan named Geneva Douglas to chair the newly formed Governor's Advisory Committee on Volunteerism, whose focus was to discover and coordinate volunteer leadership and activities within the state of Nevada. In just a few months, Geneva had coordinated several workshops on volunteer resources and training, and organized the first statewide Conference on Volunteerism, with representatives from business and service organizations and government agencies.

Geneva also served on the steering committee of the Friends of Nevada Wilderness from 1985–1987. This coalition of environmental groups functioned to lobby the state and U.S. Congress to retain Nevada wilderness areas, and to encourage the state to purchase public lands for statewide protection. In her capacity as chairperson, she helped the group organize and focus their efforts on preparing statements and congressional testimony relating to wilderness preservation.

—*Sally Wilkins*

Anna Neddenriep Dressler

Anna Engel Dorathea Neddenriep was born, the fifth of nine children, to Anna Dreier and Christian Friedrich "Fritz" Neddenriep. Both parents were born in Germany but came to Carson Valley as young children.

Anna Neddenriep's early education was at the Fredericksburg School; she walked the one mile to and from school each day. Anna attended the Douglas County High School, where she formed a strong friendship with Fred H. Dressler that led to a marriage of 60+ years.

Anna did not graduate from high school, because her oldest sister got married and moved to Oakland, California, and her mother needed Anna at home to help prepare food for the large hay crews, to can fruit and vegetables, and, no doubt, to baby-sit her youngest brother, Fritz.

After her marriage, Anna moved to the Dressler Ranch, just three miles down the road from her home. She and Fred had two children. As the wife of a rancher, she put all the skills she had learned at home to good use.

When Fred started a purebred Hereford herd, it was Anna who took charge of the tedious record keeping. Her knowledge of ranch operations and the cattle business led her to help organize the Western Nevada CowBelles, whose purpose was to promote the beef industry. In 1956, she was elected president of the American National CowBelles at their New Orleans convention.

On October 8, 1958, 44 women met in Elko to organize a Nevada State CowBelle group and chose Anna as their first president. They became affiliated with the American National CowBelles in 1959. (The name "CowBelles" was later changed to "Cattlewomen.") In 1982, at the age of 84, Anna was welcomed into the Hereford

1898–1987
RANCHER,
WOMEN'S CLUB MEMBER

Heritage Hall of Fame. Her picture was seen in numerous newspaper and magazine features, often shown with fellow beef industry promoters, state governors, and other well-known dignitaries.

Anna was instrumental in organizing a Mother's Club for mothers of students attending the Minden Grammar School. Her expertise in sewing was displayed in the many costumes she made for the school plays.

Along with Grace Dangberg, Anna was involved in organizing the Carson Valley Historical Society and was elected to serve as its first president. A favorite project was the restoration of the Genoa Courthouse into a museum.

Anna and Fred were active members of the Republican Party and hosted many parties "for the good of the Party."

Anna Dressler died in March of 1987 and is buried in the Mottsville Cemetery in Carson Valley at the foot of the Sierra Nevada Mountains that she loved.

—*Jean Ford*

Edna Crauch Trunnell Eddy

D r. Phillip Grable Trunnell and his wife, Harriet Virginia Hatzell Trunnell, of Louisville, Kentucky, had two children, Bradley H. Trunnell and Edna Crauch Trunnell. Edna attended the Nazareth School for Girls in Nazareth, Kentucky, and after her graduation was employed by the *Courier General* under Henry Watterson, a famous southern orator, statesman, and writer living in Louisville. Edna also studied nursing in Kentucky.

It was in 1898 in Chattanooga that Edna met Louis Byron Eddy, then a member of Company H, 7th U.S. Infantry, who would become her husband in Salt Lake City, Utah, on June 11, 1900, and whose name she would use for the rest of her life. Their only child, a son named Hallie, was born March 19, 1902. Although a divorce decree was never located, a second marriage to Edna Eddy was recorded on June 18, 1914, It was apparently a somewhat rocky marriage since a Complaint for Divorce was filed on May 5, 1917, another on May 11, 1917, and the final one on March 18, 1918, with a Decree of Divorce rendered on June 1, 1918, all in Humboldt County, Nevada.

1876–1962
EMBALMER, MORTICIAN

Edna Eddy also had a difficult time obtaining a Nevada State embalmer's license. In a letter of October 5, 1916, addressed to George E. Kitzmeyer, Secretary for the Nevada State Board of Embalmers in Carson City, she said that she had California State license No. 1224, and asked that it be transferred to Nevada so she wouldn't have to travel to Tonopah to take the required test. The letter also stated that she had a diploma from the Worsham School of Embalming in Chicago, Illinois and listed two professional references: Sid Evans, an undertaker in Salt Lake City, Utah, and Professor F. A. Sullivan, "who edits the Embalmer's Manual, published by St. Louis Coffin Co., St. Louis, Mo."

It was Nevada custom at that time to accept licenses from other states on a discretionary basis, but the board arbitrarily denied Edna's application. She sought the protection of the law and sued the Board of Embalmers, finally appealing to the Supreme Court of the State of Nevada. In Case No. 2273 of the January Term, 1917, the Supreme Court noted, in a long and interesting discussion of practices and language, that Edna had received a California license that required "a rigid written examination and actual demonstration on a cadaver," and so Mrs. Edna T. Eddy's certificate as an Embalmer was issued effective September 1909, and she became the first lady funeral director and mortician in Humboldt County and possibly in Nevada.

In 1915, Edna opened and operated the Eddy Funeral Parlor in Lovelock and later, when she learned that there was no funeral parlor in Winnemucca, she opened one there, too. Eddy's son, Hallie, became an active partner in the embalming business in 1925, and the name changed to "Edna T. Eddy & Son, Inc." Edna became Secretary of the State Board of Embalmers on July 9, 1927, in Reno. She obtained a chauffeur's license so she could transport deceased persons from other towns to her funeral parlors for embalming and burial. The last renewal of that license was in 1942 when she was age 66. In February 1943, Edna also began flight lessons through the Fillmore Flying School at the Winnemucca Airport; her last lesson there was logged on September 14, 1944.

On July 26, 1918, Edna married John C. Foster at the Lovelock Parsonage. Foster had been a resident of Nevada since 1906, first living in Rawhide, then becoming Lovelock postmaster in 1926, and state senator from Pershing County in 1936. He drafted the Resolution adopted by the Nevada legislature requesting that silver be included in the metal basis for our national coinage. Edna and John were divorced on March 17, 1926, and Foster died in a Reno hospital on

March 31, 1940. It is interesting to note that Edna was listed as a widow in Who's Who in Nevada, 1931–32, probably to avoid the political stigma attached to divorce in those days.

Edna was very active politically and ran unopposed for Pershing County Administrator in 1920 under her married name of Foster. In 1922 she resumed her former name of Eddy and began a four-year term, successfully running again in 1926. In 1930, 1934, and 1938, she ran unopposed as a Democrat for Humboldt County Administrator.

Edna served on the Pershing County School Board and was also very active in the Order of the Eastern Star Rebekah Lodge, eventually being initiated into the Past Matron's Association of that Order, as well as the Macabees, Women of Woodcraft, and the American Legion Auxiliary. The *Humboldt Star* frequently noted the dinner parties, "Dagwood Spreads," and other social events held in her "country home east of Winnemucca" during the early 1940s.

In the late 1940s, Edna purchased property in Placerville, California, and began to spend much of her time there at her home called "Yankee Jim's," finally giving up active interest in the funeral parlor around 1960. In 1962, she was confined to a hospital and later a convalescent home in Auburn, California, where she died on April 27th. Order of the Eastern Star Rebekah Lodge took charge of her final rites, and she was interred in the Masonic section of Winnemucca Cemetery.

—*Janet E. White*

Charlotte Rowberry Ellsworth

Charlotte Rowberry Ellsworth was a room reservation manager and executive at the Flamingo Hotel, Frontier Hotel, MGM Grand Hotel, and Bally's Grand Hotel from 1948 to 1998. Born in Cardston, Alberta, Canada, Charlotte was the daughter of Thomas Clark Rowberry and Jane Ann Hartley Rowberry, among the first group of Mormon farmers to settle in that region of Canada.

When Charlotte was two years old, her father died. Her mother, devastated by this loss, was unable to keep her portion of the family enterprise. She left Canada and struggled for the remaining years of her life to support and keep her three children, Hyram, John, and Charlotte, together. Survival became the family business, and Charlotte began working at the age of eight. When Jane cooked for road gangs and Salt Lake City fraternity houses, the three children assisted her in the work and then washed dishes for as many as 30 men three times a day. Charlotte was working in her school offices as soon as she was in high school.

Charlotte's mother was determined that Charlotte would attend the private L.D.S. High School and learn secretarial skills. As secretary to President Feramorz Young Fox, Charlotte mastered graciousness, tact, and the qualities of a true professional. So rigorous was Fox's tutelage that Charlotte maintained that no work was ever so hard again.

A quick study, Charlotte graduated from high school at the age of 17. Her mother died of cancer six weeks before the graduation ceremony. She had lived long enough to ensure each of her children a living. In Charlotte's case, her office skills carried her well through the Great Depression.

As the years passed, Charlotte worked in the Salt Lake City area and then spent a year in Washington, DC. While there, she renewed an acquaintance with Elmo H. Ellsworth. He had determined to marry her when they were both students at L.D.S. High School. Elmo had completed a mission, was working for the government and, at twenty-four years of age, finally convinced Charlotte to marry him. He transferred to San Francisco, California, and they were married there on October 16, 1936. A daughter, Jane, was born in 1938.

When World War II broke out, Elmo found work in Clark County at the newly constructed

1912–1998
Casino Manager

Basic Magnesium Plant. As there was no housing, he lived in the plant's tent city. Charlotte and Jane joined him in April. They found a room at the Walipai Lodge and stayed there until the Henderson homes were available. Their second daughter was born shortly after that move but was very ill and died at ten months of age.

Elmo's friend Jack Walsh suggested that Charlotte work for him at the El Rancho Hotel in Las Vegas. At the hotel she was given a "flunkey's job," helping out in any and all of the departments of the hotel. This would prove to be a wonderful opportunity. She learned the needs and demands of the entire hotel operation and soon became secretary to the president. When Sanford Alder took over the casino, Charlotte was made head of the room reservation department. The demands and details of the work were extraordinary and, according to Charlotte, one reservation manager was hauled to jail for overselling the hotel. She left the El Rancho to stay home and enjoy her new baby boy, John Elmo, who was born on May 18, 1947.

Charlotte had to be hospitalized for six months after the baby's birth. By the time she had recuperated, the family finances were stretched to the breaking point. Again, Jack Walsh called and wanted her at the new Flamingo Hotel. In November of 1948 she agreed to go to the Flamingo to manage the room reservations department.

She moved on to the Frontier Hotel in 1967, where she stayed for ten years. Elmo died in December of 1971, and so her work became a kind of refuge. At the age of 65 Charlotte was persuaded to join her associates for the opening of the MGM Grand Hotel in Reno, Nevada. She remained at the Grand until her retirement at the age of 76. She had been a room reservation manager for 40 years.

Charlotte had certain qualities that made her invaluable to hotel owners. She was willing to work 12- and 14-hour days, seven days a week, as many of the owners themselves did. She recognized the needs of the entire operation and gave balanced opinions that were always pointed to the success of the enterprise. She was loyal to her bosses, and they were very protective of her.

Stories of her brilliance and graciousness abound. Once, she went to one of her bosses to ask for raises for her staff. She was told that she could have the raise for herself or for her staff, not both. Charlotte chose the raise for "her girls." As the decades passed, she trained hundreds of men and women in the hotel business.

Charlotte could remember the guest's names, and many details about their lives. Guests loved her and hundreds became her personal friends.

—*Jane Ellsworth Olive*

Ruth Mary Cooper Ferron

Ruth Mary Cooper Ferron arrived in Las Vegas, Nevada, as a bride in 1917. What a shock it was for the young lady from Salt Lake City to arrive in the little desert town with "unpaved streets, wooden sidewalks, and scarcely any trees." But before long, Ruth Ferron was a part of the social and civic society of the town.

She was born Ruth Mary Cooper on July 20, 1893, in her grandmother's home in Minneapolis, Minnesota. Her father, William Payne Cooper, was from Towson, Maryland, and her mother, Mary Alice Thomas, was from Stowe, Vermont.

When Ruth was three years old, the family moved by train to Salt Lake City. The relatives viewed the Far West as so distant and unknown that they were fearful whether the family could survive. But Ruth's father had secured a job as the manager of the R.L. Polk Publishing Company in Salt Lake.

When Ruth was six years old she was enrolled in Rowland Hall, a private Episcopal school for girls, and stayed there through high school. Her class of 12 girls graduated in a ceremony at St. Mark's Cathedral in Salt Lake in June of 1912.

1893–1990
TEACHER

Ruth then enrolled in the University of Utah and completed her teaching degree in two years of Normal School training. She taught second grade for three years.

On February 7, 1917, at high noon, Ruth was married to William E. Ferron in St. Mark's Cathedral. He was a graduate of the Philadelphia College of Pharmacy and had just returned from three years as purchasing agent for a gold mining company in Colombia, South America, where his brother-in-law was superintendent.

William had saved some money and was looking for a place to begin a business for himself. He saw an ad in a pharmaceutical journal about a drugstore for sale in Las Vegas and took the train down to find out about it. Less than 2,000 people lived in Las Vegas at that time. He met Dr. Roy W. Martin and together in 1916 they bought the pharmacy on the corner of First and Fremont. The first floor was William's drugstore, and Dr. Martin's hospital was on the second floor. In 1916, pharmacists combined most medicinal ingredients by hand, since there were few ready-made drug preparations. This meant many long hours of preparation at the store.

The newlyweds settled in a tiny four-room rented stucco house on Third Street just off Fremont Street. The ladies of the town dressed up in their very best and called upon Ruth. Soon she was a part of the social life of the town.

Ruth had not been in Las Vegas very long when she was asked to play the part of Yum-Yum in the Gilbert and Sullivan comic opera *The Mikado*. The director traveled from town to town with a large van of costumes and scenery, using local talent in a benefit production.

The opera production was to raise money to promote the need for the Arrowhead Trail to go through Las Vegas. The new automobile route from Los Angeles was being proposed because in 1917 it was hard driving over a dusty road for two days through Searchlight and Needles.

Ruth's first child, Barbara, was born in March of 1918, and was followed by Shirley Elizabeth, born on December 15, 1919. In 1918, the Ferrons moved to a larger house at Fourth and Fremont. The Ferrons lived in this house for 24 years. In 1941 they built a new house at 1107 South Fifth Place.

In 1920, Ruth became a member of the Mesquite Club, a federated women's club dedicated to social, cultural, and philanthropic interests for the public welfare. Ruth was the club's President in 1922–1923.

During her presidency, the Mesquite Club gave a banquet for 300 people honoring a group of forty congressmen and their wives and Nevada Governor Scrugham. They were in Las Vegas to visit a site for the proposed Boulder Dam to be built on the Colorado River. Las Vegans took them in their best automobiles over the dirt-rutted road out to the river government campsite. Bill Ferron was one of the local dignitaries hosting the group. After viewing the Black Canyon site in boats, the visitors were brought to Beckley's Hall for the banquet. The Mesquite Club members had been busy cooking the meal in their own kitchens and then carrying the food to the hall. They set the sawhorse tables with their own best linens and table servings to impress the dignitaries.

Ruth Ferron was a gracious hostess and good cook. Ruth helped organize the Tuesday Bridge Club in 1918, which met for more than 60 years. She and her husband were charter members of the Knife and Fork Club, and she was a member of the first Delphian group, raising money for the new city library. She was also an active member of St. Agnes Guild of Christ Church Episcopal. Ruth served as a board member of the American Red Cross and supported cultural projects such as the Bird Cage Theatre and Community Concert Association.

—*Betty Miller*

Anna Mariza Fitch

Anna Mariza Fitch was born in Vermont in 1838. At an early age she became one of many people immigrating across the nation to California, where gold had been discovered in 1849. San Francisco was the art and cultural center of the West during the mid-1850s, and it was here, at the age of 20, that Anna founded and edited California's first woman's literary magazine, the *Hesperian*. It focused not only on literature but also on women's place in society, home, and family, as noted in this excerpt from its first edition:

"Woman holds in her hands the leading-strings to guide coming generations—and let her be equal to the task. Let her enlarge her apprehension, let her cultivate her range of thought, through the improvement of those divine gifts which may fit her for the fulfillment of her noble destiny…."

The year 1863 was a busy one for Anna. She divorced A.M. Schultz (about whom little is known) and married Thomas Edward Fitch, a lawyer, whose varied interests included politics, journalism, acting, architecture, and mining. He was also known as a prolific orator. When they married, Thomas had recently become a California Assemblyman and was to be involved in politics over the course of many years. Later that same year, the Fitches moved to Virginia City, Nevada. There they lived among such literary notables as Rollin Dagget, Dan DeQuille, Joseph Goodman, and Mark Twain. Here, Anna and Thomas published the *Weekly Occidental*. Years later, Twain would write humorously about the magazine that failed after only three issues. He refers to Anna as "Mrs. F" in his work *Roughing It*, apparently regarding her work as having little value and not to be taken too seriously: "An able romanticist of the ineffable school—I know no other name to apply to a school whose heroes are all dainty and all perfect."

Around 1865 the Fitches once again picked up roots, this time moving to Washoe City, Nevada, where they helped to found the Washoe Dramatic Association, Nevada's first amateur theatrical group. They both enjoyed acting in the productions, and it is believed Anna may have written for the group. It was during this time that she wrote several poems, among them a Lincoln eulogy entitled "The News" (not much

1838–1904
WRITER

appreciated by the critics) and "Song of the Flume." The latter was included in Bret Hart's anthology of Western poetry, *Outcroppings*, and once again in May Wentworth's *Poetry of the Pacific*. This poem depicts the necessity of running water and the flume to the mining industry.

It is obvious that, though Anna possessed no great talent, she did reveal a sincere love of writing. Her depth of emotion and patriotism is exhibited in "The Flag on Fire," a poem also included in Wentworth's anthology.

In 1869, Thomas was elected to Congress as a Nevada Representative, and while living in Washington, DC, Anna wrote a letter published in Virginia City's *Territorial Enterprise* maintaining that home and family should be uppermost in a woman's mind rather than suffrage and such worldly decisions as the Vote. Her philosophy, however, did not prevent her own literary pursuits, and in 1870 she wrote her first novel, *Bound Down, or, Life and Its Possibilities*. It was a typically Victorian book in keeping with the tenor of the day.

In the ensuing years, Anna wrote another play entitled *Items: A Washington Society Play*. It was based on her experiences as a Congressman's wife. A large part of Anna's life was devoted to traveling with Thomas. They journeyed from coast to coast and even to Hawaii. In an interview in 1881 with a New York newspaper, Anna

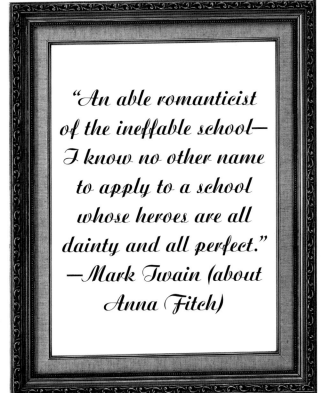

"*An able romanticist of the ineffable school—I know no other name to apply to a school whose heroes are all dainty and all perfect.*"
—*Mark Twain (about Anna Fitch)*

told of crossing the country 36 times by stage and rail, and one trip to California by ship. The traveling however did not slow her writing, and her second novel, *Better Days: Or a Millionaire of Tomorrow*, was published in 1891. It seems time had mellowed Anna's strong feelings about women's rights and civil needs. A passage from the book as spoken by Ellen (one of the principals) illustrates this point:

"Many years ago I conceived a prejudice against the popular cry concerning the wrongs of woman, a movement affirmatively named 'woman's rights,' for while it undoubtedly aided some women obtaining justice, its aim was largely the gratification of some hysterical ambition or some love of conspicuousness."

Anna caught the changing tide of the day and *Better Days* became one of her more popular works. It remained in print until 1912. As the years passed, her production of work decreased, and Anna died at the age of 66 in Los Angeles, California.

Anna Mariza Fitch faced the social constructions of her day and in true pioneer spirit overcame both physical and emotional obstacles to pursue her heart's desire—to write and to publish. Her body of work, though not widely acclaimed, was diverse and plentiful. She was a woman to admire, respect, and remember.
—*Lynn Murphy*

Imogene (Jean) Evelyn Young Ford

Jean Ford was a wife, mother, and home-maker when she arrived in Nevada without fanfare in 1962. Raised to fill a traditional woman's role, Jean expected nothing more than to find a home where her husband could work as a dermatologist, her daughters could attend school, and she could enjoy a community of friends and neighbors. Fortunately for Nevada, Jean adopted her new state with gusto. First, she explored it, from the Strip in Las Vegas to the backroads of ghost towns, ranches, mines, and wilderness areas. She camped and hiked with her family, and grew to love everything about Nevada, with its scenic desert vistas and colorful wildflowers.

Next, Jean became involved. In discovering Nevada she saw things that needed to be improved, so she volunteered to help with various projects, such as preserving Red Rock Canyon as a park and creating the Clark County Library. From volunteer and citizen activ-ist, Jean quickly moved into the Nevada legisla-ture, serving first in the Nevada State Assembly (1972–1976) and then in the Nevada State Senate (1978–1982). Between those two legislative terms, she earned a master's degree in public administra-tion from the University of Nevada–Las Vegas. Improving the legislative system intrigued Jean, and she fought for openness in government. She supported the Equal Rights Amendment, and, after that was defeated, she helped introduce a variety of bills to eliminate discrimination based on sex and to create services for women. Those were just a few of the issues she addressed while serving in the legislature, but her interest in Nevada did not end with her final senate term.

Following her days in the legislature, Jean contin-ued traveling throughout the state and serving Nevada in many capacities, from public servant and private entrepreneur to educator. Her list of accomplishments includes:

1929–1998
POLITICIAN, TEACHER, COMMUNITY ACTIVIST

- Director of community relations for the Clark County Library, 1979–1980
- Owner of a consulting business and co-owner of Nevada Discovery Tours, 1981–1986
- Appointment by Governor Richard Bryan to the first Nevada Commission on Tourism and Economic Development in 1983
- Director of Nevada Office of Community Services, 1985–1989.

In 1991, Jean temporarily filled the position of director of the Women's Studies Program at the University of Nevada–Reno. When she discovered a lack of information on Nevada women, Jean proposed a statewide campaign to create the Nevada Women's Archives at the Special Collections Department of the University of Nevada library. She completed the bibliography to the collection before she died.

Through this work, she became immersed in recovering Nevada women's history, and she discovered many with like interests. By February 1996, Jean had co-founded the Nevada Women's History Project (NWHP), a private, nonprofit organization under the umbrella of the Nevada Women's Fund. The NWHP was designed to gather and disseminate information about the roles, accomplishments, and activities of Nevada women from every race, class, and ethnic background who contributed to shaping the state's destiny.

Jean started her life in Nevada as wife, mother, and homemaker. Over the years, she expanded her role to include citizen activist, legislator, businesswoman, public figure, educator, mentor, and role model. She contributed greatly to the legacy of Nevada.

—*Victoria Ford*

Katie Christy Frazier

Katie Christy Frazier, a member of the Pyramid Lake Paiute Tribe, was widely known throughout Nevada. She received many awards in recognition of her work, among them National Indian Educator of the Year in 1985, the Governor's Award for Excellence in Folk Arts in 1986, and Outstanding Senior Citizen of the Year in 1989.

When Katie was born, Indian births were not yet officially recorded. It was still early in the settling of northwestern Nevada by the white man. Katie's grandmother had grown up in the old ways, when The People (Nimi) were free to go about in their own land as they pleased. Katie was close to her grandmother, and they slept side by side together under a rabbit-skin blanket. For many years, Katie spoke only her native language, Northern Paiute. Because she had been born prematurely, she was small for her age and was called Titzipoona, which means "small and very lively."

Her mother and grandmother, like many other Native Americans at that time, worked for white settlers to supplement the dwindling supply of wild foods available to them. Yet the family preferred to follow the old ways when it could, and in the summer they might be found encamped with relatives near the shores of Pyramid Lake or digging camus (yapa) on the Madeline Plains to the north. In the fall, they traveled north to the Pine Nut Range for the pine nut harvest. Winters were spent in Honey Lake Valley, where acorns, game, and wood for fires were abundant, and ranch work could be obtained. Their winter home was the same efficient construction that had been in use for thousands of years, the conical willow house (kani) built anew each year by Katie's mother.

By 1900, the population of white settlers in Nevada had exploded, and the Northern Paiutes who survived years of deprivation and disease were pushed onto reservations. Titzipoona had been given another name, one that could be written in English, Katie Christy, and she was required by state law to go to a military-style boarding school for Indian children. Established by the Nevada State Legislature in 1887, Carson Indian School (later renamed Stewart Indian School) operated under a federal policy to acculturate and educate Indian children to the ways of the white world. Katie was about eight years old when, in 1900, her mother took her to Carson and left her.

1891–1991
EDUCATOR, ARTIST

74

Following her graduation in 1908, Katie married John Hicks, and they had three children. She worked for white families in Virginia City and Reno; in 1918, John Hicks enlisted in WWI. Their marriage ended after the long separation caused by the war, and in 1921, Katie moved to the Pyramid Lake Paiute Reservation. She later married her second husband, Harrison Frazier, and they had four children together.

Katie was an enthusiastic advocate for the traditional Indian ways, not only because she enjoyed them, but because it was important to her that knowledge of the Northern Paiute culture be passed on. In 1989, she said this about dancing:

"I just love to dance! I'd be dancing yet today if I could. Us Indians used to have lots of dances here at Pyramid Lake. A long time ago, people would come from all around and make a big camp by the Truckee River where Wadsworth is now, and they would circle dance a whole week. People did this in the fall, before they went to the mountains to pick pine nuts. They were dancing for a good harvest. Pine nuts meant a lot to us because it was our winter food. I was little then, but I remember how the dance kept going, night and day. Some dancers would go off to rest, but the dance kept going. Us children would always run and play. Sometimes we'd get into mischief! In the winter, people would come to fish along the river where it goes into the lake, and they danced then too. Later some of us here at Pyramid Lake formed a dancing group. We danced at pageants and ceremonies, hospitals and schools, wherever we were invited. My husband was the singer. We did the Antelope Dance, the Owl Dance, the Bear Dance, lots of dances."

Katie Frazier's life is a fascinating saga of survival during a period of rapid and drastic change. Whether tanning deer hide to make cradleboards and moccasins, or teaching dances, songs, and the Paiute language to schoolchildren at Pyramid Lake, Katie embodied strength, practicality, and wisdom. Those who knew her remember another delightful quality: her droll sense of humor and wit.

On August 5, 1991, Katie spent most of the day stitching together squares of cloth, making another of her beautiful patchwork quilts. She had recently celebrated her 100th birthday, and both Nevada Senator Richard Bryan and President George Bush had sent engraved cards of congratulations. She joked, "Well, I'm glad they know how old I am, and I might be older though." At that advanced age, her health was still good: she read, sewed, and loved to go places. In July, she had gone with her family to Fallon to spend the day at the All-Indian Rodeo. And so, on August 5th, a Tuesday, when the time came and Katie was called Home, she went easily and gently, smiling.

—JoAnne Peden

Maude Frazier

The pioneering spirit was bred into Maude. She was born on a farm in Sauk County, Wisconsin. Her Scottish heritage and her environment stressed self-sufficiency and resourcefulness. Maude was subjected to the stern discipline of the late 19th-century educational system, and this gave her the foundation she would need to deal with the wide-open spaces of Nevada.

Maude graduated from the State Teacher's College and began her teaching career in a small Wisconsin town. Soon she began writing letters of application to schools in the west and was offered a teaching principalship in Genoa, Nevada. The fact that she couldn't even find Genoa on a map did not deter her. She boarded the train for Reno, then on to Minden, the end of the railway line. Next was a horse-drawn coach to Genoa. Her new position was principal and teacher of the upper grades in a two-teacher school.

Her early Nevada teaching career took her to Lovelock, a new mining camp at Seven Troughs. Maude next went to Beatty for $100 a month,

1881–1963
TEACHER, LEGISLATOR,
LIEUTENANT GOVERNOR

but the mining activities in Beatty were slowing, and in 1912 she moved to Goldfield. In 1917, she had her first administrative job as principal of the Sundog School. All the mines were in a slump, and Maude took advantage of an opportunity to go to Sparks, where she became a member of a 19-teacher staff. In 1920 she was named principal of the Sparks Eementary School.

Because of changes in the State Department of Education, new administrative positions became available, and Maude, always eager for advancement and adventure, applied for the position of supervisor over the public schools of Lincoln, Clark, Esmaralda, and Nye Counties, an area of 40,390 square miles. In 1921, to the amazement of the male candidates, Maude was selected for this assignment. The area to be covered was desolate, hot, virtually inaccessible, and a challenge even for a seasoned man. Maude was undaunted by all the skeptics; she was no longer a "tenderfoot girl from the east."

To meet the requirements of her new position of supervising 75 schools in 63 school districts,

with an enrolment of 2,824, Maude purchased a Dodge Roadster and a set of tools, took a course in auto mechanics, and went forth to fulfill her assignment. She traveled the deputy superintendent's circuit for six years. In 1927 she was the logical choice to become the superintendent of the Las Vegas Union School District, and principal of Las Vegas High School. Maude was responsible for many innovative programs and initiated the first major permanent building for Las Vegas, after the construction of the county courthouse.

The Boulder Dam project was approved not long after, and an increase in student enrollment was inevitable. A school bond issue was passed that provided the $350,000 needed to build the "ultra-modern" Las Vegas High School at 7th and Bridger. During Maude's administration, six new elementary schools were constructed and there were many additions to the existing ones. Maude served as superintendent of Clark County Schools through the growth period before and after World War II, finally retiring in 1947.

Even though Maude had planned on relaxing and just taking it easy, she found that it was not the life for her. In 1948 she ran for the state legislature but was not elected. In 1950 she again ran and led the ticket from Clark County. She was appointed to the committee for education and became known as a champion of public education. She was instrumental in getting the appropriations to establish a branch of the state university in Las Vegas. The first building on the new Nevada Southern University campus (now UNLV) was named in her honor. In 1955 she received an honorary doctorate of letters from the University of Nevada.

On July 13, 1962, at the age of 81, Maude was appointed Lieutenant Governor of the state to replace Rex Bell, who had died in office. This was the highest political position ever occupied by a woman in the state.

Maude Frazier died in her sleep on June 20, 1963. Governor Grant Sawyer said: "I was shocked and greatly saddened by the news of Maude Frazier's death. In her long career of public service, I can think of no one who contributed more to the welfare of the citizens of Nevada."

—*Jean F. Spiller*

Mary Freeman

In 1875, Mary Freeman—daughter of John Watt and Hannah Swain—was born into one of the most prominent families in Woodland, California. Her Freeman ancestors were pioneers who had followed the American adventure, moving from Virginia to Kentucky to Missouri and, finally, to California. Her father, a veteran of the Mexican War, had headed for the goldfields and established himself in Yolo County as a man with extensive land holdings and a profitable ranching and mercantile business.

Mary's mother had come to California from Michigan. She became a teacher and also settled in Yolo County. Her marriage to John Freeman brought her into a family that was a major force in the social, political, cultural, and economic circle in Woodland. It was into this vibrant and active life that Mary Freeman was born.

When Mary was twelve, her father bought into a cattle and sheep ranch in Stillwater, Nevada, where the family enjoyed extended visits while still maintaining their home base in Woodland. Although she was used to a more sophisticated environment, Mary learned to appreciate the rural life in Stillwater.

1875–1923
PHOTOGRAPHER

As a member of the first family of Woodland, Mary was educated at local schools and then entered Stanford University, receiving a B.S. degree in 1897. Then, like many young ladies from her social background, she embarked on a grand tour of Europe, where she recorded her experiences in sketches. Upon her return, she spent summers at the Freeman ranch in Stillwater, returning to California during the colder weather.

Mary and her mother spent long periods of time there, taking advantage of the city's cultural offerings, including a study of literature under the tutelage of a Professor Morrow.

Mary Freeman married late for a privileged young woman of her time. But the years before her marriage were busy ones that saw her commuting between the family ranch in Nevada's high desert, the lush surroundings of Woodland, and the cultural life of San Francisco.

Mary made several new friends during her years visiting San Francisco, but she also reacquainted herself with people from Woodland. One of those people was Edward M. Armstrong, a prosperous businessman and mining engineer who had been raised in Placerville. Mr. Armstrong had lived in Woodland for a number of years, first making a success in the nursery business and then amassing a fortune from mining investments. He had moved to San Francisco to attend business school. He had married, but his wife died of cancer. After her death, he traveled widely through the gold country, enjoying his financial success. His sophistication and wealth made him a suitable marriage prospect for the daughter of one of Woodland's first families.

Mary Freeman's marriage to Armstrong lasted fifteen months, much of it spent on the east coast, with an extended stay in Chicago. When they returned to Woodland for the winter of 1903–1904, Mary's husband became involved in a legal dispute concerning a mine. While traveling by train to Auburn, Edward Armstrong was shot and killed at point blank range by a man who claimed that Armstrong had brought him to financial ruin.

Following the death of her husband, Mary continued to travel between her homes in Woodland and Stillwater, with frequent stops in San Francisco. During this time, she met a local news reporter named J. Hammond Crabbe. A native of Prince Edward Island, Crabbe had moved with his family to Chico, California, where he received a public school education followed by an entry into the newspaper business. He later studied law in Berkeley and San Francisco, and served as an apprentice in the law offices of John O'Gara. He and Mary wed in 1908 in San Francisco, and in 1910, Crabbe was admitted to

"Her artistic touch and her 'joie de vivre' live on in her photographic glimpses of life in Stillwater."
—Dr. Catherine S. Fowler

the California State Bar. The couple bought a home on Washington Street, where Mary lived until her death in 1923.

Mary had started photographing her father's ranch in the 1890s and early 1900s. Although she did not live there full-time, her photographs are an eloquent chronicle of life in turn-of-the-century Stillwater. Her Stillwater years seem to have been a relaxed phase. And her photographs reflect not only life on a substantial cattle and sheep ranch but are permanent records of the Paiute people. Dr. Catherine S. Fowler says of Mary Freeman's photographs, "Her artistic touch and her *joie de vivre* live on in her photographic glimpses of life in Stillwater."

In 1992, Dr. Fowler, professor in the department of anthropology at the University of Nevada, published a book about the Northern Paiutes of Stillwater Marsh. In the course of researching her book, she found photographs of Mary Freeman's examination of everyday life on the family ranch. Dr. Fowler used some of the photographs—the first time they had ever been published. Although Dr. Fowler focused on Mary's studies of Indians in transition, Churchill County Museum staff members located the original Freeman album in Fallon and were able to view many other subjects that Mary had captured on film. The result of this discovery was the first catalog and traveling exhibit of Mary's work.
    —*Fran Haraway*

Frances Gertrude Friedhoff

Frances Gertrude Price was born at Stockton, California, on June 9, 1895, but came to Carson City, Nevada, at an early age. While Frances was quite young, her mother died, and Frances was raised as a member of the family of former Governor R.K. Colcord. She received her early education in the schools of California, Oregon, and Nevada, and later attended the University of Nevada.

Frances married George W. Friedhoff in 1912 and moved to Yerington, where her husband was active in the construction business and operated several ranch properties. They had one son, George, Jr., who also attended the University of Nevada and returned to live in Yerington.

Her public activities were numerous. For the entire duration of World War I, Frances served on the Council of Defense and the Red Cross, and as secretary of the Lyon County Four-Minute Men.

1895–1958
POLITICIAN,
CIVIC ACTIVIST

Frances represented agriculture and home economics education on the State Board of Vocational Education for 12 years. In 1921, she was appointed by President Harding to represent Nevada at the Agricultural Conference called by the President in Washington, DC, one of the sixteen women appointed throughout the United States.

In 1924, Frances was elected as a delegate from Nevada to the National Democratic Party convention in New York. From 1924 to 1928 she served as Democratic national committeewoman for Nevada.

Frances was elected the first State President of the Home Makers' Clubs of the Nevada State Farm Bureau, serving for two years, and in 1928 was a member of the State Advisory Board for that organization. Later, she was a member of the National Speakers' Bureau of the American Farm Bureau Federation and attended several National Conventions.

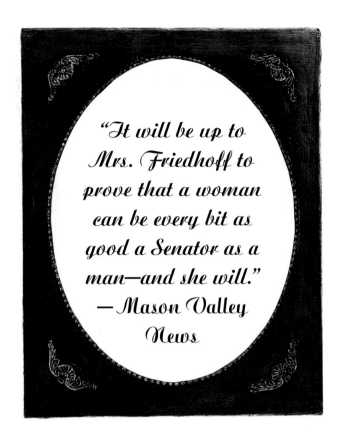

"It will be up to Mrs. Friedhoff to prove that a woman can be every bit as good a Senator as a man—and she will."
— Mason Valley News

She was a charter member of the American Legion Auxiliary, Lyon County Unit #9, serving the local unit and department in every capacity.

Frances served many stations during her years of membership in the Order of the Eastern Star, culminating in her election as Worthy Grand Matron in June, 1928.

In March 1935, Frances' husband, in his third term as a State Senator representing Lyon County, resigned his position to accept a federal appointment as Nevada's Federal Housing Administrator. The following week, the Lyon County Commission appointed Frances to succeed him in his Senate post, and she was sworn in on March 16 as the first woman to serve in the State Senate.

A March 22 article in the *Mason Valley News* stated: "The list of ladies who have been elected to the Nevada Assembly and who have made fine records in that legislative body is quite long . . . . It will be up to Mrs. Friedhoff to prove that a woman can be every bit as good a Senator as a man—and she will."

Frances's particular interest that session was in the advancement and betterment of rural schools. On being asked her stand on the pending assembly bill regarding the state assuming the medical and financial care of expectant mothers, she stated that she favored any legislation that was beneficial to the welfare of womanhood. She would not state definitely her stand on any pending measures but promised to act as much as possible in the way the people would have had her husband act.

Frances became a semi-invalid in her later years, which stopped her public appearances, but her Red Cross record in World War II showed that "many hours were spent working to be of use to the world." Frances Gertrude Friedhoff died on March 8, 1958, in Reno and was buried in the Masonic section of Mountain View cemetery.

—*Jean Ford*

Dr. Mary Hill Fulstone

Mary Hill was born in Eureka, Nevada, the second child of John and Ella Riley Hill. John Hill worked for Reinhold Sadler as manager of his large mercantile store. After Sadler became governor of the state, he offered Mr. Hill a position as head of the commissary at the Nevada State Prison, so the Hill family moved to Carson City in 1896.

Mary's elementary education began at the North Ward School and then Central School. She graduated from Carson High with the class of 1911 and enrolled that fall at the University of California–Berkeley. While at Berkeley, Mary changed her career aspirations from math teacher to medical doctor. After graduating from medical school in 1918, she served her residency period at San Francisco's County Hospital and Children's Hospital. The nationwide flu epidemic hit San Francisco hard that year. Mary remembered that period as "a dreadful time," one that she could never forget. Mothers and children would arrive in the morning and be dead before nightfall. In those days, there was little any doctor could do to help a person stricken with this particularly virulent form of the flu.

In July 1919, Mary married Fred Fulstone. When she finished with her training, Mary moved to Fred's ranch. The 600-acre ranch sat in the heart of the valley and was the center of Fred's sheep ranching operation.

Fred Jr. was born in 1920 in the house where the family lived. Over the next nine years, four more children—David, Richard, and twin girls Eleanor and Jeannie—were delivered in the Children's Hospital in San Francisco.

Dr. Fulstone's career as a medical doctor began slowly but grew steadily. There are conflicting accounts regarding her acceptance at the beginning of her career. One account states that at first "none of the white people in the valley would have dreamed of seeking her services." But in her oral history, Fulstone gives an opposite view: "On the whole, I think the people in Smith Valley started right in and came here." Before Mary arrived in the valley, the nearest doctor was 25 miles away in Yerington. Most residents were pleased to have a local doctor, although there was no doubt some resistance to a female doctor.

1892–1987
PHYSICIAN,
EDUCATION ACTIVIST

Dr. Mary, as she was called, had a government contract to care for the Indians. She was paid $90 per month to minister to the Indians in a wide-ranging area that took her out of the valley to Topaz, Coleville, Bridgeport, and Sweetwater. One major function was delivering babies, but she also performed many other duties. Mary was never satisfied when her work could not produce a positive outcome.

Since modern antibiotics had not been introduced at that time, she had little more than morphine, chloroform, and aspirin to relieve pain. Many died from illnesses that today could be easily treated. Mary's house had no electric lights, and the nearest phone was in Wellington. According to one tale, even though Dr. Mary had one of the few cars in the valley, at times the roads were poor and nearly impassable, so she occasionally made house calls with the old reliable horse and buggy.

During the depression of the 1920s and 1930s, cash was scarce for the farmers in the valley. Patients who could not afford to pay would trade animals or other farm products for Mary's services. The family also traded her fees for goods from the local merchants. Mary never refused treatment to anybody based upon their ability to pay. Some say that she did not even begin formal billing until sometime during the 1950s.

Starting about 1938, Mary began traveling to Yerington three days a week due to a shortage of doctors. In the early 1950s, Mary began a crusade to get a new hospital built in Yerington, and in 1954, the voters passed the bond issue that authorized it. One wing of the Lyon Health Center was later named the "Doctor Mary."

Because of her deep interest in education, Mary was elected to the county school board. Despite resistance, her first major project was to consolidate the several small schools in Smith Valley into one central school. Dr. Mary considered that one of her major achievements. Later, she was elected to the Nevada State Board of Education to continue her interest in improving education.

After 60 years, Dr. Mary Fulstone formally retired at age ninety-one with the distinction of being the longest-practicing physician in the state. Even then she did not willingly quit, but glaucoma had been narrowing her vision for years and finally made it impossible to continue.

Dr. Mary was Nevada's Mother of the Year in 1950 and Nevada's Doctor of the Year in 1961, and was named a Distinguished Nevadan by the University of Nevada in 1964. She was a member of state and county medical societies, and active in the civic and educational organizations of Smith Valley and Yerington.

Mary Hill Fulstone died at her home in December 1987. She left behind five children and eleven grandchildren. She was a true Nevada pioneer woman who broke down barriers, fought for causes, and remained dedicated to her family and her profession.

—*Terry Bunkowski; Nancy Sansone, ed.*

Laura Kitchen Garvin

Edward Noles Kitchen, father of Laura, left his family home in Mt. Pleasant, Iowa, when he was 16, and made his way to Goldfield, Nevada, arriving during the mining boom of 1904. Laura's mother was visiting friends in Lida in 1912 and met Mr. Kitchen. They were soon married, and Laura was born a year later. She was the first of three children, the only white children in town. In 1913, Goldfield had a population of about 20,000. Most of the time the family lived in Lida, 30 miles from Goldfield. Laura's parents spent the rest of their lives in the area.

In an autobiographical article by Laura, "What It Was Like to Grow Up," she reminisces about Lida. It was the "...home of a fairly large cattle spread, had a post office and general store, an Indian camp and a scattering of cabins, and various old bachelors." Her mother had an Indian girl helper for a couple of years, and Laura and her brother and sister learned as many Shoshone words as English. There was a doctor and a drugstore 30 miles away and no fresh milk. "You can't milk range cows." The family seldom had fresh meat except for her mother's chickens or the rabbits her father shot. For holidays, her father killed a turkey, and her mother cooked a company dinner and invited the "old fellows."

Laura started school at four, because Nevada law required at least five students to start a school, and there were only four in the area. The teacher and Laura's mother decided that Laura could drop out in a few weeks after the school was established, but later the teacher asked her mother to let Laura stay because she was doing so well.

When Laura was seven, the family moved to Hornsilver, 20 miles away, where her father was the mine manager. They had a larger house, larger school, and playmates. The biggest drawback was that water had to be hauled from Lida at $2 a barrel, a lot of money for water in 1920.

Laura and her siblings loved the freedom of living in Hornsilver. They roamed the desert for hours, and if they kept very quiet they could watch the wild animals drink from the depression in the limestone hills where rainwater collected. Hornsilver had only an eight-month school, so the students had to go to Goldfield for one month to pass their grades. The family moved back and forth from Hornsilver to Goldfield to accommodate the children's school requirements.

1913–2000
NURSE

When Laura started high school the family moved to Goldfield permanently since there was no high school in Hornsilver.

Goldfield was no longer a booming mining town. The mines and mills were closing. In 1929, when Laura graduated from high school, the population had dropped from 20,000 to around 2,500. There were no jobs or future in the area, especially for girls. On a summer visit to Los Angeles, Laura saw a tall white building on a hill and was told it was the Queen of Angels Hospital. Laura had always loved reading books about nurses and decided that she wanted to be one. Since Laura was only 16, and the age requirement for nursing school was 18, the school principal and the doctor in Goldfield made the six look like an eight on the school application. Laura entered nurse's training in the fall.

Laura completed her training in the early 1930s at Queen of Angels Hospital. Her first job was at the Boulder City Hospital. Construction on the Hoover Dam had recently begun, and the nurses worked ten-hour days, seven days a week, and were paid $8 a month. In addition to the work-related injuries, there was a lot of pneumonia and flu among the dam workers and the Boulder City residents.

The Depression was in full swing, and there were bread lines in Las Vegas. Laura recalled that the road between Las Vegas and the Dam had many bars and gambling clubs. Liquor was illegal, but the locals know when the "revenuers" were coming and closed up shop until they were gone.

Laura remembered the early days in Las Vegas, especially the swimming pool at the Stewart Ranch. The Nevada Test Site was responsible for a large payroll in the area, but in those days the only hotels on the Strip were the El Rancho and the Flamingo.

Later, Laura worked at the Tonopah Mines and was director of nursing at the Las Vegas Hospital until it closed in 1974. She moved to Southern Nevada Memorial Hospital before retiring from nursing at Saint Rose de Lima Hospital in October 1979.

Laura attended UNLV during the 1960s. She was an avid reader and student of history.

Laura's husband, Don Garvin, had lived in Goldfield from 1934 to 1938. He was born north of Reno, in California, and educated in Oakland. Don worked as an engineer in Los Angeles, and the couple lived there during World War II before returning to Las Vegas in 1946. Don was Chief Engineer at the Flamingo from 1947 to 1972 and worked there until his retirement in 1979. The couple had four children: two daughters and twin sons.

—*Jean F. Spiller*

Wuzzie George

Wuzzie George, a Northern Paiute woman, learned tribal customs from her grandmother and spent an important part of her life working to preserve those tribal traditions by teaching and demonstrating her skills and knowledge. She also preserved Paiute customs through her work with Nevada anthropologist Margaret Wheat. Wuzzie was born sometime between 1880 and 1883 to Sam and Suzie Dick, who were in the Nevada mountains on a fall pine-nut gathering expedition. Her Paiute name was Wizii, which means "Small Animal" and is pronounced similarly to Wuzzie, the white man's version of her name. Her ancestors were of the group of Paiutes called "Cattail-Eaters."

During her childhood she lived near "Indian Village," about 60 miles east of Reno near the Carson Desert. Wuzzie's grandparents, who were known as Stovepipe and Mattie, played a major role in shaping her life.

Wuzzie's father Sam Dick worked for a rancher named Charles Kaiser herding sheep, building fences and laboring as a general ranch hand. Wuzzie's mother Suzie washed dishes at

BETWEEN
1880 & 1883—1984
ARTIST

John Sanford's hotel in Stillwater. While her mother worked, Wuzzie spent her days with Grandmother Mattie, who taught Wuzzie the traditional skills of the "Cattail-Eaters."

Wuzzie and Grandmother Mattie began each day by gathering greasewood for the hotel's kitchen stove. In exchange, they were given breakfast. Afterwards, they spent their days walking to the sloughs and rivers to fish. They gathered berries and tules, dug roots, and collected pine pollen and honeydew from the cane. Wuzzie learned to make the baskets that were used to carry water, berries, nuts, and seeds, and her grandmother taught her how to hunt ducks and gather duck eggs.

While they worked, Grandmother Mattie told Wuzzie stories about her life and her tribe's first contact with whites, such as this one:

"Before the [1860] war at Pyramid Lake, the Indians lived in tule houses for miles along the Carson Slough. Indians lived everyplace. Smoke all over when Indians built their fires in morning. When the soldiers threw poison in river lots of them died. My people stay in the mountains that time. That's what my grandma and grandpa always say. Stay over there on the mountains all winter, make

86

house over there on mountain. That's why they never catch it, the poison. We call that place, where Indians died, 'people's bones' . . . ."

When Wuzzie was ten years old, her parents separated. Wuzzie moved away from her grandmother and went with her mother Suzie to the Ernst ranch. There she worked for white people for the first time. Her job was to iron towels, and being a small child, she had to stand on a box to reach the ironing board. She also watched a herd of sheep. Her wages were ten cents a day, which she spent on candy at Jim Richard's store. Mrs. Ernst talked to Wuzzie while she worked, so Wuzzie began to learn English.

When her mother died, Wuzzie's father took her to live with his mother in Virginia City. She was not there long before she was taken to Carson City to enroll in the new Indian School, but her father removed her from school after just six months, fearing an epidemic of measles would harm her. "That is why I never got my schooling," Wuzzie told Margaret Wheat. Her father took her home to Fallon, and she returned to her grandmother's instruction.

Between 1909 and 1915, Wuzzie's life went through several changes. She married and divorced her first husband, Joe Springer. Their two children stayed with their father. Wuzzie then worked at a restaurant owned by a Chinese man. It was there that she met Jimmy George, and they were married a year later. After the restaurant burned down, Wuzzie went to work in the home

of Marge Harmon, a job she continued off and on until 1928.

Wuzzie and Jimmy had eight children together, and five survived to adulthood. Jimmy worked as a ranch hand, but he also had another important calling as a medicine man or shaman. For about 40 years, Jimmy worked as a doctor and treated more than 1,000 people. Wuzzie traveled with him and served as his interpreter until he lost his "powers" in the mid-1950s.

At about that same time, Wuzzie and Jimmy began working with anthropologist Margaret Wheat to document the Paiute culture. Wheat's book *Survival Arts of the Primitive Paiutes* features Wuzzie harvesting pine nuts, making cradleboards for babies out of willows, and working with her husband to make a house of willows. The book also shows traditional Paiute fishing with hand-made harpoons and making items like a boat and duck decoy out of cattails and tules, cordage for nets out of hemp, blankets from rabbit skins, and clothing from soft plant fibers.

Her work was filmed, and many of the items she made are still in the Nevada State Museum in Carson City and the Churchill County Museum in Fallon.

Wuzzie was reportedly 104 years old when she died on December 20, 1984. Wuzzie guarded and saved the traditions of "the old ones" to pass on to future generations.

—*Victoria Ford*

Mary Louise Grantz

Mary Louise Grantz (originally "Grenz") was born on December 4, 1879 to German parents who farmed at Tigerton, Wisconsin. According to author Sally Zanjani, Mary couldn't wait to leave the farm, and early in her life began working for a local doctor. A scandal brewed when she was accused of having an affair with the doctor, and Mary left town in disgrace with her sister Emma. The two moved to Florida where they both became hairdressers. From there, they moved to Montana, where Mary's brother Walter and his wife had homesteaded a ranch near Butte. Emma got a job teaching at a nearby school and then met and married a shoemaker. The couple returned to Wisconsin, but Mary stayed in Montana with her brother and his family.

Records indicate that she probably met her first husband in Montana. Joseph P. "Perry" Clough formed a corporation while in Montana called the Northern Nevada Charleston Hill Mining Corporation. It seems that Mary and Perry both moved to Nevada at about the same time, because when Mary staked her first claims in 1919, Perry

1879–1970
MINING PROMOTER,
PROSPECTOR

also had claims recorded, and it wasn't long before they were married.

Mary and her husband were very aggressive in promoting their Nevada mining property, as well as real estate they owned in Florida, Arizona, Seattle, and California. They traveled on promotional tours, enjoying the good life along the way. Mary was known for always being well-dressed and for buying expensive clothing and jewelry. Perhaps it was her taste for riches that earned her the nickname "Queen Mary." Or perhaps it was her unapproachable personality that made people give her this title.

No doubt her promotional efforts did not help her reputation. Relatives who invested and lost money were not complimentary to Mary. Her sister Emma brought her family back to Nevada to help operate the Charleston Hill Mine. They were struggling to make a living while Mary was enjoying the high-life on her promotional tours. Finally, Emma and her family moved to Seattle, where Emma succumbed to cancer. Mary's family was so disgusted with her that her father refused to have anything more to do with her.

Perhaps it was her taste for riches that earned her the nickname "Queen Mary." Or perhaps it was her unapproachable personality that made people give her this title.

But by the late 1930s, Mary's situation had changed. Perry had died, and their mines were not producing. To earn a living, Mary moved to San Francisco and worked as a housekeeper.

Like many others, her fortunes took a turn for the better with the arrival of World War II. Suddenly, the world needed magnesium and tungsten, and Mary had mines that could produce them. Her Black Diablo mine produced an estimated 90,000 tons of magnesium and may have earned her as much as $150,000. However, true to the gambling nature of miners, Mary lost most of her new fortune through further prospecting. One of her prospecting partners, Duane Devine, described Mary's prospecting method to author Zanjani: "Mary would work her way up a gulch or a hillside, looking for float, trying to trace any float she found to a ledge, doubling back when the disappearance of specimens suggested that the ledge might be somewhere behind her.... She was pretty wise on that line. She done pretty good on that for a lady. And she wasn't scared—she was a working little scamp. . . . No grass growed under her."

In spite of her mining knowledge, Mary was known around Winnemucca as a woman who kept to herself. Alienated from most of her family, she had grown close to her brother's son, Leon. When Leon married, Mary apparently took offense and was then left with only one niece who stayed in contact with her. June, daughter of Emma, made an annual visit to the Charleston Mine. For companionship, Mary finally married Max Magnussen, a handsome man who was 25 years younger than her. She also continued to lose money on her mines by making large, unwise investments in equipment that she thought would help her mines become productive.

During this period of time, another woman miner, Josie Pearl, was also operating in the area around Winnemucca. Local residents agree the two were competing on some level to be the best woman miner in the area, a competition to become the "Queen Bee," according to Zanjani. Although Mary's World War II successes won the competition for wealth, Pearl's easier personality eventually resulted in more recognition and fame.

—*Victoria Ford*

Glenn Edna Park Grier

In 1935, Glenn Edna Grier became White Pine County's only woman representative to the Nevada State Legislature, sitting as an Assemblywoman during the 37th session. It was the middle of the Great Depression, and Mrs. Grier was of the opinion that a woman's touch could only make things better.

Retired from J.C. Penny Company after 13 years working in its Ely store and needing a fresh outlet for her energy at the age of 66, Glenn decided to go into politics. Through the store she had made many friends who trusted her, and so, brushing aside the objections of her family, she filed for the Assembly on the Democrat ticket and set out to canvas the voters. Driving her own car, Glenn visited every ranch, sheep camp, prospector's hole, and mine in White Pine County. She carried with her news of the latest budget and soundly reasoned opinions on the political issues. The voters elected her, and she served them well. During the legislative session the usual number of lobbyists courted the legislator's support for all sorts of projects. Glenn made it a rule to accept nothing whatsoever from these people, not even a cup of coffee, so there would be no

1868—1957
POLITICIAN, TEACHER, WPA MANAGER

misunderstanding that her support of a proposed bill was based only on its merits.

Glenn Edna Park was born in Forrest, Ohio, on April 16, 1868, the eldest daughter of Rosolvo H. and Mary Ellen Bradshaw Park. The family soon moved to Kansas, where her father homesteaded land opened to veterans of the Civil War. Glenn grew up in Kansas and at the age of 16 passed the state teacher's examination. After teaching for two years in Kansas, she moved to Indianola, Nebraska, where her clear handwriting made her employable as a copyist in one of the county offices. There, she met and married Charles L. Grier. Charles took his bride to Provo, Utah, where he was in business. Three children were born to the union: Harriet Elle; Charles Park, who for many years worked at the *Ely Daily Times* and who became a newspaper man in Antioch, California; and Robert Emmett, who became manager of the J.C. Penny store in Anchorage, Alaska. Glenn's husband Charles died in Ely in 1930.

Glenn was a gifted and outgoing person with a jolly nature. She was an excellent wife, mother, and homemaker who always had plenty of energy

left over for church and community service. There was always at least one personal project on hand, from fancy chicken-raising to painting in oils and watercolors. Her flair for style and love and appreciation of fine fabrics led Glenn to become a very adept dressmaker. After moving to Ely in 1911, she engaged in this work for several years. She once was commissioned to create a beautiful bridal trousseau, complete with a gray dove satin ball gown. This gown had a long train that was draped over the left arm and controlled by a concealed cord, truly an intricate piece of work. The bride was going east to meet her husband's relatives for the first time, and both she and the trousseau were met with approval.

In about 1920, Mrs. Grier went to work for the J.C. Penney Company in Ely. She was in charge of the ladies' ready-to-wear department, which she built into one of the finest in the West. In 1930 the company offered a prize to the best salesman in its western district—an all expenses paid, two-week trip to New York City. Of the fifteen prizes awarded, two were won by employees of the Ely store, and Glenn was one of them.

When the legislative session ended in the spring of 1935, Mrs. Grier was appointed by U.S. Senator Key Pittman to take charge of the Nevada women's division of President Roosevelt's Works Progress Administration (WPA), headquartered in Reno. Glenn traveled all over the state, often alone, inspecting projects designed to provide paying jobs for those who were on relief due to the Depression. The close of the WPA project after several years ended her time as a pubic servant.

Even in her 70s Glenn's amazing drive was a source of wonder to her family and friends. She made her home in Ely for several more years but finally consented to live with her children, who were concerned about her health. She visited each one in turn and was with her son Robert in Coos Bay, Oregon, when, at the age of 87, her strong heart faltered and a long life of service for others came to an end. She is buried in the family plot in Ely, Nevada.

—*Glenn Taylor Robertson, Harriet Grier Morrill and Doris Drummond*

Doris Virginia Hancock

The petite schoolteacher known as "Miss Doris" came to Las Vegas by train on December 29, 1924 to take a temporary kindergarten position expected to last four months. During the train ride, Doris was warned never to speak to railroad men. A well-informed and kindly railroad conductor knew that she was the new kindergarten teacher in town and offered to carry her bags to the hotel across the street from the train station. Doris relented, realizing that her teaching position carried with it dignity and respect. Thirty-nine years later, Doris Virginia Hancock retired from teaching after a full and successful teaching career in Las Vegas.

Doris was born in Belfast, Washington, on April 24, 1895, but grew up in Clarion, Iowa, where her father was in the mercantile business. After high school graduation Doris passed the State Teachers' Examination and taught for two years in a one-room schoolhouse in Belmont, Iowa. Doris said, "Like other rural teachers of the time, I had to walk miles to school in the snow and had to build a fire upon arrival. We carried water from a well across the road in an old oaken bucket from which we all drank using the same dipper." That assignment was followed by another one-room school before Doris felt "a calling to specialize in the primary grades," rather than teaching all eight grades. She received a Normal School Diploma from Peru State Teachers College in Peru, Nebraska, where she was enrolled in a program of kindergarten education and supervision; she also graduated from Colorado State College of Education with an AB degree in Kindergarten Supervision and received further education from Utah State Agricultural College, Arizona State, the University of Nevada at Reno and Las Vegas, and the University of Southern California.

After teaching in Iowa for eight years, Miss Hancock's pioneering spirit garnered her teaching positions in Idaho, Washington, and Nebraska before she arrived in Las Vegas. Nineteen years of her Nevada teaching career were spent in Las Vegas at the Fifth Street School, and twenty years were spent at John S. Park School. The list of Miss

1895–1987
TEACHER, ARTIST,
COMMUNITY ACTIVIST

Doris's students reads like a Who's Who of Las Vegas history. The daughter of a pupil of Miss Hancock's, in a letter to the Doris Hancock School staff, wrote, "It is my understanding that she was quite a disciplinarian; it was understood that each child would carry a handkerchief and that left handedness [sic] was forbidden. As the Christmas party neared Miss Hancock told my mother she *would* bring sugar cookies and they *would* be in the shape of reindeers. My mother responded, 'I do not have a sugar cookie recipe!' Miss Hancock promptly provided the recipe to be used."

Doris believed that "creative teaching arises from varied sources," and she pursued many interests beyond teaching. She studied art under painters of international reputation and also in Taos, New Mexico, where her paintings were exhibited and sold.

An avid reader and student of Western history, Doris had a large collection of out-of-print books and first editions. In 1940, with the help of artist Robert Capels and writer Walter Van Tilburg Clark, she sponsored the first exhibit of original paintings at the Fifth Street School. "Miss Doris" spent her own money to purchase art works to brighten her classrooms because she felt that children should live with beauty to enrich their lives.

When asked why she chose teaching as a career, especially kindergarten, Doris replied "…little children are such fascinating people! The work of a teacher at all levels is far-reaching. At the kindergarten age our children are in their most impressionable age." In an article written for the *Nevada Education Bulletin*, of May 1960, Miss Hancock said, "A kindergarten teacher must give comfort and assurance."

Doris Hancock was dubbed "the first lady of education," and on November 9, 1965, she was given the highest possible honor when an elementary school was dedicated in her name. Governor Richard H. Bryan declared the 24th of April 1985 to be Doris V. Hancock Day. After her retirement in 1963, Hancock moved to Wesley Palms, near San Diego, California, where she passed away on April 8, 1987.

—*Jean F. Spiller*

Grace Hayes

Grace Hayes was born in Springfield, Missouri on August 23, 1896. When she was just a young girl, her mother took her and her four sisters to live in San Francisco, where they experienced the 1906 earthquake. As a teenager, Grace landed her first job as a singer at the Moulin Rouge, a nightclub on the infamous Barbary Coast. Her salary was the nickels and dimes that rowdy men would throw on the stage floor. When her mother found out where Grace was performing, she put a quick end to it.

In 1912, at the age of 15, Grace married entertainer Joseph Lind. She remembered that they worked their way across the United States to Chicago, working anyplace they could earn two or three dollars so they could eat. They worked for a few months at a restaurant in Chicago until Grace became pregnant. At that point they decided to make their way back to San Francisco so Grace could be close to her mother. Her son,

1896–1989
ENTERTAINER, SINGER

Joseph Conrad Lind, now known as Peter Lind Hayes, was born in 1915. Gracie was widowed a year and a half later, but her resolve to have a future in show business remained strong.

Soon, Gracie's career began to blossom when more people in the entertainment industry took notice of her wide-ranging talents. Gracie starred in many Broadway shows and has the distinction of being one of the first stars of radio. She made several movies but is perhaps best remembered for her comedic turn in the 1930 Technicolor musical *King of Jazz* with Paul Whiteman and Bing Crosby. She was also one of the first entertainers to use a large fan during her on-stage performances. In 1942, Tommy Hull, who owned the Roosevelt Hotel in Los Angeles, coaxed Grace into coming to Las Vegas to headline at his popular El Rancho Vegas Hotel. She was a smash. "I was the Mary Pickford of Las Vegas," she boasted. Grace ended up doing successive 16, 8, and 12-week engagements at the hotel.

She fell in love with Las Vegas and bought the Red Rooster nightclub, about two miles south of the El Rancho Vegas and just north of where Caesars Palace now stands. She remembered, "I met an elderly couple and I gave them $15,000 and I said bid on it. It was a blind bid. I could have bought it for about $3,000. And when I came back from an engagement in Los Angeles, they turned it over to me." At the time, Grace owned the Grace Hayes Lodge in Hollywood, but she closed the property and transferred the name to her new club. All of Las Vegas's better-known personalities frequented the Gracie Hayes Lodge, from Ben "Bugsy" Siegel to Howard Hughes. She gave up operation of her lodge in 1957 because of ill health.

Gracie suffered from a chronic spinal condition and had to wear a steel brace. She was finally bedridden for a long period of time but never complained. Her doctors cautioned her that she would probably never walk again. It was a verdict she refused to accept. Her sheer determination, resolve, and hard work resulted in victory. A deeply religious woman, Gracie claimed that her faith in God gave her the power to walk again. In a newspaper story, she was christened by the press as "Lady Courageous of Las Vegas."

After a brief marriage to entertainer Charlie Foy, in 1945, Gracie married Robert E. Hopkins, who was known as the "doctor of scripts" for Metro-Goldwyn-Mayer. After traveling back and forth between Hollywood and Las Vegas, Robert, or "Hoppy" as he was called, finally retired from show business in 1960. He then moved to Las Vegas permanently to be with Gracie. Both remained active in community affairs until Robert passed away n 1966.

As traffic and hotels grew around it, the Hayes property was abandoned as a place to live and sold to the Golden Nugget for their new hotel, the Mirage. As a result of the sale, Gracie moved into a lavish suite in her downtown property, where she lived until 1987. On February 1, 1989, Grace Hayes died at the age of 93. She will always be remembered for her talents as a singer, actress, and businesswoman.

—*Joyce Marshall Moore*

Frances Gore Hazlett

Frances "Fannie" Gore was born in 1838 in New Hampshire. Her mother died when she was a child. When she was a young woman, Fannie and her brothers bought a ranch in Iowa, but, lured by the discovery of gold out west, the Gores bought wagons, found two other couples to share expenses, and trekked to Nevada. Frances was 24 years old when she left Iowa and crossed the Emigrant Trail in a covered wagon in 1862. Upon arriving in Silver City, the older brother traded his mule team for an interest in the El Dorado Canyon south of Dayton.

In her book *Pioneer Women of Nevada*, author Mildred Bray quotes from Fannie's remembrances, documented in a paper for the Nevada Historical Society to commemorate the semi-centennial of Nevada's statehood. Of her 2,000-mile wagon trip across the U.S., Fannie wrote:

"Crossing the plains was in no sense a picnic or pleasure trip. I crossed in 1862 with the usual experience of terrific thunderstorms on the Platte River, when lightening could be seen at night playing around the ironwork of the wagons; riding all day in a drizzling rain, knowing there was no warm fire of comfortable bed at night; our supper remnants of a former meal; walking miles every day; cooking over fires of brush or anything we could find; tending sick people; sometimes a funeral; sometimes fun; sometimes an Indian scare; and fording swollen streams.

We were from seven in the morning until ten at night getting across the Green River. We plodded over the Nevada deserts, often traveling at night to avoid the fierce heat of the sun and the reflection from the sand. People tired and irritable; teams worn out—so we toiled about 15 miles per day.

At last we arrived at Fort Churchill on the Carson River. A company of soldiers was on parade. We thought we had never seen anything so clean and white: we were very dirty and very happy; the long road, 2,000 miles of it, lay behind us since leaving Iowa 16 weeks before."

Fannie said that they passed several ranches making big money selling hay and grain to emigrants and local towns. She had the pleasure of listening to Brigham Young one Sunday morning and saw nine of his wives and four children.

1838–1933
SUFFRAGETTE, AUTHOR, HISTORIAN

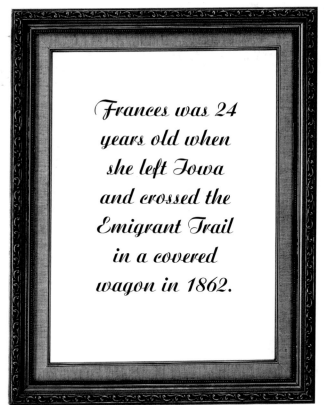

Frances was 24 years old when she left Iowa and crossed the Emigrant Trail in a covered wagon in 1862.

Brigham was sixty years old at the time.

In Nevada, Fannie lived with her older brother in a tent-like structure. She did cooking and laundry in a wood camp for $25 a month. Her brother earned good pay lumbering on his ranch. She became ill from "mountain fever" while living in the wood camp and went to Silver City to recuperate. She later returned to Dayton.

Fannie had no thought of marriage right then, even though there were twenty men to every one woman in Nevada territory, because the men were rough, drinkers and gamblers. She had hoped to settle in California where people were more civilized. But it happened that two years later Fannie married J.C. Hazlett, one of Dayton's first doctors and pharmacists. She helped open Dayton's first library, was active in her church, and raised a family. Dr. J.C. Hazlett also served as Lyon County representative in the Nevada Legislature and was Nevada's Superintendent of Public Schools in 1868.

Fannie Gore Hazlett lived in Dayton for 52 years, serving as the town's postmistress for 10 years after her husband's death in 1895. She always supported women's suffrage and wrote letters to the editors of Nevada newspapers on behalf of a woman's right to vote, including an 1895 letter to the editor of the *Gazette* and one to the *Nevada State Journal* in the early 1900s.

After her husband's death, Fannie traveled America by prairie schooner, ox-cart, buggy, carriage, sulky, automobile, railroad coach, and, in 1922, an airplane. She attended a lecture by Mark Twain and socialized with Nevada's first governors and legislators. But in Dayton, she was known simply as "Gramma Hazlett." Instead of fearing progress, she grew with it. Her youthful attitude and sense of humor stayed in the memory of all those who knew her. And Fannie served her community's history well by leaving behind scrapbooks containing early-day records and historical writings.

Fannie is remembered as an intelligent, outspoken, kind, and charitable leader and organizer, with remarkable energy and endurance, interested in everybody and everything. She was described as "short and plump . . . having inquiring eyes, being clean, tidy and well groomed but caring little for style." In later years she moved to Reno to be near her grandchildren. Fannie was 95 years old when she died and is buried in Dayton Cemetery, the same one she wrote about as she passed by in a covered wagon on her way to Carson City.

—*Phyllis Young*

Sarah Dotson Hurst

Sarah was born to Charles A. and Miriam Dotson in Iowa. She married Horton Hurst and, at age 28, gave birth to a son, Glenn. Two years later, another son, Dale, was born. After her husband passed away, Sarah and her family continued to live in Iowa for a while but moved to Reno in the early 1900s when her two sons developed an interest in "theatrical enterprises."

Once established in Reno, Sarah became a busy clubwoman. In January 1915, she was elected president of a newly organized Women's Citizen's Club, representing "women of every political and non-political faith." Its constitution called the club a "nonpartisan association for the study of questions of general interest and the promotion of any movement for the betterment of society." Among the club's first activities were circulating petitions in opposition to a bill requiring six months' residency for divorce and to a proposed racetrack bill. In 1914 and again in 1916 Sarah served as president of the Washoe County Equal Franchise Society, the purpose of which was to promote women's right to the vote. In October 1916, she joined the newly organized Women's

Republican Committee of Washoe County, as well as the Twentieth Century Club.

Shortly after her 61st birthday, Sarah decided to run for the State Assembly as a Washoe County candidate. The press wrote little about her, and she did not campaign much. Her announcement read that she was "endorsed by the club women of Reno." This included a resolution from the Women Citizens' Club stating in part, "Mrs. Hurst has given strong adherence to all moral issues and has a broad knowledge of the state's needs." She won on Election Day in 1918. On January 1919, Mrs. Sarah Hurst was sworn in and became the first female legislator in Nevada. Apparently there was much discussion in the Assembly how to properly address the Honorable Sarah Hurst. Some chose to refer to her as "Assembly Woman," while others called her "Gentle Lady." She reported that her one pledge was "to vote for the ratification of the federal prohibition amendment." She stated that she also expected to give particular attention to legislation designed to benefit women and children. While sitting in the legislature, Sarah served on three

1857–1952
POLITICIAN,
COMMUNITY ACTIVIST

committees: Education, State Institutions, and Federal Relations.

Mrs. Hurst introduced eight bills into the Assembly, including one granting the right of suffrage to women. Others bills dealt with the registration and licensing of nurses, the guardianship and estates of a minor child of a deceased father, the requirement of a wife's consent to the disposal of community property, and an act for the prevention of cruelty to animals. Her bills apparently fared somewhat better than those of other freshman legislators. However, Sarah was opposed to a bill granting the right of marriage between Caucasians and Indians stating, "I do not believe in the intermingling of races." The measure passed, however, and became law.

News articles reported that Sarah was excluded from some of the social activities afforded her male colleagues. One was a dinner at Governor Boyle's mansion, and another was a moving picture and lecture at the Grand Theater. Conversely, during the very important special session of the Assembly acknowledging the passage of the Federal Suffrage Amendment in February, 1920, Sarah was asked by the Speaker to preside because she was the only woman representative in the legislature. After the voting passed in the house, she quickly resumed her place on the floor and addressed the speaker, noting that a number of suffragist leaders were present and requesting that they be allowed to speak. In August 1920, Mrs. Hurst spoke on "Women's Part in the Ratification" at the amendment's ratification ceremony.

Although unsuccessful in her bid for reelection that same year, Sarah had opened a wide door for Nevada women in politics. Since her service in the state legislature, only three sessions, in 1931, 1933, and 1947, have not had a woman represented in that body.

Mrs. Hurst remained active in club work. She was put in charge of the Information and Reciprocity Bureau of the State Federation of Women's Clubs and continued to give lectures that demonstrated her intimate knowledge of Nevada laws concerning women and children.

Sarah made her home with son Glenn and his family in Reno but, in 1922, moved with the Hurst family to California, where her sons pursued their interests in the theater. In 1952, at the age of 94, she passed away in Pasadena.

—*Dorothy Bokelmann*

Thelma Brown Ireland

Thelma Brown Ireland was one of Nevada's most prolific published poets. Acknowledged nationally and internationally, she wrote eloquently about the Nevada frontier, transforming her impressions into poetry that was enjoyed by many people in the western states and beyond.

Thelma was born in Creighton, Nebraska, to Willis and Clara Brown in 1899 and had the typical conservative Midwestern upbringing. The "Roaring Twenties" were not even a murmur. It was an environment of no dancing, no card playing, and no fun for a young attractive woman.

"Brownie," as she was called by her friends, started teaching at age seventeen in rural Nebraska schools. For her it was a deadly existence, and her only remedy was to leave. She opened a map, and, in a haphazard way, put her finger on Nevada. She wrote to the State Superintendent of Schools in Carson City, who told her of a teaching position in McGill, Nevada. She naively theorized that if she became bored with McGill, she could spend the weekends in the town of Cobre, not knowing that Cobre consisted only of a water tank for the steam trains

1899–1997
TEACHER, AUTHOR

and a depot for passenger and mail transfers on the Southern Pacific Railroad. Those who got off the train often asked, "Oh, God, what have I done?"

Lured by the promise of good pay and the excitement of a boom town, Brownie sent her application along with a flattering photo to the school board secretary at the Nevada Consolidated Copper Company office. She later learned that the young men in the office picked the applicants from their photos rather than their qualifications. Of course, the prettiest teachers were selected. These pretty teachers would arrive via the Nevada Northern Railway from Cobre. Soon, they would marry one of the bachelors and become housewives and mothers. Custom did not allow married women to work.

On a summer night when the moon was full, Thelma Brown arrived in McGill. It was 1922. She watched moonbeams dance on a huge lake below the town and delighted in the possibility of leisurely boat rides. Little did she know the magic lake was in fact the tailings pond from the mill. (Tailings are tiny particles left as residue from the milling process. When dry, the wind raised these par-

100

ticles into towering clouds, a housewife's nightmare as dust crept under doors and windowsills.)

Thelma also did not know that the huge five-acre mill—the reason for the town's existence—had burned to the ground in July. However, the rebuilding of the mill brought many educated personnel, skilled workers, and bachelors to the area. The predicted pattern of social life and romance followed, and in 1924, charming and talented Brownie married William "Irish" Ireland, who was to become the purchasing agent for the company's mining and smelting operations. They had two children: Patricia and Willis (Bill). She returned to teaching for two years in McGill during the teacher shortage caused by World War II.

It was on the shore of the magical McGill tailings pond that Brownie directed her energy and talent into becoming a poet. Where others saw ugliness, she saw beauty. In her short, lyrical, witty, and simple poems, she observed the humor, beauty, foibles, virtues, and foolishness of the human experience. Her children inspired many of her poems that were read on "Don McNeill's Breakfast Club," the national radio program originating in Chicago. She had more than 3,000 verses published in over 50 national and international magazines, including *Better Homes and Gardens* and *Ladies Home Journal*. She compiled three poetry books: *Home Work*, *Once Upon a Rhyme*, and its sequel *Twice Upon a Rhyme*.

She was a board member of the Girl Scouts local council and the McGill Library. She was a member of the Order of the Eastern Star, the Knife and Fork Club, and the Visitors' Board of the University of Nevada. In 1962, her beloved husband died. Brownie continued her pursuit of adventure by teaching conversational English in Kuwait during the summer of 1963 and by traveling widely in Europe, Africa, the Middle East, and the Orient.

In 1975, Brownie moved to Reno, where she was instrumental in forming the Reno Poetry Society. She was listed in *Who's Who of American Women* (1961–62), *Who's Who of the West*, and the *International Who's Who of Poetry*. Her haiku was accepted for publication in Japan. In 1960, she was awarded the degree of Honorary Master of Humane Letters from England's International Academy, the Sovereign Order of Alfred the Great, and she received the Poetry Award of Excellence presented by the Delta Kappa Gamma Society, but her most treasured award was from the University of Southern Mississippi, a 1972 Bronze Medal inscribed "Thelma Ireland. Her talents have been used to enrich the lives of children."

It is doubtful that Brownie ever regretted her journey to Nevada. There, she developed a deep understanding and love of the desert and the people who lived in it. Those who knew her were the better for it, as are those who read her poetry.

—*Doris Drummond*

Theresa Smokey Jackson

Theresa Smokey Jackson was born on July 1, 1916 in Minden, Nevada, to William and Sadie Joe Smokey, Washoe Indian natives. Theresa was one of twelve children. As times changed, the Washoe people and the Smokey family changed their way of life from hunting, fishing, and gathering to working as laborers on nearby farms and ranches. In 1917, a man named Fred Dressler donated 40 acres to be used as the Dressler Indian Reservation, so that the Washoe Indians would have a home base rather than being scattered throughout the area. Eventually, the Smokey family moved to Dresslerville, approximately six miles south of Gardnerville. There, Theresa and her siblings learned the Washoe culture, traditions, and language, often traveling to Lake Tahoe and nearby hills to gather the traditional foods of pine nuts, acorns, wild onions, and berries. The children participated in the food preparation, pounding nuts into powder and danced in Washoe ceremonies, including the girls' puberty dance, the rabbit dance, and the pine nut dance.

Because Washoe native children were not allowed to attend school in Gardnerville, an elementary school was built for them in Dresslerville. They learned to speak English, as they were not allowed to speak their native language at school. After completing elementary school, Theresa attended Stewart Indian School, south of Carson City, but because she was lonely and prone to crying, she was sent back to her family.

Growing up in the Carson Valley, Theresa had many positive experiences with her family, church, and school. Basketry was an important part of her life. When she was a teenager, she learned to weave baskets by watching her mother and older sister. Later in life, basketry became one of her major interests and talents. Unfortunately, she also experienced the prejudice, segregation, and curfews of the local townspeople.

1916—1999
EDUCATOR,
BASKET WEAVER

When Theresa was 18 or 19 years old, she married Scotty Fillmore. They were married in "the Indian way," by just saying, "We are married." At the time, this was considered a legal marriage, as this was the way it was always done in this Indian community. Early in their marriage, Theresa and Scotty worked and lived on ranches in the area. In the 1930s, homes were being built on the reservation for the Washoe. Theresa and Scotty moved into their own home on the Dresslerville Reservation in 1939. Helping to build the house had been their payment. Two children, William Elwood in 1949 and Pamela Susan in 1950, were added to the Fillmore family. Nine years later, Scott Fillmore died. Theresa later married Donald Green but was divorced four years later. In the early 1970s she married Ronald Jackson, a Kiowa Indian.

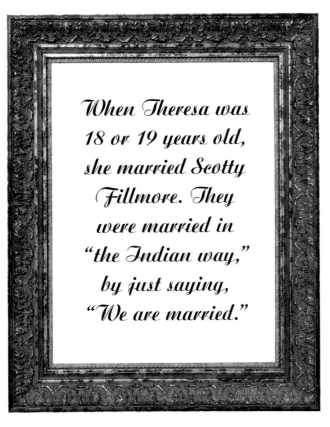

When Theresa was 18 or 19 years old, she married Scotty Fillmore. They were married in "the Indian way," by just saying, "We are married."

Tahoe, and the opening of the U.S. Forest Service Lake Tahoe Basin Tallac Historical Site, where the Washoe natives traditionally spent the summer months. She was the interpreter for the Washoe Blessing at the Governor's Breakfast in 1991 and 1992, and was recipient of the Governor's Arts Award in 1995.

Later in her life, Theresa again picked up the willow and began making beautiful baskets, specializing in the cradleboard or baby basket. She became a master weaver and demonstrated her techniques at educational and historic events throughout the aboriginal areas of the Washoe people. As a delegate for the Washoe Tribe Basket Exhibition, she participated in the Festival of American Folklore in 1989 at the Smithsonian Institute in Washington, DC. She also worked in schools teaching and demonstrating basketry and the folkways she practiced. In 1991, Theresa was granted the Folklore Basket Weaving Award by the Nevada Humanities Commission. She was a member of the Hawaii Cultural Exchange Program and was honored as a grand marshal of the 1992 Fourth of July parade in Carson City.

As a speaker for the Washoe Tribe, Theresa offered prayer blessings in the Washoe language on many occasions, including the Special Olympics, the opening session of the Nevada State Legislature, the Presidential Forum at

Theresa was extremely active and involved in the Senior Center Program at the Dresslerville Community Center, chairing the Advocacy Council for that program. She was also a director of Building Traditional Homes at Lake Tahoe Baldwin Estates. But most importantly, she was a spiritual person. She never forgot the teachings of the Baptist missionaries who came to the reservation when she was a young woman. She knew she had a special gift and became a spiritual leader for the Washoe tribe. Many people from all races came to her home asking her to pray for them. No one was turned away. If necessary, she traveled to people's homes to pray for them. From 1984 to 1994 she was a teacher at the Washoe Baptist Church Sunday School. These are but a few of the many contributions made by this Washoe woman who received countless state and national honors and awards. On October 29, 1999, Theresa Smokey Jackson, age 83, died at the Washoe Medical Center in Reno, Nevada, respected, admired, and loved by so many.

—*JoAnn Martinez and Doris Drummond*

Lubertha Miller Johnson

Lubertha Johnson was born in Ackerman, Mississippi, in 1906 to Golden and Mary Miller. She was born on a farm that her father had inherited from his father Joe, who had been a slave.

During many of her early years, Lubertha lived with her grandmother about ten miles from her parents. This grandmother, whose father had been murdered by white men, enjoyed having her granddaughter live with her while Lubertha's parents worked hard to get ahead—it was also easier for Lubertha to attend school near her grandmother's place. From her grandmother, Lubertha learned many skills, such as how to use a spinning wheel and how to use various plants to dye cloth different colors. On the farm, the two women raised rice, corn, and a small amount of cotton; they also tended a large orchard.

The Millers were working hard in the South at a time, the 1920s, when the KKK membership was growing by leaps and bounds, so the family made the decision to move north to Chicago. They decided to travel by train, but the stationmaster for the railroad in Lubertha's town would not

1906—1989
NURSE,
COMMUNITY ACTIVIST

sell them tickets; friends took them by wagon to another town from which the family left.

The move to Chicago, with its tall buildings and more sophisticated lifestyle, opened up a whole new world for Lubertha. Seventeen years old when she arrived in Chicago, Lubertha landed in a neighborhood that was mostly Italian. It was her first real interaction with whites. At home in the South, blacks and whites did not mingle. A year later, the family moved to a suburban area, Maywood, a steel mill town where her father worked.

Johnson found race relations in the North much better than in the South, even though she refused to go to school with white children at first. Finally, she enrolled at Chicago Music College and the Y College, where she met not only white people from her area but also white people from the South who wanted to be friendly, a new experience for her. Following high school, she enrolled in Roger Williams University, an all-black school in Nashville, Tennessee. She planned to pursue a teaching career, but the Depression forced her to leave school and get a job to help support her family.

She remained in the Chicago area when her parents moved to Pasadena for Mr. Miller's health.

In 1943, Lubertha moved west to be with her parents and immediately got a job in public housing for the Urban League. She remained there only a few months before moving to Las Vegas, where the family had purchased a 24-acre ranch in Paradise Valley on which they raised chickens. It was located near Eastern Avenue and Sunset Road. Many blacks found the ranch to be a favorite picnic and recreation spot since they were still barred from most other public accommodations. The family finally sold the ranch in 1979.

Lubertha worked as recreation director of the Carver Park Housing Project in Henderson. She served as president of the local NAACP chapter and was a signee of the Consent Decree to end employment discrimination in the hotel and casino industry. She was a member of Gamma Phi Delta Sorority and the National Conference (formerly the National Conference of Christians and Jews), as well as a board member of the Caliente School for Girls and founder of Operation Independence Pre-school Learning Center.

Lubertha was sometimes compared to the famous educator, Mary McLeod Bethune, in that she had access to powerbrokers and often used that to push for social change. During her lifetime, Lubertha Johnson was a recipient of numerous awards in recognition of her contributions to the community and to the state of Nevada. She left a legacy for all: "Education is the key to independence." She was southern Nevada's first black nurse, but it is felt that she really made her mark after becoming active with the NAACP's Las Vegas chapter in 1945. She served two different terms as president of the organization. Her many accomplishments included helping to expand employment opportunities for blacks in the school district, hospitals, and hotels. She is also credited with helping to enact open housing legislation and helping in the fight to enact Nevada's civil rights law.

One of her proudest achievements was the founding of the county's first anti-poverty self-help initiative, Operation Independence. It included a Head Start program, a Manpower program, and the Operation Independence child development centers, and was the first black non-profit agency to receive funding from the United Way of Southern Nevada.

On February 6, 1989, Lubertha died in a Las Vegas nursing home.

—*Sally Wilkins and Jean Ford*

Laura Belle Kelch

Laura Belle Kelch was born to Arthur and Gertrude Gang in Cincinnati, Ohio, on September 13, 1912. Laura Belle earned an associates degree in interior design from the University of Cincinnati and then moved first to New York City and later to Hollywood, California, where she met Maxwell Kelch. Laura Belle and Max married in Carson City, Nevada, and moved to Las Vegas in 1939.

In 1940, Laura Belle and Max started KENO, the first radio station in Las Vegas. Until that time, few people in Las Vegas even had radios because reception from the west coast cities was poor. With the advent of KENO, all of the stores in town quickly sold out of radios. Laura Belle had her own daily talk show on KENO, "Listen Ladies," and helped staff the station during the difficult war years when they were on constant alert for a Japanese attack on the west coast. KENO was declared a "vital industry" in WWII and had to monitor a certain radio frequency 24 hours a day to be prepared to shut down instantly so the Japanese couldn't hone in on the signal and bomb Boulder Dam or the Basic Magnesium

1912–2004
BROADCASTER, ARTIST, COMMUNITY ACTIVIST

plant or the Las Vegas Aerial Gunnery School. The station would have also been the only way of controlling the influx of refugees if the Japanese bombed Southern California.

During WWII, Laura Belle became the first women to join the local Rotary Club. In 1953 she became a charter member of the First Presbyterian Church. She was a fine watercolorist, and in 1958 Laura Belle became a charter member of the Nevada Watercolor Society and received numerous awards and prizes, including national recognition when she was invited to display her work with the American Watercolor Society at an exhibition in Riverside in 1976. In 1950 Laura Belle joined the Las Vegas Art League.

Laura Belle's dedication to the children of Las Vegas was one of the highlights of her life. The fact that the Boy Scout building is named the Laura Belle and Maxwell Kelch Scout Service Center is witness to that dedication. In 1979, she was awarded Scouting's highest council award, the Silver Beaver. She was also active in Girl Scouting and escorted a troop of girls to Europe for three months in 1959. For over 30

years she served on the Board of Directors of the Boulder Dam Area Council of the Boy Scouts.

In 1977, Laura Belle was chosen Nevada's Mother of the Year by the American Mother's Association. The Clark County Community College selected her as one of its first two recipients of Honorary Associate Degrees in Humane Letters. She served on its Advisory Board for many years. She was a member of the Chamber of Commerce and served as secretary for its Prospectors Group.

Laura Belle and her husband Max Kelch, a physicist and engineer, were entrepreneurs whose business interest contributed in substantial ways to building the community. They manufactured cinder blocks; Hyde Park is built of those blocks. They built apartments and owned the Foodland chain of grocery stores in Las Vegas, North Las Vegas, and Henderson. When they sold KENO, they purchased the local franchise for Muzak and formed the Nevada Music Corporation, which provided background music in banks, offices, hotels, stores, and homes, and was the most productive franchise in the country.

Her husband was a private pilot, and Laura Belle earned the America Aircraft Owners and Pilots Association "Pinch Hitters" award, proving that she could take over the controls of an aircraft in flight, navigate to an airport, and land the aircraft safely.

Laura Belle saw Las Vegas at every stage of development. When asked which stage she liked best, when it was most exciting, and when it was best to live in Las Vegas, she said, "Every period of Las Vegas was wonderful and now is the best and most exciting time to live here. We're growing in every area, and we're growing well."

She served on several organization boards including the Salvation Army Advisory Board for nearly 20 years, the Community College Board for 15 years, the Las Vegas Chamber of Commerce for 20 years, the Mesquite Club, and the PEO Sisterhood, Chapter G, a philanthropic organization to further higher education for women.

Laura Belle passed away July 13, 2004, at the age of 91. She was survived by her daughter, Marilyn Kelch Gubler, and her son, Robert Maxwell Kelch.

—*Mollie L. Murphy*

Bertha C. Knemeyer

Bertha C. Knemeyer (known affectionately as B.C.K.) belongs to Nevada
and to the West. Born in Carson City
on October 30, 1885, during a brief visit by her
family to the area, Bertha was the daughter of one
of the sturdy groups of German immigrants who
settled in the Carson and Mason Valleys from
the 1870s through the 1890s. Her father, Franz
H. Knemeyer, and her mother, Marie Heidlage
Springmeyer, came to the fertile Carson Valley
in 1882 at the instigation of relatives and friends
who had preceded them. The family settled
permanently in Mason Valley after spending a
few years in "Old Empire" on the Carson River,
where Bertha's brother, Edward, and sister, Erma,
were born, and in Carson City.

Bertha received her early
education in a little country
school. Quiet and shy but
very bright, she displayed a
definite talent for mathematics. Defying all obstacles,
Bertha earned the equiva-
lent of a high school diploma by being tutored by
Dr. G. E. Leavitt, who took it upon himself to
teach the girl everything he knew—mathematics,
Latin, science, and German.

1885—UNKNOWN
EDUCATOR

In 1902, after completing her education
with Dr. Leavitt, Bertha applied in person to the
University of Nevada in Reno without a single
actual high school credit. Dr. Thurtell, a professor
of mathematics, agreed to be responsible for the
girl while she was at the University. Dr. Stubbs,
the president of the University, proved to be kind
and understanding, and there were others whom
Bertha remembered with gratitude. One was Dr.
J.E. Church, a long-time professor of classical
languages, later famous for his snow surveys.

Following her graduation in 1906 as the
youngest member of her class, Bertha began a
30-year professional career in Elko County. She
became a teacher in the local high school. Not
only did she teach her beloved mathematics, she
also conducted classes in
German, Latin, science, and
physical education.

By the time she was
thirty, Bertha was appointed
Deputy Superintendent
of Public Instruction for
northeastern Nevada, the first woman in the state
to hold that position. During the years as Deputy
Superintendent, she traveled to every town in her
district. She told many tales of the rides about
the countryside, in all sorts of weather and over

miles and miles of terrible roads, in her old Model T Ford, and of her encounters with the various problems that arose in the tiny schools of those early days. She felt her adventures were exciting as well as satisfying; through it all she left a trail of wonderful, loyal friends whose kindness and hospitality helped her over rough spots, and whose companionship she cherished for years.

During the years of World War I, Bertha became the target of discrimination by those who were resentful of her German origins. A younger brother was still in Germany—he had been too young to travel to America—and many bigots felt that the Knemeyer's ties to Germany were too strong.

In 1919, Knemeyer resigned her Deputy Superintendent position to become teacher and principal at Metropolis High School; a year later, she accepted the opportunity to become principal of the new high school in Elko, a position she held for 15 years. During that time, the student population expanded from 80 in 1920 to 200 in 1936. Although Bertha's duties expanded proportionately, she continued to reserve for herself the privilege of teaching the classes in higher mathematics.

Bertha worked zealously within the community as a whole. She was instrumental in bringing the Chautauqua and other lecture series to Elko.

Bertha acquired a master's degree by attending several universities during summer sessions, including Harvard, the University of Chicago, the University of California at Berkeley, and the University of Berlin. She was elected a delegate to the Convention of the World Federation of Education Associations in Geneva, Switzerland, and in 1934, was elected one of the 12 national vice-presidents of the National Education Association.

Bertha was an active citizen in Elko, her adopted home. She was a charter member, in 1912, of the Elko Twentieth Century Club, a member of the first PEO chapter in the state of Nevada, and a member and Past Matron of the Elko Chapter No. 17 of the Order of the Eastern Star.

An outspoken person, Bertha faced a major crisis in 1935; she was asked to resign her position of 29 years because she took a strong stand in favor of scholastics over athletics. The community submitted a petition with over 1,000 signatures demanding she keep her job.

Following her retirement in 1936, Bertha traveled throughout the world, pursued a Ph.D. program at Columbia University, and taught once again at the Chadwick School in Rolling Hills, California, the Montezuma School for Boys in Los Gatos, and finally at the Sarah Dix Hamlin School for Girls in San Francisco. She was convinced that girls were as bright at mathematics as boys, when given the chance.

Bertha traveled to Europe again and to Asia for the first time. She was gone for over six years before returning to the United States.

—*Sally Wilkins from an article by Gertrude Badt*

Molly Flagg Knudtsen

Thyrza Benson Flagg, "Molly," was born in New York City into a privileged life, with great family wealth and travel in the highest social circles. She was privately schooled, took riding lessons in Central Park, and vacationed in Europe. Her formal debut in New York society was in the fall of 1933, and the following spring she was presented at the Court of St. James in London. She attended the University of London's King College, intermittently touring the Continent.

Molly was married to Robert Gibb in 1937. Seriously injured in a horse-riding accident that same year, she spent nearly two years recovering at the home of friends in Cannes, France. Here, she often dined with the recently abdicated Duke of Windsor and his wife. In 1939, Molly returned to the U.S. and, two years later, went to Reno, Nevada, to obtain a divorce from Gibb. Staying at an outlying dude ranch, she helped train racehorses, no problem for one who had earned a diploma from the prestigious Royal Institute of the Horse in London. At this dude ranch, she met handsome Dick Magee, trainer of thoroughbred horses, owner of the huge Grass Valley

1915–2001
CATTLE RANCHER, POET, UNIVERSITY REGENT

Ranch northeast of Austin, graduate of Princeton, and member of one of Nevada's founding families. Molly and Dick married in 1942. Thus, she began her second life in one of the most remote valleys of the state.

In 1931, Dick had purchased a herd of registered purebred Hereford cattle developed by the University of Nevada's College of Agriculture. This herd became the cornerstone of success for his ranch in the years that followed. Molly learned how to register purebred Hereford cattle and about bovine psychology. She improved and preserved the lineage of the herd. Later this purebred Hereford line was brought back to the University. From her observations of cow behavior, Molly wrote *Cow Sense*, published in 1977.

She published articles in *Vogue*, *Family Circle*, Austin's *Reese River Reveille* newspaper, and various archaeology magazines. In cooperation with Smithsonian Institute, the University of California, the Nevada State Museum, and the Desert Research Institute, Molly found archaeological sites as she rode about the ranch, collecting and documenting artifacts and mapping sites. These pursuits led her to become a trustee of the Nevada State Museum.

Her interest in Lander County's history resulted in a campaign to re-roof Austin's Episcopal Church and to preserve Stokes Castle. In 1971, businessmen thought of moving the mysterious Stokes Castle from Austin to the Las Vegas strip. This prompted Molly to buy the Roman watchtower-like building and its underlying gold mine so it would remain in Austin. Ironically, the "castle" had been built in 1897 by Molly's wealthy New York cousin, Anson Phelps Stokes, a nineteenth-century mining and railroad baron. He lived there during his early business stays in Austin.

In 1960, concern about limited educational opportunities in rural areas led Molly to seek a position on the Board of Regents at the University. Against advice from friends who said she could not win, rancher Molly McGee ran a ranch-to-ranch campaign in the cow counties. She won by a landslide. Facing the hostility of eight male regents, the hard-working and charming Molly was soon acknowledged as "one of the most articulate and best informed persons" to hold the regent position. She was instrumental in establishing the University of Nevada Press (1961), the Department of Anthropology UNR, the community college system (1968), and an expansion of the College of Agriculture and thence the creation of the total University of Nevada system. Molly played a key role in the complex and difficult decisions facing the regents, using her

wit, humor, and "cow sense." Continuing her many roles of public service, she wrote and spoke about archaeology, literature, poetry, historic preservation, agriculture, and ranch life. In 1973, Molly was awarded an honorary Doctorate of Science degree in archaeology-anthropology from the University.

After becoming more involved in horse racing in California, Dick Magee moved himself and his horses to a ranch in that state. Molly bought the Grass Valley Ranch from him; they were divorced in 1969. Molly increased the size of the ranch as well as the size of its purebred and commercial herds. Her purebred bulls brought top prices at Western auctions. She worked with the cattle daily. In 1969, Molly married William C. Knudtsen, a California rancher and stockman.

Molly's life again took a big turn in 1987. While chasing a calf, her horse stepped into a badge hole, and she was thrown. The horse landed atop her, and she was badly injured. Her recovery was long and hard. After this accident, Molly remained in Reno but with Bill's help continued to manage the ranch from a distance. In 1995, she sold the 9,000-acre Grass Valley Ranch and all the cattle yet still continued her writing, research, and public service until her death in 2001. Excelling in all she did, former socialite Dr. Molly Knudtsen, rancher, environmentalist, educator, participated extensively in building the new Nevada.

—*Doris Drummond*

Therese Laxalt

Therese Alpetche was born in 1891 in the Germiette quarter of St. Etienne de Baigorry, in the Basque province of Basse Navarre in France. She spent her latter youth in Bordeaux, France, where her family operated the Hotel America and one of the early travel agencies from Europe to the Americas. A graduate of the Cordon Bleu in Paris, she came to the United States after World War I to take home her brother, Michel, who was dying from the lingering effects of a poison gas attack he faced as a soldier in the French army. Michel died in Reno in 1920, and Therese chose to remain in the United States.

In 1921, Therese was married in Reno to Dominique Laxalt, who had also emigrated from the Basque country and was part owner of the Allied Land and Livestock Company, which had sheep and cattle holdings in Nevada and California and crops growing on five ranches and farms.

The livestock crash of 1922 caused Dominique to take his herds of sheep to northern Washoe County, where a hard winter destroyed the remainder of his investment. In the following year, Therese accompanied her husband as he worked as sheepherder and ranch hand for various ranching outfits in California and Nevada. She also worked, cooking three meals a day for as many as 30 ranch hands.

The Laxalts moved to Carson City in 1926, where they operated the French Hotel and owned the original Ormsby House. Dominique Laxalt returned to owning sheep as Therese tended to their joint business interests and assumed much of the task of raising their family of six children—John who became an attorney in Las Vegas; Susanne; who became Sister Mary Robert, a nun with the Holy Family Order; Peter, a Reno attorney; Paul, who became a Nevada governor and senator; Robert, who became an author and director of the University of Nevada Press; and Marie Bini who became a teacher. Therese's dream was that, somehow, they could give all of their children a college education so that they might earn their livelihoods with their minds rather than their hands.

In 1967, the Leisure Hour Club of Carson City nominated Therese Laxalt to be "Mother of the Year." This nomination led to her being called Mother of the State of Nevada for 1967 by the Nevada Committee of the American Mothers Committee. In 1976, Therese Laxalt was again honored as one of twelve Nevada Mothers Of

1891–1978
BUSINESSWOMAN

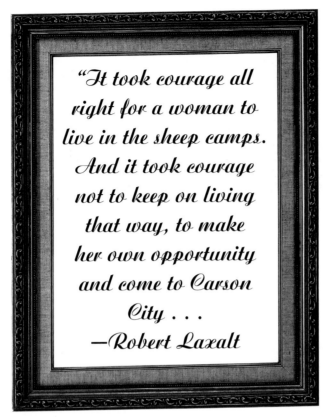

"It took courage all right for a woman to live in the sheep camps. And it took courage not to keep on living that way, to make her own opportunity and come to Carson City . . .
—Robert Laxalt

Achievement in a national publication, entitled *Mothers of Achievement in American History, 1776–1976*. In the nominating letter, Mrs. W. MacDonald Smith said:

"It is not often that one individual can be found who so well embodies the many traits of character which have come to be highly regarded in mothers; our nominee exemplifies to a rare degree the qualities of courage, cheerfulness, patience, affection, understanding, and homemaking ability . . . .

Dominique Laxalt died in 1971, after a return to the hills as a sheepherder. Therese followed him in 1978. At the time of Therese's death, the *Nevada State Journal* published the following excerpt from Robert Laxalt's book, *Sweet Promised Land*, which dealt with the life of his mother: "A Son's Tribute to His Mother"

"It took courage all right for a woman to live in the sheep camps. And it took courage not to keep on living that way, to make her own opportunity and come to Carson City as she did, out of an old brown board cabin in the desert, with four children and a hundred dollars, to start another life in the little hotel, doing all the cooking for the workingmen boarders, on her feet from four o'clock in the morning until midnight, and with only half enough sleep at night. And it took courage for a pretty woman to watch slender legs become purple veined forever from standing on her feet until the last day of the ninth month, and then deliver her child and go back to work.

Even after we left the hotel and my father had gone back to the hills with his sheep, it took courage to face a life with six children who could have gone one way or another, and do it with an iron rule, without fear ever once showing, and with a love that was there in little things like a touch of the hand or an unguarded glance, because if she had every shown fear or weakness or too much love, she would have been lost.

It took courage, all right, but it took something else, too. It had to do with forty mornings of Lent, up when the sky was still dark and the snow was piled high on the ground, trudging a narrow path to the church, with her brood strung out behind her, little dark patches moving slowly through the white snow, huddled deep in their coats, shivering, and with eyes still stuck with sleep.

It had to do with winter nights when the big trees outside the house moaned fearfully with blizzards, and long after the children had gone to bed, a single candle burned in the living room, and a wife prayed for her husband in the hills."

Therese died in Santa Clara on May 11, 1978. A Requiem Mass was held at St. Theresa of Avilla Catholic Church in Carson City and burial was in the family plot in the Lone Mountain Cemetery, also in Carson City.
—*Fran Haraway.*

Moya Olsen Lear

Moya Lear was born in Chicago, Illinois, to Lillian and John "Ole" Olsen. Her father was a well-known comedian who was half of the famed comedy duo, Olsen and Johnson. Moya attended Ohio State University and later went to New York City's Pratt Institute before taking over as her father's accountant and secretary during the Broadway run of Olsen and Johnson's hit, *Hellzapoppin*.

In 1938, backstage at the show, Moya was introduced to William P. Lear, the inventor of the first workable car radio. She later recalled that she had been "totally unimpressed." In spite of this opinion, Moya accepted William's offer of a drink at the famed Stork Club. Four years later they married.

Soon after came children John, Shanda, David, and Tina. The young family traveled the world with Bill, who pursued his career as an inventor/designer. They lived everywhere from Santa Monica, California, to Geneva, Switzerland, always enjoying the company of scientists, aviation experts, entertainers, and fellow inventors. After a most successful career, Bill Lear died of leukemia in 1978. His most famous inventions included the Lear jet, the autopilot, and the eight-track tape.

Moya had promised Bill that she would see his Lear Fan—a revolutionary experimental airplane—to flight status. She said publicly that she had learned from her husband "by osmosis," so, surrounding herself with loyal employees, she took over the management of the Lear Aviation Corporation and guided the early production of the Lear Fan prototype. Unfortunately, the project failed because of lack of funding, but Moya made sure that the plane flew at least once after Bill's death.

Moya lived at River House, a 50-acre estate on the Truckee River in Verdi, Nevada. At the time of her death, she was on the Board Emeritus of the Nevada Policy Research Institute and served as an honorary member of the Nevada Women's Fund. Moya was awarded six honorary doctorate degrees and was a member of several halls of fame, including Women in Aviation Pioneers and the United States Achievement Academy.

A lifelong Christian Scientist, Moya was known for her generosity to a variety of groups. Her father gave free performances for charities

1915–2001
BUSINESSWOMAN,
PHILANTHROPIST

and military groups, and her mother helped others in accord with the principles of Christian healing. Moya continued this tradition by, among other projects, giving a $1.1 million matching grant to the Reno-Sparks Theater Community Coalition, which turned the First Church of Christian Science building on Riverside Drive into a home for the performing arts.

Moya also gave hundreds of acres of Lear land to Washoe County. The land was used for a Boy Scouts of America venue and for the perpetuation of wetlands.

Rollan Melton, a *Reno Gazette Journal* columnist and Moya's eulogist recalled "...her myriad gifts of education. For instance, year after year she underwrote Christmas programs at Verdi elementary school, goodies and clothing and books and winter fund equipment for little kids."

Moya served on the board of directors of the Nevada Opera Association, the Nevada Festival Ballet, the Sierra Arts Foundation and Embry-Riddle Aeronautical University, the board of trustees of the Nevada Foundation, Truckee Meadows Community College, the YWCA and Museum of Flight in Seattle, the university advisory board of the University of Nevada Reno, and on President Reagan's International Private Enterprise Task Force.

Moya Lear's awards include the Anti-Defamation League's 1990 Torch of Liberty Award, the Nevada Lung Association's 1989 Silver Lilly Award, and the National Jewish Hospital and Research Center's 1981 Humanitarian Award. The Nevada Chapter of Contractors presented her with their SIR award, and she was also given the Kathryn Wright award, which honored her as an outstanding woman in the field of aviation.

Moya received honorary law degrees from Clemson and Pepperdine Universities. Although she was not trained as an aviator or businesswoman, Moya performed outstanding work in both areas. Congressman Jim Gibbons said of her, "She believed that in working to achieve her dreams, she could help others achieve theirs."

Moya Lear's remembrance service was not only devoted to her achievements. Friends had personal stories too. Some recalled her tendency to drive too fast. She was stopped several times, but every time the officer approached the car, Moya would pull out her honorary Deputy Sheriff of Washoe County card and say, "Look here, officer, it says right here—I'm a law-enforcement person just like you...." Evidently it worked every time.

Moya Lear's autobiography, *Bill and Moya Lear: an Unforgettable Flight*, was published in 1996. Although her adventures spanned the globe, and she could have chosen to live anywhere, she remained in Nevada. She said, "Home means Nevada, and I'll never move from my beloved home."

—*Fran Haraway*

Jessie Callahan Mahoney

essie Callahan Mahoney was born in
Austin, Nevada, to Eliza and Dan
Callahan, local ranchers of Irish descent.
When Jessie was three months old, her father
died in an accident, leaving Jessie's mother alone
to raise four children. A loan from her brothers
allowed Jessie's mother to keep the ranch, where
she sold beef, corn, grain, and pork to the nearby
Cortez mining community. Two years after her
husband's death she married Hugh McAfee, a
hired hand on area ranches.

Jessie attended school in Austin, Nevada, and
then at St. Mary's of Wasatch Academy in Salt
Lake City. For a short time she became a teacher
at the Waltis ranch near Grass Valley, Nevada.
There, she met William
Mahoney, a native of County
Cork, Ireland, and man-
ager of a huge estate owned
by William Dunphy, an
Irishman who now lived in
California. Dunphy's property encompassed 151,000
acres, with 8,000 head of cattle and horses and
other personal property valued at more than two
million dollars.

Jessie and William Mahoney were married in
1915 at a Catholic cathedral in San Francisco. They
established their residence at the White House
Ranch in Dunphy, Eureka County, Nevada. Jessie
got a saddle as a wedding present. She loved riding
and ranching and managed the household affairs of
the ranch, including supervising the Chinese cooks
who prepared meals for the hands who were off
branding or working on hay crews.

Jessie was responsible for entertaining the
ranch's many visitors. Business people, neighbors, cattle buyers, miners, traveling clergy,
relatives, and other people from all over stopped
by the White House Ranch. Often, the guests
included state politicians such as Tasker Odie,
Pat McCarran, and Judge Eather from Eureka.
Members of the Dunphy family, who owned the
ranch, occasionally visited
for an inspection. But after
a week of roughing it they
would return to their life in
San Francisco. For a time
she was even the postmis-
tress of Dunphy. Miners,
prospectors, trappers,
railroad workers, and people on other ranches
retrieved their mail from her.

Jessie and William had four children: Aileen,
Mary, Dan, and Theresa. Because William was
often off managing various ranch properties,

1887–1956
RANCHER, TEACHER, POSTMISTRESS, EUREKA COUNTY COMMISSIONER

Jessie would travel to San Francisco before each birth and stay for a time afterward. Later, because Aileen's rheumatic fever required constant medical care and attention, she took the children to live in San Francisco for a year. Aileen recounted in an oral history of the family that, "Wherever my mother was, was a lovely place to be. No matter what she was doing, she put magic in it." Aileen especially remembers her mother putting bouquets of wild roses on the dining-room table.

Having grown up on the banks of the Callahan Creek, Jessie enjoyed living near the Humboldt River and frequently took her children fishing there. She was always a teacher at heart and gave her children books for gifts, encouraged them in their studies, and filled their home with up-to-date newspapers and magazines.

In 1938, the Dunphy estate owners split up their holdings, and William found himself without a job. So, Jessie and William purchased a ranch near Beowawe, Nevada. The ranch was much smaller than the Dunphy spread, but at least it was their own. They had their own cattle and their own brand. The Mahoneys took an active interest in local politics by participating in Fourth of July parades and political rallies in Eureka and by supporting Democratic candidates for state offices.

William was elected to the Eureka County Commission, where he served several terms in the late 1930s and 1940s. When he died in 1945, Jessie was appointed by Governor Carville to finish his term. She was then elected for two more terms on her own. After her husband's death, Jessie took over running the Beowawe Ranch with son Dan and daughter Theresa. Daughter Mary also lived on the ranch while teaching school in Beowawe. Aileen reported, "Mother had always wanted to manage a ranch of her own and especially loved this one with its wide-open views." Jessie demonstrated a knowledgeable interest in every aspect of the ranch and cattle operation and was a very shrewd business person. As others at her table were figuring out cattle prices and tonnage for hay on paper, Jessie could figure it out in her head, all while serving everyone coffee.

She and Aileen used to ride together and walk through the fields close to the house looking for turkey's nests. Jessie loved picnics and could always come up with an excuse to cook steaks over an open fire or eat watermelon on the banks of the Humboldt River. She was nevertheless very feminine. Her daughter recalls that Jessie often wore earrings and a ruffled apron around the house

Jessie died on June 12, 1956, and was buried in Elko, Nevada. On her tombstone is the inscription *Manos in prosperitate, major in adversitate*. Translation: "Great in prosperity, greater in adversity."

—*Mary Gafford*

Lillian Malcolm

Lillian Malcolm was born in 1868, grew up in the eastern United States, and started a career as an actress on Broadway. But when the 1898 Klondike gold rush gave the nation gold fever, Lillian packed up her show costumes and headed "North to Alaska." It was the beginning of her new career as a mining prospector—one of the very few women who took up what was considered at the time to be strictly a man's job.

Alone, Lillian took a sled and dog team over the treacherous Chilkoot trail to Dawson City in the Yukon, a death-defying feat, but not the only adventure she would encounter. She also took a dip in the frozen Bering Sea while jumping between chunks of ice and came close to starvation when she ran out of provisions. She wore a pistol in her belt but, unfortunately, was not able to fend off the men who jumped her claim in Alaska.

After a year in court battling to retrieve her claim, she left Alaska completely broke but not discouraged. She continued to follow gold strikes for the rest of her life, always a little bit too late and never striking the big bonanza, but blazing a trail for other women to follow nonetheless.

In her book, *A Mine of Her Own*, Sally Zanjani shares some of Lillian's own works: "The grandest and healthiest life known is this rough pioneer life. And I don't see why more women are not out in the hills. It ought to be as easy and natural for women to read rocks as it is for astronomers to read the stars. The day will come when they will not sneer at Miss Malcolm. They will not pick up their skirts when I come around. Disgusting conventionality must pay the penalty in any pioneer work. . . . Woman can endure as much as a man. Comply with the law, and you will have man's responsibilities and man's reward."

From Alaska, Lillian traveled to Nevada to join the new gold and silver strikes at Goldfield and Tonopah in 1902. Since she had no money, she paid for her room and board along the way by telling stories of her Alaskan adventures. She missed the heyday of the

1868–UNKNOWN
MINING PROSPECTOR

big strikes at Goldfield and Tonopah, but staked a claim at nearby Silver Peak in Esmeralda County. She then went to Pittsburgh to raise money from eastern investors and formed a company called the Scotch Lassie Gold Mining Company. When she returned to Nevada, the *Tonopah Bonanza* reported her success in raising funds on November 2, 1907: "She is a hustler of no mean ability, and has done prospecting on her own account, both in Nevada and in Alaska." Unfortunately, her Silver Peak claims did not pan out. The gold she was looking for was not there.

Lillian also lived for a time in Rhyolite, which served as a home base while she prospected in Death Valley. There she met Death Valley Scotty, an eccentric miner and scam artist. She took an option on a claim held by his partner Bill Key. When she became involved in defending Key against accusations that he was involved in a murder plot, she lost precious time and also her option on his claim.

She spent some time in Mexico, then moved back to northern Nevada to work in the Slumbering Hills mining district. In 1911, she moved to Jarbidge in northeastern Nevada and continued her prospecting. Because Lillian had been scorned by other women and preferred the company of men, she told a newspaper reporter that she had no close female companions. Sometimes she prospected with men, and often she wandered the Nevada desert alone.

No one knows what happened to Lillian after she moved to the rugged mountains around Jarbidge. Perhaps she moved to another state or located another stake to pay for her prospecting. To curious newspaper reporters, Lillian always voiced her strong belief that women should be able to work as prospectors in any mining occupation anywhere. However, women were considered bad luck in the underground mines, a stigma they were unable to break until the 1970s, more than 100 years after Lillian Malcolm's birth.

—*Victoria Ford*

Mildred Mann

Mildred Mann was born in 1910 in St. Joseph, Missouri, where she spent her youth and early adulthood. During the Depression and World War II years, she worked in many different jobs—as a telephone operator, coil winder, electrical worker, fountain manager, marker and counter person in dry-cleaning plants, and city and county surveyor. After the war, she and her husband Arthur moved to Nevada and settled in North Las Vegas. They homesteaded property on Bassler Avenue, and Mildred immediately became active in community affairs.

As a newly developing area in Southern Nevada, the North Las Vegas property had no public services. Mildred volunteered her time and energies to serve on the newly formed Arrowhead Water Board, eventually taken over by the Las Vegas Valley Water District. She also fought hard for paved roads and streetlights in the area. Her dedication extended to canvassing neighborhoods to increase voter registrations. She served for more than 40 years on local election boards and was awarded many citations for her service.

Mildred was a founding member of the North Las Vegas Ground Observers Corp. On July 5, 1957 she was elected to represent North Las Vegas on the Board of Directors for the newly created local chapter of the National United Fund for Clark County.

In 1956, she became involved in ceramics, and in 1960 she was asked to set up a ceramics program at the Blind Center in Las Vegas. She welcomed the opportunity and served as the director of that program until her death. In 1964, along with other ceramic enthusiasts, she founded the Nevada State Ceramic Association of which she was a life member.

In 1966, Mildred was awarded the "Decoration of Chivalry" by the Odd Fellows Sovereign Grand Lodge for her work with children and the blind. She was honored with the

1910–1996
SURVEYOR, COMMUNITY
ACTIVIST

120

Governor Bob Miller bestowed the "Senior Samaritan Award" on Mildred in 1991.

Fred DeLiden Award for outstanding achievement in the field of arts and crafts. That same year she also received the Outstanding Service Award for selfless service and talent with a unique capacity for empathy that was presented by the Southern Nevada Association of Life Underwriters.

On May 15, 1972, the American Business Woman's Association honored Mildred as "Boss of the Year," and in 1977 she was honored with the Carnation Community Service Award. In 1978, she was invited to be a guest of the city of Raleigh, North Carolina, and to set up a workshop for the handicapped at Pullen Park Art Center. In 1979, Mildred was employed as the supervising teacher for the CTEA program "Project Earth" at the National Ceramic Association Educational Foundation in Cosby, Tennessee, to train the disabled through art. That same year she was awarded the Distinguished Service Award given by the Governor's Committee on Employment of the Handicapped. Governor Bob Miller bestowed the "Senior Samaritan Award" on Mildred in 1991.

Over the years, Mildred worked not only at the Blind Center but also operated Mil-Art Studio out of her home and taught porcelain art at the Clark County Community College. She was involved in may craft programs for the Parks and Recreation Department and designed craft projects for the Sears Company. She was an associate member of the National Federation of the Blind and attended the organization's national conventions as a guide to their delegates. She drafted and set up craft projects for the handicapped in many states and was the subject of stories in many national publications.

In addition to her tireless work on behalf of the handicapped, Mildred was also a member of Eastern Star, Rebekahs, and the Ladies Auxiliary of the VFW, and volunteered for the Home League of the Salvation Army.

Mildred exemplified the meaning of the word "humanitarian" and took great joy in promoting the welfare of the people of Nevada and of the nation.

—Joyce Marshall Moore

Anne Henrietta Martin

The first woman in the United States to run for the office of U.S. Senator was Nevada's dynamic political activist, Anne Martin. In 1918 and 1920, Anne ran unsuccessfully in Nevada for the U.S. Senate on the Independent ticket.

Anne Martin was born on September 30, 1875, in Empire, Nevada. Her father was a member of the Nevada Senate from 1875–1879 and was involved in a mercantile store in Empire City and later became president of the Washoe County Bank, Reno Water Company, and Reno Flour Mills. Anne and her sisters attended Reno's Bishop Whittaker School for girls. Because of her upbringing, Anne was well-educated, enjoyed physical comfort, and had independent wealth and intellectual stimulation throughout her entire life.

In 1891, Anne and her classmates were told they needed an additional year to graduate. Anne enrolled in Nevada State University, entering classes as a sophomore. After claiming her B.A. from NSU at the age of 19, she earned a B.A. and M.A. in history at Leland Stanford Junior University.

**1875–1951
EDUCATOR, POLITICAL
ACTIVIST, SUFFRAGETTE**

She returned to Reno, founded the Department of History at Nevada State University, and served on the Nevada State University faculty from 1897–1901. During a leave of absence from 1899–1901, Anne traveled abroad to study at the Universities of London, Leipzig, and Columbia, and was a student at Chase's Art School in New York City from 1899–1900. She traveled and studied in Europe from 1904–1907 and in the Orient from 1909–1911.

A stay in England brought Anne Martin to the cause of feminism. She was associated with the Fabian Socialists and was affiliated with the Women's Social and Political Union (WSPU). She participated in political activism with the Parkhurst sisters, England's leading feminists.

In 1910, Anne, 114 other women, and four men were arrested in Great Britain for their political demonstrations. They were sent by the WSPU to the House of Commons to request that the Prime Minister facilitate the Conciliation Bill, which would extend the franchise to British women in a limited way. Oddly enough, Herbert Hoover was sent by his wife Lou, Anne's friend since Stanford days, to pay her bail.

Anne returned to Nevada in 1911 after hearing that the Nevada Legislature had passed the suffrage amendment that year, to be voted on again in 1913. She was elected President of the Nevada Equal Franchise Society in 1912, organized county equal franchise societies, and led a successful statewide campaign that won women's suffrage in Nevada by popular vote on November 3, 1914, adding Nevada to the few states at the time that allowed women to vote.

Now, Anne transferred her energy to the national scene, becoming Legislative Chairman of the Congressional Union for Woman Suffrage and the first chair of the National Woman's Party in 1916. In this capacity, she urged Congress to propose a suffrage amendment to the U.S. Constitution that would take women out of the category of second-class citizens. She and others were arrested and jailed in 1917 for picketing the White House in a suffrage demonstration. They were released three days later through a legal appeal that freed all women incarcerated for suffrage activities. The suffrage movement was finally successful when the Nineteenth Amendment was proposed by Congress in 1919 and ratification was completed in 1920, giving all women who were citizens the right to vote.

Anne Martin's other accomplishments include: first female member of the Nevada Educational Survey Commission (1915); presi-dent of the Nevada Women's Civic League; first state woman tennis champion; organizer and delegate to the Women's International League for Peace and Freedom; member of the executive committee of the National American Woman Suffrage Association; chairperson of the National Woman's Party; and Independent Party candidate from Nevada for the U.S. Senate in 1918 and 1920.

In 1921, Anne and her mother sold their house in Reno and moved to Carmel, California. For the rest of her life, Anne lived mostly in Carmel but frequently returned to Reno to work on articles in the Washoe County Library. She wrote for magazines (including *Good Housekeeping*), newspapers, and the *Encyclopedia Britannica* regarding politics, economics, women's equality, and children's issues.

In recognition of her leadership in the fight for national and state suffrage, as well as her work in other fields, the University of Nevada in 1945 conferred upon Anne the degree of Doctor of Laws, with this citation: "Anne Henrietta Martin . . . native daughter, distinguished alumnus, student and scholar, inspiring teacher, disciple of world peace, pioneer in the triumphant struggle for women's rights, leader of womankind . . . Doctor of Laws."

—*Holly Van Valkenburgh*

Mila Tupper Maynard

She only lived in Reno for only a few short years, but as possibly the first female minister in Nevada, Mila Tupper Maynard's impact and influence on the community was noteworthy.

Mila Frances Tupper was born in Washington County, Iowa, as the Civil War was drawing to a close. Mila's sister, Eliza Tupper Wilkes, 20 years her senior, was active in organizing many new churches, and Mila assisted Eliza with church business during summers in her college years. This early experience encouraged Mila to later become one of a group of women ministers who provided effective leadership to Unitarian and Universalist churches throughout the Midwest.

Mila graduated from Cornell University in 1889 with a Bachelor of Letters and a special diploma in philosophy. She was ordained as a Unitarian minister that same year. She then served as the pastor of churches in La Porte, Indiana, and Grand Rapids, Michigan. During this time she received "small stipends" from the women's auxiliary of the Western Unitarian Conference to support her in a "part-time" pastorate.

When Mila was the minister of the Unitarian Church in Grand Rapids, Michigan, she was called upon to counsel Rezin Maynard, a member of the board of trustees. They formed a strong attraction and soon married in Chicago.

In 1893 Mila was also a representative at the World's Congress of Representative Women, which was held during the Columbian Exposition in Chicago.

During the early years of her marriage and career, Mila Tupper Maynard's liberal ministry became identified with Christian socialism. With her husband, she served New York's Broadway Temple, a church founded by Christian Socialist Myron Reed.

The Maynards arrived in Reno in 1892. In the fall of 1893 the Rev. Mila and Rezin Maynard became co-pastors of the newly organized Reno Unitarian Church. At the time, Mila was 29 and Rezin was 41. By 1893 the couple began to offer a series of lectures at the church, and Mila also taught courses at the University of Nevada.

In 1894, Nevada's governor appointed her to attend the Congress of the National Prison Association. In that same year, she was also invited to present a paper on Social Reform at the Women's Congress at the Midwinter Fair.

1864–1926
UNITARIAN MINISTER

Both Mila and her husband were leaders in the woman's suffrage movement, and Mila played a critical role in a temporary 1895 victory in the struggle. The 1894 election was a clean sweep in the Assembly and guaranteed that the 1895 legislature would support reforms of several kinds. One was women's suffrage, which had been an issue in the 1894 election. In the fall of 1894, the first in a series of pieces on woman's suffrage was published in the *Reno Evening Gazette*. Rezin wrote a passionate plea for the right of women to vote and predicted that allowing them to do so would bring about "a complete revolution in government, religion, and social life."

On February 11, 1895, Mila was given the highly unusual honor of addressing the Nevada State Assembly on the topic of woman's suffrage. .

Unfortunately, no newspaper printed Mila's address, but it was described by reporters as "eloquent" and as eliciting "a number of rounds of merited and appreciative applause." Her talk was followed by a vote against the woman's suffrage amendment, but later the resolution was revived and passed both houses. Unfortunately, the 1897 Legislature did not repeat the actions, a necessary step before a proposal to amend the state constitution could be presented to the voters. Success for the women's suffrage movement was finally achieved in 1914.

Mila was also the chief organizer of the Twentieth Century Club of Reno, an important organization in the 1890s. The Twentieth Century Club is credited with helping to organize the first kindergarten in Reno and with the establishment of the city's first public library.

The Maynards left Reno in 1895. It is speculated that the main reason for their departure was Mila's support for Alice Hartley, a woman who had shot her lover, Reno banker and legislator M.D. Foley, after he abandoned her when she became pregnant. Although Ms. Hartley was not a member of Mila's congregation, Mila paid pastoral visits to the accused before and during her trial. Much of the public, including members of her own congregation and other ministers, criticized her, interpreting her behavior as condoning the crime.

After leaving Reno, the Maynards moved to Salt Lake City, where they served as ministers of the First Unitarian Church. Following their time in Utah, they moved to Denver, Colorado. Rezin preached at the People's Temple there, and both Mila and Rezin contributed to Denver newspapers.

In 1907, they returned to Los Angeles. Both were active in the Socialist party and the women's suffrage movement, and Mila's focus shifted from the pastoral ministry to education. In 1918, Mila left the Socialist Party to support the country's involvement in World War I. From 1918 until her death in 1926, she devoted herself largely to teaching.

Jean Sybil McElrath

Jean Sybil McElrath was born on June 8, 1917, in the mining camp of Chloride, Arizona, to Mabell Paddock McElrath and Fenton Morrill McElrath. In 1924, the family resettled in the small town of Wells, Nevada, where Jean lived, always in the same house, until her death on October 7, 1967. She had two sisters, Anita Cory and Marjorie Klein, and one brother. Her father died in an accident in 1936, which left her mother to raise the four children alone. She graduated from Wells High School as valedictorian.

At the age of 16 she developed progressive rheumatoid arthritis and by 1938 was bedfast and unable to walk. Except for medical treatments in Idaho and surgery in Kansas City, Jean seldom left the house for the remainder of her life. Her mother and older sister Anita took most of the responsibility for her round-the-clock care, but many friends and the rest of her family helped in other ways.

Jean lost her sight by 1950, and by 1958 she had become so paralyzed and weak that she began using an electric typewriter that she nicknamed "Simon Legree." She taught herself Braille and members of her family made Braille caps for her typewriter keys.

1917–1967
AUTHOR, POET, COLUMNIST, HISTORIAN, JOURNALIST

Jean's mother and sister helped to organize, proofread, and type up the items she sent in for publication. She enjoyed listening to Talking Books from the Library of Congress and friends and family often read books to her. She would even record brief reviews and critiques of the books in her private journals. At the hospital bed in her room Jean set up a "newsroom," where she processed news items and information of all kinds and then sent it out by phone or mail to the appropriate newspaper or magazine. She often "scooped" other reporters because of the loyalty of her sources of information. She usually knew of news before it broke, but she was very careful to always verify her stories. Sometimes, Anita would transport Jean to the scene of a story on a gurney nicknamed "The Zephyr."

In January, 1966, Jean wrote in a letter, "As for the word 'handicap,' it seems to me that to the person concerned, a handicap is pretty much a matter of attitude. It depends, too, I'd say, on what you are trying to do. Nearly everyone is handicapped in some way. Hardly anyone is handicapped in every way . . . 'Boondoggling' will not do. It is an insult to adult self-respect."

Jean's memory was remarkable, as was her gift for writing. She especially enjoyed the stories of "old timers," which she collected and retold with humor and compassion.

She never lost her thirst for knowledge. After high school, Jean took correspondence courses in journalism and freelance writing. She had tutoring in Latin and Spanish. Until she lost her sight, she read omnivorously.

Famous people, such as Joel McCrae, the movie star who had a ranch in Ruby Valley, befriended Jean. Robert Laxalt, author, professor, and director of the University of Nevada Press, was one of her mentors and was instrumental in getting her book *Aged in Sage* published. In the foreword, he wrote, "In this book, author Jean McElrath has done a remarkable thing. Not only has she breathed life into fine old stories that would otherwise have been left to die, but she has done so with a true storyteller's gift of narrative, with kindness, and a deep understanding of the people she writes about."

Jean received many awards, but the highlight was when she was named Distinguished Nevadan in 1965. She was transported to the University of Nevada–Reno, where she accepted the award in person from her gurney. She was then 48 years old and had been unable to walk for 27 years and blind for 15. At the ceremony she received a congratulatory telegram that was more than eight feet long and covered with signatures from her friends.

She received the National Certificate of Award for the State of Nevada from the United States Commission for the Celebration of the Two Hundredth Anniversary of the Birth of George Washington, 1932; 1954 Winner– American Association of University Women, Nevada State Division, Pioneer Nevada Woman Essay Contest; Distinguished Nevadan award, 1965; Most Valuable Correspondent from the *Salt Lake Tribune*, 1954–1961; Certificate of Merit from the Nevada Press Association, 1966; and the Rose Award from Nevada Future Homemakers of America, 1967.

She was president of the state's Girl Scout Association (1946–56) and was an Associate Intermediate Troop Leader for three years. She belonged to the Nevada State Historical Society, Nevada Federation of the Blind, League of Women Voters, The Westerners (Los Angeles Corral), and the National League of American Pen Women.

In September, 1967, she told the editor of the *Nevada State Journal* that he should get someone else to do her job. When he refused to accept her resignation, she wrote that she would try to continue, but she signed the note "Square Wheels." Soon she was sent to the hospital in Elko, Nevada, where she slipped into a coma, and, as the editor of the *Nevada State Journal* wrote on Oct. 7, 1967, "Saturday morning death claimed Jean McElrath, newspaper reporter, author and, indeed, Distinguished Nevadan."

—*Esther Early*

Laura Mills

aura Mills devoted her entire life to the principle that a busy youngster is a happy youngster. For fifty years, Laura taught art and Nevada history in Churchill County Schools. She was, among other things, a Sunday school teacher at Epworth Methodist Church, a member of its choir, a community photographer, a contributor to western magazines, a skiing and swimming instructor, and a readily available field-trip guide.

Mills was born in Meadowvale, Minnesota, the eldest of seven children. Her mother was an enthusiastic botanist and taxidermist. Each of the Mills children, under the direction of their parents, laid out, planted, and tended individual gardens. As a result of her parents' interest, Laura was a nature enthusiast from early childhood.

Laura's parents farmed in Elk River, Minnesota for several years before moving to the Wildes District of Nevada in 1908. They later transplanted their homestead to the Sheckler District and began, again, to farm.

In 1912, Laura graduated from the original Churchill County High School. Having decided to become a teacher, she passed her examinations and began her first teaching job in Tobar Station, Elko County, in a one-room school with nine students for $65 a month. She stayed for one year during which time she "traversed the fields of Clover Valley and hiked the valley's rugged mountains as hunter, fisherman, camera bug, rock-hound, and naturalist." The following June Laura headed home to teach school in the Smart District School in Churchill County.

Never content with her education, she enrolled by correspondence in the University of Nevada–Reno in 1918, focusing on art, music, and natural history. In 1924, she was admitted to the Yosemite Field School (now Yosemite Institute), a select group of 20 pupils

1893–1973
TEACHER, WRITER, CIVIC
LEADER, PHOTOGRAPHER,
TAXIDERMIST

who wandered the high Sierra Nevadas. They lived in Yosemite for six weeks, instructed by professors from the University of California at Berkeley. She studied there for several summers, which gave her an expanding knowledge of the natural history of the West. She soon became a recognized authority in this field.

Mills was appointed an honorary curator of ornithology in 1941 by the Nevada State Museum Board of Trustees. Between 1941–43 she gave the museum a total of 114 mounted birds on which she had done the taxidermy herself. Many of them were native to the West.

Laura Mills officially retired from teaching in 1953. Her students remember clustering around to make plans for the next field trip to Virginia City, to go on the latest hunt for bug specimens, to identify various flora and fauna, or perhaps to receive some needed direction and guidance. As a photographer, she took many of the pictures for *Here is Nevada* by Sawyer and Mack, *The Past in Glass* by the Ferraros, and *The Antique Bottle Collection* by Kendrick, all books widely sought after by collectors. She frequently presented photo programs on various tours around Nevada and was a member of the Reno Colorfoto Club. She also led youth activities for 4-H clubs, Campfire Girls, church and musical groups. Laura Mills received the Distinguished Nevadan Award in 1968. She died on December 25, 1973.

—*Sally Wilkins*

Emma Wixom Nevada

Emma Wixom was born in Nevada City, California, but in the spring of 1864 she moved with her family to Austin, Nevada, where her father, Dr. William Wixom, started a practice as a physician. Emma soon became a center of attention in what was then Nevada's second-largest city, an isolated silver mining boomtown in the rugged mountains of central Nevada.

Emma first received public applause at age five, when she marched in the historic Gridley Sack of Flour Parade. The parade is significant because it may have led to the first national fundraising gimmick for a charitable organization. The Gridley parade started as a result of a political bet between Austin grocer Rueul Gridley and Dr. R.C. Herrick. The loser of the wager was to buy and deliver a fifty-pound sack of flour to the winner. Gridley lost the bet, and consequently, with the Austin Brass Bend tooting, city officials cheering, flags flying, whistles blowing, and an assembly of enthusiastic fun-loving Austin residents following him, Gridley marched the length of the city's main street to Clifton in lower Austin. Little Emma Wixom joined this entertaining parade and sang "John Brown's Body," to the great pleasure of the crowd, In Clifton, the parade

1859–1940
LYRIC SOPRANO
OPERA SINGER

stopped at the Bank Exchange Saloon for refreshments and then retraced its steps back uphill to the Grimes and Gibson Saloon. Here the patriotically decorated sack of flour was auctioned off, then given back to the auctioneer and sold repeatedly, raising $4549 for the Sanitary Fund, a fund to help Civil War wounded and sick. Emma's father may have been one of the auctioneers.

This story hit the newspapers, and upon the urging of Mark Twain, an old friend from Missouri, Gridley brought the sack of flour to the Comstock area and, with great pomp and hilarity, again sold the sack of flour many times. From the Comstock area he proceeded to Sacramento and San Francisco, where he sailed to the East Coast. His journey ended one year later at the St. Louis World's Fair. In the interim, Gridley had raised as much as $275,000 for the Sanitary Fund, forerunner of the American Red Cross. The Gridley Sack of Flour can be seen at the Nevada Historical Society in Reno.

After Emma's debut in the parade, her father encouraged her singing, and she was often found vocalizing in the doorways of the town's streets. At age ten, her pure soprano voice was again noticed when she sang with international vocalist

Baron von Netzer in Austin's Methodist Church. Emma was a member of the church choir and attended Sunday School there.

When Emma was twelve, her mother died, so Dr. Wixom sent Emma to Mills Seminary [College] in Oakland, California, where she was further educated in music and language. She studied German, French, Italian, and Spanish; this background as a linguist eventually led her to learn to sign for the deaf and to speak Washoe, Paiute, and Shoshone. It was at Mills that Emma Wixom, not too scholarly, not too pretty, near-sighted, and somewhat stout and having questionable taste in clothing, sang whenever and wherever she was asked. Soon she was attracting enthusiastic crowds from Oakland and San Francisco to listen to her beautiful crystalline soprano voice.

Emma became friends with a music teacher at Mills, Dr. Adrian Ebell. Dr. Ebell and his wife arranged to take Emma with them to Europe, where she could receive serious training as a singer under the direction of Madame Marchesi in Paris and Vienna. When Dr. Ebell died during the trip, Emma remained in Europe to complete her training. She was sustained by funds given by friends in California and Nevada. In 1880, Emma made her singing debut in London and adopted the stage name of Emma Nevada in honor of her birthplace and home state. She continued touring engagements in France, Germany, and Italy. Her father went to Europe to handle Emma's tours, and she became an instant success

in operatic and musical circles throughout the world, often singing for kings and queens. Once, Queen Victoria gave Emma, a favorite of the queen, a diamond necklace said to be valued at $100,000.

In 1885, she returned to the United States with the Mapleson Opera Company. Dr. Raymond Palmer, an Englishman living in Paris, was now her manager. She sang to sold-out crowds throughout the country. Her performances in San Francisco were met with wild enthusiasm. She returned to her beloved Austin on a special train and was met by all the townspeople. Emma gave a concert to an overflowing crowd in Austin's Methodist Church, where old-time miners again came down from the hills to hear her sing.

That same year, Emma and Dr. Palmer were married in Paris but soon moved to London. Emma returned to the United States several times with opera companies and concert tours. In 1902, she honored Nevada City and Mills College with concerts, again attracting old-timers who had heard her as a child. Soon after, she retired from her brief but brilliant operatic career—with the one exception of singing at the coronation of George V in 1910. Emma had a daughter named Mignon whom she trained for a singing career. Emma Wixom Nevada lived in quiet retirement until her death in Liverpool, England, on June 26, 1940 at the age of 81.

—*Doris Drummond*

Sarah Thompson Olds

Sarah Elizabeth Thompson, the youngest daughter of nine children, was born in Iowa in 1875. Her father, Alexander Thompson, had come to America from Scotland by way of Canada, and her mother, Mary Anne Harper, had emigrated from Ireland. The Thompsons settled on a farm near Ottumwa, where they had children over a spread of many years. By the time Sarah was a young girl; several siblings were already out on their own.

One of Sarah's brothers, Dave, had been drawn to the mining boom out west, and the accounts of his adventures prompted several family members to follow his example and head for the camps. Sarah's older sister Nettie had also gone west to escape the criticism that resulted after her divorce, considered shameful in those days.

In 1890, Sarah's parents became ill, and Sarah, as the youngest daughter, stayed home to care for them by working as a dressmaker, one of the few acceptable occupations for a young woman from the Bible Belt. By 1891, her parents had died, and 21-year-old Sarah was free of responsibility, so over the objections of family,

1875–1963
HOMESTEADER, DUDE
RANCH OPERATOR

friends, and hopeful young suitors, she headed west like her disgraced sister Nettie.

Nettie, who made a living as a cook and housekeeper in Modesto, California, knew that the mining camps of the southern motherlode would appreciate anyone who could cook and sew. Sarah set out for Sonora but eventually chose a camp in California called Stent. There she met A.J. Olds, a prospector and miner.

A.J.'s father had been a member of the Constitutional Convention of California, and his grandfather had extensive landholdings, but A.J. and his brother were lured by the gold fields, traveling from camp to camp until both were failing in health, suffering from silicosis, in those days known as miner's consumption or "miner's con."

After Sarah and A.J. married, they continued their search for riches. Their first three children were born in the promising camps of the time—Edson in Confidence, California, Jessie in Bisbee, Arizona, and Alice in Virginia City, Nevada.

Their last three children—Leslie, Albert and Martha—were born in Reno, where the family settled in 1906 after A.J. became too ill to work underground. The Olds homestead consisted of

a three-room board-and-batten house with a shed roof. There were no fences, so the live-stock slept next to the house, which was surrounded by open range with Tule Mountain to the east and Dogskin Mountain to the west. The nearest neighbor was twelve miles away.

By 1926 the Olds children were away at school or had married and moved on, so Sarah, know as Mom Olds to the local ranchers and cowboys, launched a new career. Pyramid Lake featured a popular fishing camp called Sutcliff or The Willows. The camp was located on one of the few privately deeded pieces of property on the Paiute Reservation. The owner, Maggie Sutcliff, had died, and her husband could not run the operation, so Sarah and A.J. took over the ragtag conglomeration of tent houses and shacks. Sarah tended to the needs of the camp while A.J. entertained their guests with tales of early days in the mines. They replaced the main building and got rid of the tents. Indian women helped Sarah with the dishes and laundry, and the three youngest Olds children pitched in during the summers.

In 1927 the Nevada state legislature changed residency requirements for divorce from six months to three months. Would-be divorcees flocked to the Reno area, and their need for housing sparked the creation of several dude ranches.

Sutcliff, too, became a dude ranch but also kept its fishing camp activities going.

In 1931, Sarah sold Sutcliff and moved to Reno, where A.J., who had been bedridden for years, died. The Great Depression had come to Nevada, and Sarah was able to buy part of the Waltz Ranch near Virginia Lake. She planned to operate it as a dude ranch, but the "Winter of the Big Hungry" changed her plans. She found herself playing hostess to un-employed cowboys and out-of-work locals, so she leased the ranch house and built a smaller home nearby (where the Lakeside Plaza shopping center now stands).

Sarah spent her time revising her memoirs, *Twenty Miles from a Match: Homesteading in Nevada*, which she had written during her sojourn at Sutcliff. She was active in the Unity Church. Alert and energetic until the end, Sarah died in 1963 at the age of 88, having attained her goal of educating her six children without outside help. Her daughter, Leslie Olds Zurfluh, speaking of the accomplishments of her mother and her siblings, remarked, "Not a bad record for a bunch of homesteaders' kids and a woman who started from scratch."

—*Fran Haraway*

Mary Leitch Oxborrow

Mary Leitch was born in West Bromage, Staffordshire, England on October 17, 1852. Her parents—natives of Germany—had moved to England in 1850. Her father was a band teacher who had once conducted the Kaiser's band. Her mother was a harpist and singer. The Leitch family also owned a music store in England and once even entertained the King and Queen, mother singing while the father accompanied on violin.

Mary's mother died when Mary was ten months old, and her father, who had been visited by Mormon missionaries and had become a member of the Church of Jesus Christ of Latter Day Saints, died five years later as he was making plans to sail to America, where he hoped to open a music store.

Mary finally did leave for America on May 3, 1864, in the company of her stepmother's family. The voyage took five weeks and four days. Upon arriving, they steamed across the Great Lakes and then took a train to the Illinois frontier where they joined an overland wagon train and headed west.

Although their journey had been difficult, those hardships did not compare to the family's

1852—1935
MEDICINE WOMAN,
MIDWIFE

trek across the plains to Utah. Mary walked the entire distance next to the ox team. She and the other girls wore aprons in which they gathered buffalo chips to burn for light and warmth at night. Mary recalled that by the time the company had reached a stream in which to bathe, she would be covered with body lice, and, having no shampoo, she would try to wash her hair with the smooth, black mud from the river bank.

The family arrived in Salt Lake City but remained there only three weeks before heading to the new settlement of St. George, Utah. Mary began to earn her living by hiring out to large families to help with the washing, ironing, baby tending, cooking, dishwashing, sewing, and quilt making. With no evenings or afternoons off, she received top wages of $2.50 per week.

Mary also sang in church choir and began to meet people her own age, but on June 21, 1870, the 17-year-old girl was persuaded to enter into a plural marriage with Joseph Oxborrow, 52 years of age and already husband to one wife, Jenette. Mary was already acquainted with Jenette, and they got along fairly well. Like many young women of the LDS church, Mary accepted polygamy and understood the seriousness of her undertaking, faithfully maintaining her marriage vows and working to overcome the many problems of plural marriage.

Mary and Joseph had eleven children, four of whom died while very young. Joseph passed away in 1895, and, 1899, Mary was chosen by the church to travel to Nevada to work as a midwife and nurse to the settlers of the Tom Plane Ranch—now the town of Lund. In Nevada, Mary at once became active as a medicine woman and as a counselor and teacher in her church. Her skills in midwifery and nursing made her in great demand, since the nearest doctor was 35 miles away by horse and buggy.

In 1908, Mary was sent to Salt Lake City by the Lund Ward of the LDS Church to study obstetrics under the supervision of Dr. Ramona B. Pratt, but her plan was sidelined by her brother, who sustained a spinal injury while working on the battleship *Utah* on the docks of New Jersey.

Mary spent two years nursing her brother back to health before returning to Nevada to continue her work in medicine. Sometimes entire days were spent tending to the cuts, carbuncles, dislocated bones, kidney infections, burns, and other problems of the Lund locals. Often, instead of sitting through the night at a patient's home, she would bring the afflicted person into her own home.

Two hundred and thirty-seven babies were brought into the world by Mary Oxborrow, including two of her own great grandchildren. She never lost a mother, and only two of the babies were born dead.

Mary made great use of natural herbs. The druggists in Ely counted her as one of their best customers. They knew her recipes for salve, canker medicine, hand lotion, and other cures made from local healing ingredients.

An energetic, vital woman, Mary's one vanity was wearing shoes too small for her feet. She was consequently slightly bowlegged. Mary wore at least four petticoats each day, one of these her money-pocket petticoat. Moving close to the counter in each store she patronized, she would carefully lift each skirt until she came to the one which held her small coin purse. Nobody had the nerve to tell her that this was an unladylike gesture.

A widow for forty years, Mary remained in her own home with at least one grandchild spending the night with her each night until her death on January 10, 1935. Those who knew her affectionately called her Grandma.

—*Sally Wilkins, from information provided by Effie O. Reed, Mary Leitch Oxborrow's granddaughter (Fran Haraway, ed.)*

Mary Belle Park

Mary Belle Viley grew up in Kentucky and attended the Central University of Kentucky, where she met fellow student William Park. Park's father, John S. Park, moved his family from Kentucky to Las Vegas in 1905, where he established the First State Bank and founded the city's first power company. Young William Park worked with his father in the bank, but on a visit back to Kentucky, he became reacquainted with Mary Belle, and they were married on August 17, 1909.

Dr. William Park and his bride made Las Vegas their home and lived with Park's parents in a large stone house at Fourth and Fremont. Dr. Park quit his job at the bank and opened a dental practice, which he continued until his death in 1946.

In 1905, John S. Park purchased the Kiel Ranch, located in what is now North Las Vegas. He used this property as a "working ranch," but as Fremont Street became the business center of the new community, John S. built a new home for his family at the Kiel Ranch. This mansion, known as "The White House," was the scene of many of the area's social events and, after John S. sold it, became known as Bolderado, a dude/divorce ranch patronized by the rich and famous.

In 1920, William and Mary Belle built new house of their own at 622 East Charleston Blvd. This home was the showplace of the growing community, set back from the street and shaded by large cottonwood and mesquite trees. Mary Belle was famous for her beautiful gardens. It was the first "ranch-style" home built in the area.

Dr. and Mrs. Park had only one child, a son. John William graduated from Stanford University with a degree in aeronautical engineering and was killed in the crash of an experimental bomber during a test flight in 1940. He had one daughter born several months after his death.

The primary community involvement of the Park family centered around Masonic organizations and civic groups. During their entire lifetime the couple were devoted leaders in promoting educational and cultural enrichment in the city. Mary Belle was particularly interested in horticulture and Dr. Park in Southwestern Indian archeology. Dr. Park became a student of Dr. E.M. Harrington, who was associated with the Southwest Museum of Los Angeles. The museum was excavating the Basketmaker tribe artifacts in

1879—1965
COMMUNITY VOLUNTEER

the Lost City area, which was soon to be covered by Lake Mead. Dr. Park accumulated one of the area's finest collections of Indian pottery and other artifacts. After his death, Mary Belle donated this rare collection to the museum in Overton.

Mary Belle was an avid gardener and early in her years in Nevada began experimenting with desert plants. Her flowers, especially her roses, almost always won a prize in local garden shows. Mary Belle was also active in Eastern Star, where she was elected Grand Matron of the Grand Chapter of Nevada. She served as President of the Mesquite Club, was a charter member of PEO, and served as PEO president from 1956 to 1957. Among her other social activities were the Daughters of the American Revolution and the Rose Unit of the Trowell and Trellis Garden Club of Las Vegas. Mary Belle Parks died at the age of 86 on September 10, 1965, in Sand Point, Idaho, and was buried in Forest Lawn Cemetery in Glendale, California.

—*Jean F. Spiller*

Maria Garifalou Pavlakis

Maria "Mama" Pavlakis knew how to run a bakery. But this was only one of the reasons why she became a beloved businesswoman and unforgettable personality in White Pine County, Nevada. Growing up in Ismir, Turkey, Maria experienced wealth, poverty, war, dislocation, the death of her parents, and the life of an orphan and refugee—all before the age of seventeen.

Maria was born in 1912 to one of the wealthiest export businessmen in Turkey. But, in 1922, Greeks living in Turkey had a sudden change of fortune. Because Greece had entered World War I on the side of the victorious Allies, a peace treaty gave Greece temporary control of Ismir on Turkey's west coast. But peace was short lived. In 1921, Greece renewed its historic war with the Ottoman Empire (Turkey). Because of the war, the 1.25 million Greeks living in Turkey had to return to Greece, and the 400,000 Turks living in Greece had to return to Turkey. The Greeks of Ismir, among them Maria's family, were moved into concentration camps prior to relocation. Before leaving, Mr. Garifalou had buried the family's gold, diamonds, and platinum to

1912–1982
BAKER, PASTRY SHOP OWNER

keep them from the Turks. On the forced march to the camp, a Turk demanded that Maria's father disavow his Christian faith and submit to Islam. He refused, and the Turk killed him with the butt of his gun. As refugees, Mrs. Garifalou and her children went on to Athens, where they had relatives. In Greece, Maria's mother died, leaving the children to raise themselves. Maria and her siblings supported themselves by picking olives.

In 1929, at age seventeen, Maria entered into an arranged marriage with Tony Pavlakis. Tony had emigrated from Greece to Ely, Nevada, nine years earlier. He had started a bakery that catered to the many Greeks who came to the area in the early 1900s to build the railroad and to work in the mines. A traditional man, Tony returned to Greece to find his bride.

Maria quickly learned about her new country and the bakery business. She soon became a well-liked member of the Ely community, and the Pavlakis bakery made most of the bread and pastries for the town's restaurants, stores, and hotels. Six children were born to Maria and Tony. After each birth, Maria started a bank account for that child's college education.

At first, the family managed the Royal Hotel and ran the Royal Bakery in downtown Ely. Tony was up at two in the morning to start baking. Maria arrived between five and six to greet the customers. The business became a family affair. From an early age, the Pavlakis children worked in the bakery and delivered baked goods by panel truck to its many customers. Five of the six children attended college—in 1956, all five were in college at the same time!

Out-of-town politicians frequently stopped by the pastry shop, not only for the fresh bread and pastry, but also to have a conversation with the owner. The talk they got was straightforward, to the point, and without pretext. Some regarded the Pavlakis bakery as the stock market weathervane for White Pine County. When the economy was good, Maria could hardly keep up with the orders. Governor Mike O'Callaghan was a frequent visitor to the shop, and Mama Pavlakis would tell him ways to solve the world's problems. She was considered a Nevada institution. Her loving spirit and complete candor made her a favorite with politicians and locals alike. Maria represented the best characteristics of pioneer women: a willingness to help others, a strong work ethic, and concern for her state, community, and family. When Tony died in 1967, Maria, with the help of her children, continued to run the bakery.

In the early 1980s Mama Pavlakis was interviewed on PBS Channel 10, appeared on the cover of Mt. Wheeler Power Company's monthly magazine, and was Grand Marshall of Ely's Fourth of July Parade. After Maria died in 1982, she was eulogized by former Governor O'Callaghan, who was also an honorary pallbearer, and by former Representative Jim Santini and State Supreme Court Justice Noel Manoukian. All commented on her positive contributions to the life and lore of White Pine County.

Kennecott Copper Corporation's huge mining complexes—the pit and mines in Ruth and Kimberly, the mill and smelter in McGill—are long gone. Nevada Northern Railway operations have ended. The good times have left these once bustling communities. The Pavlakis Pastry Shop has been torn down, and the corner where it stood is empty. But for those who knew her, Mama will still be there, smiling and waving to all who pass by.

Addendum: In the year 2000, this writer was walking through Ely Cemetery and noted one gravesite different from the others. It was piled high with wreaths and bouquets of flowers. Curious, I went closer to see who might be held in such high esteem. The name on the tombstone? Maria "Mama" Pavlakis.

—*Doris Drummond*

Josie Reed Pearl

Josephine (Josie) Reed was born in Evening Shade, Arkansas, on December 19, 1873, and lived long beyond her allotted three score and ten years to become one of Nevada's most notable characters. She and her family moved to Tennessee in 1875 and to San Luis Valley, New Mexico Territory, six years later. She loved being outdoors and developed an interest in mining in her early teens after she was shown how to pan for gold. In 1886 she filed a gold claim at Rat Creek in New Mexico that she later sold for $5,000.

After moving to Crede, Colorado, in 1890, Josie worked as a waitress in a boardinghouse until she married a young mining engineer, Lane Pearl, two years later. For the next ten years, Josie followed her husband from one mining camp to another, until they ended up in Goldfield, Nevada, in 1904. When Goldfield's boom went bust in 1910, the couple moved to Ward in White Pine County. Josie continued to work in restaurants and boarding houses while also prospecting.

Following her husband's death in 1918, Josie drifted from one end of Nevada to the other for the next four years. In 1922, she acquired several

1873–1962
PROSPECTOR, MINER

mining claims in the Columbia Mining District in the Pine Forest Range of northern Humboldt County. There, she settled down for good, building a cabin in Cove Canyon near the Black Rock Desert where she was to remain for the next forty years.

For years she hoped to make a big strike, but her claims provided only the most meager living. Nonetheless, she grubstaked other prospectors, apparently hoping that their luck would be better than hers.

Writer Ernie Pyle visited Josie in 1936 and wrote about her in his nationally syndicated column, describing her as "...a woman of the West. Her dress was calico, with an apron over it. On her head was a farmer's straw hat. On her feet a mismatched pair of men's shoes, and on her left hand and wrist $6,000 worth of diamonds! That was Josie—contradictions all over, and a sort of Tugboat Annie of the desert. Her whole life has been spent hunting for gold in the ground. She was a prospector. She had been at it since she was nine, playing a man's part in a man's game."

In 1947, selections from Pyle's columns were published in the book *Home Country*, and Josie

once again found herself on the national stage for a brief moment. However, other writers who wanted to follow up on Pyle's story were either unable to locate her place or found the cabin deserted when they arrived.

In 1953, Western writer Nell Murbarger heard that Josie was still alive and was able to get directions to her camp. In an article that appeared in *Desert Magazine* in August 1954, Murbarger described her as "not a large woman, but healthy-looking and robust, with determination and self-sufficiency written all over her." Her face was "one of the most unforgettable I have ever seen," Murbarger wrote. "Years were in that face—a great many years—but there was in it some indefinable quality that far overshadowed the casual importance of age. The eyes that bored into mine were neither friendly nor unfriendly. Rather, they were shrewd and appraising; as steady as the eyes of a gunfighter; as noncommittal as those of a poker player."

Pyle had described Josie's cabin as "the wildest hodgepodge of riches and rubbish I'd ever seen," a judgment with which Murbarger agreed. Josie kept letters from friends pinned on the walls, assay reports, newspaper clippings, tax receipts, and piles of newspapers and maga-

zines. Josie confirmed her grubstakes with other would-be mining magnates and told Murbarger of the many lawsuits she had been involved in over the years. Murbarger wrote: "She also told of loneliness, of what it meant to be the only woman in mining camps numbering hundreds of men. She told of packing grub on her back through twenty-below-zero blizzards, of wading through snow and sharpening drill steel and loading shots, of defending her successive mines against high graders and claim jumpers and faithless partners. "

When she got lonely in later years, she would drive her pickup the seventy-five miles into Winnemucca to visit Avery Sitzer, editor of the *Humboldt Star*. When her eyesight began to fail, however, she became a menace to local ranchers and other drivers, coming hell-bent for leather down the middle of the road, leaving clouds of dust in her wake. "Oh, oh, here comes Josie… head for the brush!" was the usual comment of those who saw her driving.

In the fall of 1962, she succumbed to heart disease and complications of old age, and died at Washoe Medical Center on December 29. On her death certificate, her occupation was listed as "hardrock miner." But she was so much more.

—*Phil Earl*

141

Alice Pearson

lice Pearson was born to Mabel and Elmer Lien in 1918 in the small western Minnesota town of Hendricks. Alice's parents were both first generation Americans born of Norwegian immigrant parents.

Alice's father was a mechanic at the Hendricks garage, owned by Alice's grandfather. Her other grandfather owned the local telephone company, and Alice's mother worked as the head operator in the telephone office. The family lived in the telephone office, and the main switchboard was located in their living room.

Alice was raised by her mother and grandparents and attended grade school in Hendricks. When she was high school age, her grandparents sent her to Mankato, Minnesota, to the Bethany Lutheran Academy, where she graduated in 1936. Alice then took courses in executive secretarial training at the Minneapolis Business College, finishing in 1937.

Alice's first job was working for the Sons of Norway Lodge headquarters in Minneapolis, a position she was able to obtain thanks to her ability to speak Norwegian, an important skill,

1918–2002
COMMUNITY ACTIVIST, OFFICE WORKER, PTA MEMBER, SCOUT LEADER, SALVATION ARMY LEADER

since many of the members at that time wrote their correspondence to the lodge in their native Norwegian. She started in this position at a salary of $60 per month and after five years was earning $90 per month, a respectful amount in the late 1930s.

In 1941, after America's entry in WWII, jobs were available with defense contractors in the Minneapolis area, and Alice took a job, at a considerable increase in pay, as purchasing agent for a company that manufactured gun mounts for Navy 3-inch guns.

One evening, Alice was out for dinner in a restaurant with her cousin, and they met Arthur Pearson, a young first generation American of Swedish decent on leave from the army. Art and Alice were soon very interested in one another.

Art, a graduate of the University of Minnesota, was an accountant and had been working for the Arthur Anderson accounting firm until drafted into the Army. In the Army, Art worked in the Post Finance Office. Art was soon sent overseas to Europe and remained there for several months after the war ended. When he returned, Art and Alice were

married in the Lutheran church in August 1946. Art went back to work for Arthur Anderson, and the young couple remained in Minneapolis until 1956. During this time, Art and Alice had three children: Steven, born in 1947, Nancy, born in 1956, and Mark, born in 1956. All three children eventually attended schools in Las Vegas, and all earned college degrees.

It was the policy of Arthur Anderson to select proven and reliable members for senior jobs with other firms. In 1956, Art was selected to interview with the Nevada Power Company in Las Vegas, Nevada, for the position of company treasurer. He was selected for the job, and he and Alice sold their home, bought a new Ford station wagon, and moved their family from Minneapolis to Las Vegas in December. They lived in different rental homes before finally completing their own house on Chapman Drive in 1958. Alice lived in the house until her death in 2002. Art retired from Nevada Power in 1981 after serving as both president and chairman of the board for the company. The large Nevada Power Building located at the corner of Sahara and Jones in west Las

Vegas is named the Pearson Building in honor of Arthur Pearson.

Alice was always active in the Las Vegas community. When her children were young, she was involved in the PTA, Boy Scouts, Girl Scouts, and many church groups. After her children were grown, Alice became more involved in community activities, serving on the advisory board of the Salvation Army and as president of the Salvation Army Women's Auxiliary. In 2000, she was awarded the Salvation Army's prestigious Life Membership Award.

Alice started the Altar Guild, a service group in the First Good Shepherd Lutheran Church and was a charter member and president of the Assistance League of Las Vegas and president of the Mesquite Club. She was also an active member of the Nevada Women's History Project and served on the PEO state board for seven years, conducting the organization's state meeting as president in 1987.

—*Mollie L. Murphy*

Marjory Gusewelle Phillips

arjory Phillips, longtime Las Vegas resident and civic leader, made significant contributions to the growth of Nevada.

Marjory Gusewelle was born on October 1, 1920, in Las Vegas Hospital to Juanita Clark and Frank Weldon Gusewelle, both schoolteachers from Missouri. The newly married couple had moved to Searchlight, Nevada, in 1918, where Frank had a job driving trucks for Juanita's uncle. At that time Searchlight was a larger town than Las Vegas.

They moved to Las Vegas in 1923, and Frank worked as a distributor for Texaco service stations. With the trucks and equipment used in the construction of the Boulder Dam, gasoline distributors were kept busy. The family's first home was at Fourth and Bridger. In 1936 they moved into a larger home on Sixth Street.

Frank was a role model for his daughter in civic leadership and responsibility. He was a county commissioner and a leader in the Elks, Rotary Club, and Chamber of Commerce.

Marjory attended the Las Vegas Elementary School (Fifth Street School) and graduated from Las Vegas High School in 1937 as salutatorian of her class. She spoke at the commencement services on "World Problems, Our Problems." She had been student body treasurer in 1936-37 and in the Honor Club and Torch Honor Society, and was business manager and associate editor of the school newspaper, *The Desert Breeze*, and editor of the yearbook, *Boulder Echo*.

Marjory graduated from the University of Nevada–Reno in 1941 with majors in journalism and English. She was women's editor of the *Sagebrush*, a student publication and a member of the Kappa Alpha Theta social sorority; the Cap and Scroll honorary scholastic society; Chi Delta Phi, a women's national honorary literary society; and the Press Club.

After graduation, Marjory got a job with the *Reno Evening Gazette*. On March 9, 1944, she married George W. Phillips and moved to Las Vegas for good. Marjory and George had two children, a son, George William Phillips, Jr., and a daughter, Marjory Lynne.

In 1946, a small group of ladies founded the Service League, later called the Junior League. Marjory became its president in 1953. Under her

1920—1978
COMMUNITY ACTIVIST

leadership, the League maintained a craft workshop for the blind in association with the Southern Nevada Association for the Blind and the Lions Club, as well as thrift shop to fund the group's many projects in the community.

Marjory served on the Executive Committee of the University of Nevada Alumni Association in Southern Nevada and received the Alumni Service Award for strengthening Alumni Association memberships in Southern Nevada.

A new state university campus in Las Vegas was a dream of many community leaders in the early 50s. The 1955 state legislature passed a bill to construct a campus building with a rider requiring the local residents to raise an additional $35,000 to buy the required land for the new Nevada Southern Campus. Marjory was on the sponsoring committee for the fund drive, and, between the help of the Service League and the efforts of university students, the needed amount was easily raised.

In 1958 Marjory was asked by Governor Grant Sawyer to be a member of the Nevada School Survey Commission. This commission was to serve as a fact-finding body to investigate financial and administrative problems of public elementary and high schools in Nevada.

She was also a member of the Juvenile Survey Commission appointed by the judges of the Eighth Judicial District Court. They opposed plans for a state girl's correctional institution in Caliente and called for badly needed facilities for the Clark County Juvenile Home.

Marjory was the only woman appointed by Governor Grant Sawyer in 1961 to the Centennial Committee of the state of Nevada. She worked tirelessly as a speaker at many community clubs and organizations statewide to publicize the events of the centennial celebration and coordinated the ceremonies to unveil a commemorative medallion design on April 4, 1964. As a result of her tremendous efforts, Marjory was honored as a recipient of the Nevada Saving and Loan Association's "Outstanding Citizen Award."

She was also one of the founders of the Southern Nevada Historical Museum and a moderator in 1977 for the *Las Vegas Sun*'s Youth Forum, where Clark County High School juniors and seniors exchanged viewpoints on world issues.

Marjory, among her many talents, enjoyed painting in watercolor. Her paintings portrayed scenes of the deserts, mountains, and lakes that she loved to explore with her family.

Marjory Phillips died on January 10, 1978, after a life spent living up to her belief that "by educating themselves to the needs of the community and the problems to be overcome, women will continue to make a significant contribution to the social, educational, and cultural growth of the state."

—*Betty Miller and Alice Pearson*

Bertha Raffetto

Bertha Eaton was born in Bloomfield, Iowa, on March 15, 1885, the daughter of Enoch Henry and Susan Frances Walker Eaton. Of her early life, Bertha recalled that "appreciation of good literature was fostered by Mother's nightly Bible reading; all of the classics and fiction of that period; philosophy and science." By the age of thirteen, Bertha had read Shakespeare, Thomas Paine, and Voltaire. She and her three sisters were encouraged in their self-expression by animated discussions at the family supper table. She gave her first poetry recital at the age of three, "lisping" out a couple of verses from her grandfather's church pulpit, and wrote her first poem at age five. Music, especially sacred music, was something she enjoyed every day.

Bertha became a schoolmarm in the Ozarks. She went with the men on turkey shoots and was an independent, free-thinking woman in an era when a woman's place was supposed to be in the home.

Bertha Eaton married Henry Clyde Hough and had two sons, one of whom died at an early age. She later married Fiore Raffetto, the man who had been her Reno divorce attorney after she left Henry Hough. Bertha and Fiore were married for 30 years and had one daughter, Frances Cornelia. "In view of all the places my mother both visited and lived in for varying lengths of time, I have no doubt Mother felt and meant it when she said 'Home Means Nevada,'" said Bertha's daughter, Mrs. Frances McDonald of Reno, in 1952.

Bertha worked as a writer in Nevada. She composed music and poetry and was active in club and civic work. Her poetry, articles, and stories were published in many well-known magazines and newspapers. She was a accomplished speaker and participated actively in Republican politics in numerous

1885–1952
Writer, Poet, Political Activist

campaigns. During the 1930s she conducted the popular "Poet's Corner" feature in the *Nevada State Journal*. She was also a 25-year member of the Reno branch of Pen Women, for whom she served as treasurer, vice president, president, and state president. She was poet laureate of the Nevada Federation of Women's Clubs and was awarded the Poet's Parchment by the General Federation of Women's Clubs for outstanding work on behalf of poets and poetry.

Among her other affiliations, Bertha was a member of the Women's Relief Corps, Reno Civic Club, Nevada and General Federation of Women's Clubs, Order of the Eastern Star, Daughters of the Nile, National Poetry Society, Poets of the Pacific, and the Virginia Poetry Society. As a delegate to the national convention of the Women's Relief Corps and Grand Army of the Republic, Bertha obtained the nucleus

for the G.A.R. scholarship at the University of Nevada. She also attended the General Federation of Women's Clubs at Boston in 1950 and the Pen Women's convention in Washington that same year.

Bertha's major musical achievements include her composition "Home Means Nevada," which was made the official Nevada state song by an act of the legislature on February 6, 1933. Another musical composition was "The Spirit of Democracy," a concert march for band that was performed by the U.S. Marine Band on a national broadcast from Washington, DC.

Bertha also published a narrative poem, "The Ballad of Katie Hoskins," that was widely lauded by literary critics as "an outstanding example of fine American balladry" and was used as a text by Columbia University.

—*Sally Wilkins*

Anna Frances Elleser Rechel

Anna Frances Elleser was born into comfortable surroundings on January 1, 1884, in Pearl River, New Jersey. Her parents were immigrants from Germany who had settled in Tappan, New York, where Anna grew up in a mansion. She was only in her early twenties when both parents died, leaving Anna and her brother Walter to care for themselves. Anna married young but divorced her husband quickly when she realized her mistake. She married again in 1911 to George Rechel; when complications from her divorce developed, Anna and George moved to Nevada to complete the divorce process.

They settled on a ranch south of Fernley, where all of Anna's children were born. A prospector named Bill Stewart often stopped by the ranch to visit with Anna and talk about his mining ventures. Mining fever struck Anna, and she began reading everything she could find on the subject. When the ranch failed and the Great Depression brought hard times to the whole nation, Anna and George made a dramatic change. They moved to the small town of Rawhide, Nevada, which at the time had a population of approximately 100. George

1884–1967
MINER, PROSPECTOR

worked for the state highway department, and Anna spent all of her time prospecting. Their move turned out to be a good economic solution. The family lived very inexpensively in a two-bedroom cabin, and miners at the time could make enough money to at least buy food when most people in the country couldn't even find a job.

But people who chose mining as a profession had to be hardy. Conditions in the small mining town were primitive—no phone, no gas station or grocery store. Water was scarce, and most people saved every drop when it rained and had to haul the rest from Dead Horse Wells nearby.

Anna thrived living with just the basics and from then on worked as a prospector and a miner. Her daughter Rees described Anna's optimism in always believing that she would strike it rich: "She just knew that she was going to find it. It kept her going."

When tragedy struck, Anna was glad that she had a way to earn a living. First, her husband had a stroke, which left him hardly able to walk for several years before his death in 1938. Anna's son George died in 1937 after he never fully recovered from a burst appendix. And after her two daughters, Rees and Fern, were grown and gone, Anna

was the sole provider for her son Walter ("Pal") and her brother, whose spirit had been broken by financial problems from the Depression.

During World War II, Anna mined tungsten, which was considered a strategic metal for the war effort. She worked underground, blasting with dynamite and mucking (shoveling) the ore to be hauled out of the mine. By the 1950s, with nuclear testing and atomic energy on the way, Anna got in on the search for uranium. She also mined, polished, and sold turquoise.

Anna drove an old pickup truck when she went prospecting and often slept on a mattress in the truck's bed. When a man named Alvin Nelson offered to help her with her mines and buy her a new truck, Anna married him, but divorce soon followed when she discovered that he really wanted her to become a housewife.

In Rawhide, Anna's house was the social center. Neighbors and friends stopped to visit and play chess. Often they discussed political ideas. She was vocal in her views, especially on rights for women. She believed women should not have just two choices: working for low wages or marrying in order to support a family. She was for equal pay, government-operated free daycare, and the right to choose any work that interested her.

By the 1960s, Anna was the last resident of Rawhide. She loved her home and refused to leave. Her family finally persuaded her to move to Fallon for her own protection, because dangerous people were beginning to roam the desert. She died on August 21, 1967, having lived the life she chose, one where she was free to roam the desert and work at prospecting and mining, which she loved.

—*Victoria Ford*

Olga A. Reifschneider

Olga Reifschneider was born Olga Augusta Wuertz on a farm in Illinois in 1900. She grew up and attended school in St. Louis, Missouri, reaching the eleventh grade. She then married John C. (Jack) Reifschneider, and in 1920 the two moved to Ukiah, California. Nine years later, they resettled to Reno and opened a prospering auto body shop. In her many years in Nevada, Olga pursued botany as a hobby, eventually becoming a well-known expert on plant life in Nevada.

Olga took occasional college classes but did not enroll full-time at UNR until 1944, the year her daughter, Nita Reifschneider Spangler, graduated with a journalism degree. Olga gained a bachelor's degree in botany in 1949 and attended the Yosemite Field School for Ranger Naturalists that same year.

While taking the Botany 1 course at UNR, she learned that very little was known about the earliest botanists in Nevada. Olga began keeping a list of people whose names appeared in Nevada plant genera and species. Through the years, the names grew into a collection of biographies.

1900—1978
BOTANIST, AUTHOR

Studies under such prominent Nevada botanists as William Dwight Billings, Philip A. Lehenbauer, and Ira La Rivers continued Olga's interest in the historical and biographical aspects of botany and eventually resulted in her book, *Biographies of Nevada Botanists*, published by the University of Nevada Press in 1965. Olga pinpointed the specific years that each person was directly involved with botanical work in Nevada. The book has entries on 48 botanists, only five of whom were women—she modestly did not include herself.

Although occupied as financial manager for her husband's business until his retirement in 1968, Olga maintained a second career as botanist and nature writer until her death in early 1978. Through contact with James R. Henrichs, Agnes (Hume Scott Train) Janssen, and W. Andrew Archer, who worked on the Nevada Indian Medicine Project in the 1930s and 1940s, she developed a lifelong interest in native medicinal plants.

Reifschneider lectured and wrote articles on wildflowers, desert biology, and the environment, as well as Nevada history, petroglyphs, and Benjamin Franklin. In the field, she was an

avid plant collector and photographer. One small wildflower she collected near Pyramid Lake in 1956 was identified as a new species and given the name "Mimulus reifschneiderae." Several of her articles were published in *Nevada Parks and Highways* magazine.

Olga remained physically active most of her life. In 1974, she was still swimming a mile every day. During a month-long vacation to Hawaii in 1976, she rode a mule down a 2,000 foot cliff on the island of Molokai. Olga was a member of the Sierra Club, the Nevada State Historical Society, the Camera Club, the Nevada Horticultural Society, the National League of American Pen Women, the Nevada Corral/Westerners International, and the Order of the Eastern Star. She was one of the original seventeen sponsors responsible for creating the Northern Nevada Native Plant Society in 1975 and retired from its board of directors in November 1977, a few months before her death. An oil painting of her by R. DeMorest is in the special collections at UNR.

The women botanists Olga covered in her book include:

Alice Eastwood
— Collecting expeditions in Nevada from 1912–1941, including the Mt. Rose area and Reno.

Agnes Hume Scott Train
—Desert plant collector for museums and herbaria, 1934–1942; "Indian Medicine Project—medicinal uses of plants by Native Americans.

Desma Hall Galway
—Collected specimens in Lincoln County in 1936 and sold them to the University of Nevada Biology Department—the first specimens acquired by UN's herbarium.

Edith Van Allen Murphey
— On special assignment with the Indian Service at Stewart, Nevada, she visited reservations throughout the state to learn about the uses of native plants for food and medicine, conducting wildflower shows during her trips; learned about a plant the Shoshone women used for birth control while at Owyhee in northeastern Nevada; wrote the booklet *Indian Uses of Native Plants*.

Annie Montague Alexander
— Plant explorations in Nevada from 1939–1949, collecting specimens that she contributed to the University of California. Washoe County and Emigrant Peak were among the sites of her collection efforts. She was 80 at the time of her last expedition in Nevada.

—*Betty Glass*

Jennie O'Hare Riordan

Jeanette (Jennie) O'Hare Riordan was born in Carson City, Nevada, on May 10, 1874, the third daughter and fourth child of Michael and Margaret O'Hare. Her father, Michael O'Hare, was born in Ireland and after immigrating to America had served in the Union Artillery during the Civil War. He came to Carson City in the late 1860s and was employed first at the United States Mint and later at the Virginia and Truckee Railroad foundry. Jennie's mother, Margaret McNally, immigrated with her family to New York from Ireland at a young age. There, in 1866, she met and married Michael O'Hare and preceded him to Carson City, where her parents had moved in the early 1860s.

When she was five years old, Jennie attended Hannah Clapp's private kindergarten. The school which was operated out of Clapp's home near the governor's mansion in Carson City. Jennie graduated from the high school in Carson City in 1893.

For the next four years, Jennie taught school in Esmeralda, Nye, and Lincoln counties, beginning her teaching career at Coyote Hollow in the Cambridge Mining District. While working at the school in Nye County (White River Valley), she met James

1874–1965
TEACHER

Riordan. They were married on September 5, 1897, in St. Teresa's Church in Carson City. James Riordan was the first Anglo child born in White Pine County. His parents had emigrated from County Cork, Ireland, and had settled in the White River Valley, where they initially made their living selling milk, butter, and eggs to residents of the mining camps of Pioche and Hamilton. Later, they raised beef. The Riordan ranch became one of the best-known ranches in eastern Nevada.

Jennie and James made their first home at Lane City, Nevada, where they had some mining interests. After three years, they sold the mine, leased the O'Neill ranch in Spring Valley, White Pine County, and went into the cattle business. At the end of three unsuccessful years, the couple decided to move to the western part of the state.

Getting out of the cattle business, they purchased a hotel at Plumas Junction, about 35 miles north of Reno, in Lassen County, California. It was located at the junction of the Nevada, California, Oregon, and Sierra Valley Railroads. But when the Western Pacific Railroad was completed, the junction became obsolete, which meant another move for the Riordans.

When James' father passed away, they returned to his ranch in White Pine County and continued the operations. There they raised their six children: Francis, Emmett, Lawrence, Ethel (Fraser), Loretta (Rodrigue), and Gertrude (Gottschalk). All of their children were sent to California to be educated. After spending 34 years on the ranch, the couple retired in 1943. Their youngest son, Lawrence, became the new ranch owner. Jennie happily returned to her beloved Carson City with her husband. James died at the age of 90 in 1960 and Jennie at the age of 91 in 1965.

Jennie's four sisters also taught school in Nevada. The eldest, Minnie, taught at Wadsworth and Campbell's ranch in eastern Nevada, where she met her future husband, Josiah Miles. Tessie, the second O'Hare daughter, taught at Reese River, Candelaria, and Ione. She met her future husband, John Mayette, while teaching at Ione. Maggie, the fourth daughter, taught at the Star Mine in Cherry Creek, at Lane City, and in McGill, where she was principal and one of the two teachers employed there. She later became an operator for the telephone company in Ely, a position she held for many years. Maggie never married and lived with her mother. The last O'Hare daughter, Lyda, taught at a place called Johnny on the Phelan ranch near Currie. She married Fred Oldfield of Ely and taught naturalization classes in that area until 1959.

In 1964, when she was 90 years old, Jennie wrote a piece for the Carson City paper. In it she reminisced about earlier days, "I wonder how many Carson residents remember that Carson City once boasted a large Chinatown and quite a colony of Chinese. It was situated in the southeast section of the city, not far from Sunny Acres. I remember it best in the early 1880s when my father used to take us for a walk at night when they celebrated their New Year. The whole town would be lit with Chinese lanterns with tapers or candles in the windows. The firecrackers would be going off all around. Their funerals were another source of childhood delight, since they were so entirely different from anything we ever saw as they paraded to the cemetery moaning and beating cymbals to keep evil spirits away from the dead person." Her concluding paragraph was, "I have had a very happy life, and I look back to my school days and am glad that I lived in the best era of our country. The Gay Nineties were happy, carefree times, and we have seen so much progress over the years. I have seen Carson City grow from a small frontier town to its present population of fifteen thousand. I am glad that it has been my home."

An outstanding Nevada pioneer lady, Jennie lived her Catholic faith, raised a wonderful family, and contributed to every community in which she lived. Her biography is included in the special collections at the University of Nevada–Reno.

—*Kay Sanders*

Agnes Louise Elford Roche

In September 1927, seven young women from various states arrived to teach school in the remote copper mining town of Ruth in the mountains of eastern Nevada. The mining company, Nevada Consolidated Copper Mines, provided not only housing and medical care for the families of its employees but also elementary education. Anna Rose, secretary to the town's board of education, had written to prospective teachers stating that the board wanted women of exemplary character who would teach in the Sunday School and be active in the community, because, she said, it was a deprived community as far as children having adults to set a good example. Furthermore, the teachers were expected to remain single for the duration of their contracts.

Marriage prevented them from teaching, but in the 1940s, the board reversed its policy, and they returned to the classroom.

Agnes Elford was one of those seven women. It was near the end of her studies in Normal School at Aberdeen, South Dakota, when Agnes had learned about Ruth. The salary was very attractive. From nine months teaching she would be paid $1,500, with the added amount of $150 for summer school.

1901–2001
TEACHER, CHURCH LEADER, NEWS REPORTER, GIRL SCOUT ORGANIZER

She had no objection to the board's expectations. She signed the contract to teach sixth grade but soon began to have grave doubts about her decision.

She imagined a mining camp of black tar-paper shacks and foreigners who couldn't speak English. On the day she was to depart from her home in Los Angeles, Agnes was so distressed she could not get on the train. Her father explained to her that she had given her word. If she couldn't stand Ruth after she was there, she could come home. Agnes left Los Angeles two days later. At Cobre, Nevada, the big passenger train stopped just long enough for her to get off, then roared on toward Salt Lake City. Alone, she read the sign on the little depot, "San Francisco 522 miles." Nothing but flat desert and sagebrush surrounded her. She thought she would die.

In the station she saw another woman buying a ticket. This was Vera Moore (Mrs. Peter Norregard) from Nebraska, also going to Ruth. They sat side by side in the railroad car and talked all the way to Ely. There they boarded a coach attached to an ore car and arrived in Ruth, where they were met by five other teachers.

Three days after arriving, Agnes declared Ruth to be 10,000 times better than she expected. The Ruth Grade School was located at the foot of Grant's Hill and at the top of the hill the teachers lived together in a dormitory. It had one bathroom, four bedrooms, a dining room, kitchen, parlor, and basement. The company provided a very good cook, Mrs. Musgrove, who prepared three meals a day. The cost of board and room was $42.50 per month.

The hike up and down Grant's Hill to the school four times a day kept everyone fit. At night the company blew the curfew whistle at 9 p.m. Approximately 2,200 people lived in Ruth. There was not a blade of grass around any home or building.

Within weeks, the teachers were exploring the countryside, hiking in the hills, and going to card parties, dances, wiener roasts, dinners, movies, plays, and tent shows. They played at the company-built golf course and tennis court, and watched the Ruth team play on the baseball diamond. And they were meeting the eligible men of the community. By December they were falling in love.

The company thought the teachers should see the mining operation. They were taken to Copper Flat to see a big blast in the Ruth open cut pit and descended 700 feet into the Ruth underground mine, where Agnes saw the narrow gauge tracks, the wooden reinforcements, and the miners at work.

Agnes began teaching the high school Sunday school class at the Ruth church. The company provided a building. They put on a small steeple, then added gothic windows and two stoves. About 80 children attended.

Agnes also organized the first Girl Scout Troop in the county and perhaps the state. Agnes met her future husband, Claire P. Roche, whom she married on June 14, 1930. The couple eventually had two daughters.

For Christmas, Santa Claus came into the Ruth depot from the mining pit on a flat car all bedecked in colors and framed by Christmas trees. The company had a tradition, initiated by Claire, of giving each child a sack of fruits and nuts along with a box of good chocolates.

In the spring, new contracts came out. Raises were based on merit. Agnes's salary went from $1,500 to $1,760 a year. The superintendent of the school, Chester V. Davis, praised her work. She decided to teach another year.

In the ensuing years, Agnes became a weekly news reporter for the *Ely Record*. She organized vacation Bible schools, acted as camp counselor, became noted for her Bible studies, and taught English to immigrants. In 1955, the company sold the school buildings to make way for expanded mining facilities. Claire retired that year and moved with Agnes to California. After Claire's death in 1959, Agnes traveled extensively in the United States and abroad. She died on April 4, 2001, the last of the seven women who came to teach in Ruth, Nevada, in 1927.

—*Barbara A. Roche*

Bertha B. Ronzone

Bertha B. "Mom" Ronzone, was born on April 16, 1885, in a small town near Des Moines, Iowa, to James W. and Sarah Bishop. Her family soon moved west, and Bertha received her early education in Fowler, CA. On December 12, 1901, at the age of 16, she married A.B. Ronzone, who had come to California to prospect for gold. The young couple set out the following spring aboard a ship bound for Alaska. Blown off course in a fierce storm, they arrived in Nome three months later than anticipated only to find that Mr. Ronzone's partner had sold their business establishment and left with all of the money. Bertha's daughter, Amy, was born during their two-year stay in Alaska.

Tales of the Nevada mining boom lured Bertha and her husband to Tonopah, Goldfield, and Manhattan, Nevada. Their second daughter, Esther, was born in 1913 in Manhattan. It was during this time that Bertha began taking in the miners' laundry to help supplement the family income. It soon became evident that the miners were in dire need of socks and other clothing. On a trip to Oakland to visit her mother, Bertha made her first investment in the Ronzone store of the future. She bought, on sale, socks of odd sizes and shipped them to her daughter Amy to sell in Manhattan.

The socks were so successful that Bertha formed the idea of opening a general store to further accommodate Manhattan's urgent clothing needs. Lacking funds, she arranged to meet George Wingfield, future Nevada banker, a man she had known in Alaska. At their meeting in the Mizpah Hotel in Tonopah, "Mom" discussed her lack of funds with Mr. Wingfield, who promptly wrote her a check for $500.00 as a loan.

Bertha opened her first store in Manhattan in 1917. Her son Richard was born in that same year. In 1923 the Manhattan boom was over, and the family moved to Tonopah where they re-established the clothing business in the Elks' Building. Later, they purchased the E. Marks Clothing Store with its full complement of merchandise. News that Boulder Dam was to be built brought Bertha and her husband to Las Vegas in 1929, where they opened a new store on Carson Street that sold women's and children's wear. As Las Vegas grew during the dam construction period, Ronzone's kept pace. In 1935, the business moved to Fremont Street, and then expanded twice in the next few years.

1885–1969
ENTREPRENEUR

After the death of her husband in 1938, Bertha enlisted her son Richard to help operate the business. Richard was with her only two years until he entered military service with the Nevada National Guard and did not return until after World War II, in November 1945. He later was elected to one term in the Nevada Assembly and also to the Clark County Commission.

Meanwhile, the Tonopah store, which had been operated by Bertha's son-in-law and daughter, Mr. and Mrs. Al Adams, was sold in 1939, and the Adams family joined the Las Vegas store staff. They remained until 1943, when the Ronzones purchased the Gray, Reid and Wright department store in Reno. The Adams operated the Reno store for the family corporation until their retirement in 1964. Bertha's daughter Esther married Ed Recanzone, and the couple owned and operated the Emporium Clothing Store in Yerington. In 1946, the Las Vegas Ronzones moved into a new building constructed by Mrs. Corrine Johnson and her husband Paul at 418 Fremont. In 1968, the family opened another store on Maryland Parkway in Las Vegas in the new and modern Boulevard Mall.

Bertha believed that her success was due to the qualities of "prayer, faith, and determination." Through her own initiative and hard work, she became the head of the largest privately owned merchandising enterprise in the state of Nevada, a chain that extended into all parts of the state.

Many honors were bestowed on Bertha in recognition of her accomplishments in business and her assistance in community development. In June, 1967, during commencement ceremonies at Nevada Southern University (now UNLV), she was named as a "Distinguished Nevadan," one of the highest honors the state can bestow. She was also chosen as "Nevada's Golden Rule Pioneer Mother" in May, 1959, and was recognized by the Business and Professional Women's Club of Las Vegas, which described her as "an outstanding living example of faith, courage, and cheerfulness, all of which come through the spiritual and moral strength which makes up her character. Her greatest merit is her love of people, and she gives freely her affection, kindness, and understanding to friends and family alike." Bertha was named "Mother of the Year" by the Women's Guild of the Church of Religious Science in May, 1967. She was a founder of that church and a past president of the Guild.

Interested in education for herself and for her community, Bertha also served as a member of the school board in Tonopah and furthered her own education by graduating from the first-year course of the Church of Religious Science, where she received a bachelor's degree.

Bertha Ronzone was still active in store business until her death in Las Vegas on November 5, 1969.

—*Sally Wilkins*

Mary G. Rose

Mary Grace O'Donnell was born on February 1, 1875, on her family's ranch near Winnemucca in Humboldt County, Nevada, to Patrick and Ellen Crown O'Donnell. Her father was an Irish rancher, born in England. Her mother emigrated from Ireland to New York, then, in 1868, traveled around Cape Horn to San Francisco and eventually to Elko, Nevada, where she met and married Patrick O'Donnell on January 1, 1872. Soon after marriage, the O'Donnells moved to Winnemucca, where they bought land and ranched. They had three children: Thomas Crown, born in 1873; James, born in 1877; and Mary Grace.

Mary received her education in the Winnemucca schools and also taught there for a short time after her graduation. In addition, she served as the librarian at the Winnemucca Public Library and was active in the Winnemucca Civic Club and the P.T.A. In 1900, she married David McBane Rose and soon after had a daughter, Helen Vida, born on September 11, 1901, and a son, Donald Crown, born on August 19, 1902. In 1908, after the death of Mary's brother Thomas, she moved with her family to Portland, Oregon, where they stayed for six years. They returned to Winnemucca in 1914 to manage the O'Donnell ranches, since Mary's parents were by this time then in their 70s.

Mary registered to vote on August 12, 1918, listing herself as a housewife, 5'7" tall, Democrat, and living on the O'Donnell ranch in Humboldt County. She was a registered voter in Humboldt County until she moved to Reno in 1928.

On March 11, 1921, Mary's daughter Helen (nicknamed "Pat") died unexpectedly of appendectomy complications. She was a popular girl, and the Winnemucca High School yearbook, the *Winnada*, was dedicated to her memory and flags on the Victory and school flag poles were flown at half-mast as a mark of respect. Her funeral services were held in the Nixon Opera House in order to accommodate the large assembly of mourners. Six of her classmates, dressed in white dresses, were pallbearers, and the students of Winnemucca High School marched in a body to the gravesite, as did the Women's Benefit Association and the

1875–1935
TEACHER, POLITICIAN

Ladies of the Maccabees. Helen's death was a great shock from which Mary never fully recovered.

Mary's son Donald Crown left Winnemucca to become an international dancer shortly after graduating from Winnemucca High School in 1921. He married his dancing partner, Marian Stadler, and they toured as an act in the late 1920s all across the United States, and in France, Africa, and Greece.

The first woman legislator from Humboldt County and the second woman to appear on a general election ballot in that county, Mary Rose was elected in 1924 to the Thirty-Second Session of the Legislature of the State of Nevada. Mary was a member of several committees—Education, Internal Improvements, Enrollment, and State Library—and she introduced four bills or resolutions during her term of office, one of which provided for "free public libraries, and other matters relating thereto,'" which became the library law for the State of Nevada.

Humboldt County suffered the effects of the Depression through the 1920s and 1930s, and many ranchers, including the O'Donnells, lost their properties. Mary's mother moved off the ranch into Winnemucca, and Patrick O'Donnell went to the Veterans Home in Yountville, California.

During Mary's term in office, her mother Ellen died in Winnemucca at the age of 89, after being in ill health for some time. Mary returned to Winnemucca to bury her mother next to her brother in the Winnemucca Cemetery. Assembly Resolution No. 10 was introduced in the state legislature noting Mrs. McDonnell's death and offering Mary the Assembly's condolences. Mary and her husband moved to Reno in 1928, where he was employed as a solicitor for one of the Reno newspapers.

In 1932, Mary wrote a letter to her son in Chicago telling him that she would like to run in the Senate race that year but that money was so short she and her husband were not able to pay the $15 fee for her candidacy. She said that her friend Harriett Spann was helping her and that thirteen Democrats and nine Republicans were running for this one office. However, Mary was not successful in her bid for the Senate.

Mary's husband David was killed in an automobile accident near Susanville, California, in July of 1933, and Mary again returned to Winnemucca, burying her husband next to her daughter in the Winnemucca Cemetery.

In 1934, after again running unsuccessfully for the Senate, Mary was appointed by Governor Vail Pittman to the position of State Land Registrar, a federal position that she held until her death from pneumonia on June 1, 1935. Mary was buried in the Winnemucca Cemetery next to her mother and brother, and close to her daughter and husband.

—*Janet E. White*

Ferminia Sarras

Ferminia Sarras came to Nevada sometime around 1881, the year that she was first listed on Esmeralda County tax records and given the description, "Spanish Lady, Belleville." Much of Ferminia's story had been lost until just recently, when author Sally Zanjani worked with Ferminia's great-grandson to reconstruct her life.

Although she was often mistaken for Mexican, Ferminia always described herself as "a Spanish lady of royal blood." She was a descendant of the noble Contreras family of Nicaragua, where a relative, Roderigo de Contreras, governed during the 16th century. In her native country, Ferminia was married to a man named Pablo Flores and gave birth to four daughters—Conchetta, Conceptión, Juanita, and Emma—but when she arrived in Nevada, Ferminia evidently felt that her two youngest daughters would be safer in the Nevada Orphans Asylum in Virginia City than in the mining camps of Belleville and Candelaria. Ferminia may have traveled to Nevada to join her husband, who is thought to have worked in those rough mining towns, but, if she did, Pablo did not remain in her life for very long.

1840—1915
COPPER MINER, PROSPECTOR

Ferminia may have been married as many as five times during her life, often to men who were much younger. Her youngest son was named Joseph A. Marshall, although Ferminia was never married to anyone named Marshall. One newspaper article claimed that all of Ferminia's husbands died violent deaths, and author Zanjani speculates that she may have been interested in men who were handy with a gun because they could help protect her mining stakes. One of those men was Archie McCormack, a man twelve years younger than Ferminia and described as a Canadian-born gunman. He was killed in 1906 in a gunfight while defending one of her claims. By the end of her life, however, one of the young men Ferminia trusted stole her money from a Los Angeles bank and returned to Central America.

Ferminia did not depend on the men in her life for her livelihood. She began prospecting in the Candelaria area in 1883 and went on to file a number of claims on copper mines in the Sante Fe district. She spent a few years prospecting in Silver Peak but didn't have much luck during the 1890s, a time when Nevada was in an economic depression. She returned to the Sante Fe district in 1899, and it

was there that she eventually made her fortune. She prospected alone, wearing pants, boots, and a backpack. By the time she died in 1915, she had made several fortunes from copper mining and often stashed the gold coins from her sales in her chicken coop, where she believed it would be safer than in the banks.

Each time she made a profitable sale, Ferminia would travel to San Francisco, stay in the finest hotels, shop for elegant clothes, and enjoy fine dining and young men until her money ran out. Then she would return to Nevada's mountains and resume prospecting for another fortune.

According to author Zanjani: "One cannot resist observing that when liberated from the cloistered world of the upper-class Latin American woman in the place rightly known as a 'man's country,' Ferminia used her freedom much as a man of similar background would have done. In this tradition, wealth was to be enjoyed and generously spread among one's friends, not devoted to the civic purposes of churches and organized charities; individualism was the normal mode, not the galling restraints of team-work and joint enterprise; and a good deal of blatant philandering was both a pleasurable assertion of the self and a status symbol, not in the least damaging to one's reputation. If Ferminia had been a man, her compatriots would have admiringly called her *muy hombre.*"

Ferminia named her many mining claims after her family, friends, and lovers. She had small cabins or adobe houses in several locations but lived mostly at Luning, Nevada, between prospecting trips. Later, the town of Mina was named in her honor.

Ferminia's belief in the value of her mines eventually proved to be true. Her most valuable mines were located in Giroux Canyon, Nevada, still being mined successfully today. Likewise, her belief in herself never wavered. Ferminia arrived in Nevada as a Spanish lady of royal blood and was eventually dubbed the "Nevada Copper Queen." Now, thanks to author Sally Zanjani, her legend has been recovered.

—*Victoria Ford*

Helen Rulison Shipley

H elen Rulison was born in Dayton, Nevada, on July 23, 1870. Her father, Charles Henry Rulison, was a millwright working on the Comstock Lode at Virginia City. Helen began school in Dayton, but, due to the Comstock mining depression, the family relocated to Reno where Helen finished her senior high school year at the top of her class. She then enrolled at the University of Nevada School of Business, graduating on June 13, 1889.

Helen then became a teacher at the South Side School, across the Truckie River from Reno. At the age of 19, she earned $65 a month teaching school, a lot of money for a young girl to earn in 1889.

Helen was very close to her older brother David. He was a dentist in Reno, and she decided that she wanted to become a dentist too. After teaching for five years, she moved to San Francisco and enrolled in the University of California Dental College. She graduated as a Doctor of Dental Surgery in 1896.

Serving on the Board of Dental Examiners was a great honor in those days. In 1903, Governor Sparks appointed William Henry

1870–1955
DENTIST

Carell, Charles A. Coffin, and Helen Rulison as the new members of the Nevada State Board of Dental Examiners. With this appointment, Helen's career blossomed. Helen was the first woman to practice dentistry in the state of Nevada, but by that time there were too many dentists in Reno, so, in 1906, Helen moved to Goldfield, where she also became an investor in the Goldfield stock market. Helen did well in her investments but could see that Goldfield was on the decline, so she set up dental practice in nearby Tonopah.

Helen's 1916 marriage to Robert A. Shipley came as a surprise to her friends and family. At the age of 46, most single women at the time were considered "old maids," but love came along and on July 16 she and Robert were married. They lived in Tonopah for 10 years and then in 1926 moved to Reno when the Tonopah economy went into a slump. Helen practiced at 126 Ridge in Reno and retired at the age of 76.

Helen passed away on June 6, 1955, at the Twaddle Rest Home in Reno, preceding her husband in death by more than 11 years.

—*Mollie L. Murphy*

May Bradford Shockley

ay Bradford was born around 1881 into a traveling family. Her father, S.K. Bradford, went from mining town to mining town following each new strike and establishing his family in the local boarding house while he did surveying work. As a result, the Bradfords lived in several small towns throughout the West during May's childhood. May's mother ensured continuity in her daughter's life by having her spend time on the family farm in Missouri and seeing to it that her daughter was raised as a lady, but May was a tomboy who loved the outdoor life that her father's profession offered.

After graduating from high school, May was accepted at Stanford University. Her mother moved May, her sister, and the family furniture out to Palo Alto while her father continued to visit mining towns, looking for promising strikes.

At Stanford, May majored in art and mathematics. She was encouraged to study art in Paris and was offered a job illustrating a geology textbook, but, because her mother was ill, May took a teaching job in Palo Alto. After a year in

ABOUT 1881–1969
SURVEYOR

California, she moved to Seattle, always trying to save money for her Paris adventure.

However, a fire in her father's Tonopah office completely changed May's plans. Early on the morning of May 24, 1904, a fire started in the surveying offices of Booker and Bradford and spread to nearby buildings. S.K. Bradford (who had carelessly left a cigar burning, probably the cause of the blaze) had contracted several surveying jobs, all of which had to be redone because the records were now ashes. Luckily, he still had the good will of his customers but needed help badly, because one person couldn't redo all of the jobs. Heeding her father's plea for help, May Bradford arrived by stagecoach in Tonopah, Nevada, on July 21, 1904.

May's chores included setting up a new office, drafting maps, performing incidental surveying tasks, and keeping house for her father. After seeing to the details of the construction of her father's new building, May attacked the piles of work awaiting her. She was willing to stay at her desk late into the night, so a great deal of drafting work passed through her hands.

She also developed another source of income: She and a friend invested in burnt-leather pillows honoring Tonopah's founder, Jim Butler, and the subject of the pillows was so pleased that he took them around to the local saloons. The pillows depicted Jim Butler and his mule in a desert setting and featured the phrase, "Me and Jim founded Tonopah." Soon May and her father were using "pillow money" for weekly necessities. May's pillow-making activity also helped the Bradfords get out of debt.

Although they worked seven days a week and labored long past closing time, the amount of work was so great that May's mother came out from California to help. She took over the housekeeping and also became the family bill collector and secretary.

Her mother's help enabled May to take over the hiring of draftsmen and the overseeing of their work. And May was finally able to accept social invitations, becoming a well known figure in the Tonopah area. She joined the Spinsters' Club and was recognized as a straight shooter both personally and professionally.

May felt that with all of her experience, she should be deputized as a patent surveyor. To apply for the position, she surveyed a claim, filled out the appropriate paperwork, and sent it all into the Surveyor General. Soon she received confirmation that she had been appointed a U.S. Deputy Mineral Surveyor for the state of Nevada—the first woman to hold that title. Later, she acquired similar credentials from the state of California.

After two years of intense work, May and her father closed the Tonopah office of Bradford and Bradford. Her parents headed for California, but May left for New York and then boarded a steamer for Europe to begin the trip she had wanted to take after college. It was in Europe that May married William H. Shockley, after knowing him for only three weeks.

In 1906, the newlyweds returned to Tonopah to start their married life. For May, this was a time of relative leisure, and she enjoyed her painting, her friends, and the social life her marriage afforded. Earlier, she had made friends with Kay Pittman and his wife, and now, through her husband, she became acquainted with "Borax Smith" and young Theodore Hoover and his brother, Herbert.

May Bradford, an educated and well-traveled woman, made her mark in the largely masculine domain of mining. Her strong work ethic, her devotion to her family, and her ability to turn disaster into success mark her as an outstanding woman of Nevada.

—*Fran Haraway*

165

Fanny Soss

Fanny Goldwater Soss was a fashion-maker and retailer who became what *Women's Wear Daily* called "The finest ladies' retailer in the country." She was born in the Whitechapel neighborhood of London, England, to a confident, strong-willed mother and a father who designed and tailored extravagantly fine ladies' and men's wear. The Goldwater family came to America when Fanny was eighteen months old. They first lived in Lincoln, Nebraska, where Fanny's father opened a men's store in the Lincoln Hotel, but soon moved to a series of boomtowns in Idaho, Montana, Utah, and Wyoming, before winding up in Oakland, California, in 1906. Along the way, the family added four brothers and two sisters.

In 1897, when Fanny was 13, her mother told her that she wasn't going to school any longer because she already knew everything a proper young lady needed to know. By that time, Fanny had also assumed her father's trade. Her childhood had been secure and privileged and surrounded by fine things. Her brothers were involved in school and sports, and Fanny and her sisters spent hours dressing up, changing accessories, and impersonating their mother, their teachers, and the celebrities they read about in magazines and newspapers. Fanny was especially fascinated with a *New York World* reporter, Nellie Bly, who set out to go around the world in less than 80 days and actually made it in 72!

Fanny spent her days at home and gradually took over the duties of an Executive Housekeeper. There was a staff of servants. She never had to scrub or clean, but she planned meals, ordered supplies, managed costs, and supervised the care of clothing and the demeanor of her siblings. She studied nutrition and eventually won several awards for her creative recipes and fine cooking.

At 20, Fanny had never had an eligible suitor. Her brothers started a campaign to see that she was suitably married. Fanny was introduced to handsome Mendel Soss. Mendel's family manufactured and sold fine bench-made luggage and handbags. Fanny and Mendel were married when Fanny was 23 and Mendel was 27. They moved to Los Angeles. Fanny became a wife and a mother of a girl and boy.

Unable to reconcile differences in lifestyle and religion (she was an Orthodox Jew, and he was a Reformed Jew), Fanny divorced her husband

1884—1990
Clothing Store Owner

after twenty years of marriage and became a single parent. She rejected help from her family and worked selling coupons for photographers, cold canvassing the better neighborhoods. She also sold stockings on the street in the garment district. In 1931, Fanny was running a small clothing store in Los Angeles when she learned of the Boulder Dam Project and the boom in Las Vegas. She opened a shop on Vegas' west side that same year but couldn't make enough to cover her $15 a month rent. Fremont Street on payday was swarming curb to curb with construction workers who had just been paid, and that was where Fanny longed to be. In 1932 she moved to a house on Fremont that had previously been Watt's Café. In celebration, she and her friends participated in the first Helldorado Parade, walking down the unpaved street in bathing suits!

Her store, Fanny's, moved again in six months, but from the beginning there were salon-style touches; every purchase was carefully wrapped, and, on holidays, the outer wrapping and bows were elaborate. Alterations and complete restyling were available. This store remained for 35 glowing years. Her customers were newcomers and pioneers, and she had a loyal following of out-of-towners. As Las Vegas began to develop as a post-war resort town, Fanny's met the local need for designer women's clothing. Virginia Hill, Bugsy Siegel's paramour, came to Fanny's to shop, as did the wives of the mayor, police chief, bank presidents, and the "ladies" from Block 16. She had the first neon lights, first mannequins in the windows, and the first fashion shows of any Las Vegas shop. Buying was done in New York. Designer clothes and European imports were sold. The fur and millinery were unequalled. In 1947, she opened another store in the Flamingo Hotel, and eventually operated four locations throughout Las Vegas. The jewel of them all was on Las Vegas Boulevard and Deal Drive (now known as Fashion Show Drive). Her son Maury operated that location until 1979. When it closed, Fanny wasn't sorry or nostalgic. The high-minded business woman who worked seven days a week for years said that she was never a slave to business and moved on with her rich full life!

Achieving so much success in a man's world, Fanny never felt diminished because she was a woman and was never too busy to enjoy herself or become involved in community causes. During World War II, she volunteered with the USO. She was always a benefactress of the Blind Center. She was a member of the Royal Neighbors of America and a booster of Helldorado. In Fanny's last Helldorado Parade, at age 92, the elephant from the movie *Around the World in 80 Days* was flown in, and Fanny rode it bareback down the street, the same street where she had started out when Las Vegas was just a one-burro town!

Fanny lived to be the oldest woman in Nevada. She died at her own home while planning a party for her 106th birthday.

—*Mary Gafford and Frankie Williams*

167

Blanche Sprague

Blanche Sprague arrived in Goldfield, Nevada, from Colorado Springs, Colorado, on April 13, 1906. She came with her little daughter, Sallie, to join her husband, who was the managing editor of the *Goldfield News*. Information about her prominence in social and musical circles in Colorado Springs preceded her.

Because of the isolation of the community, women in Goldfield formed social clubs that met in the homes of their members. In October 1906, Blanche organized the 40-member Goldfield Women's Club. She was elected the first president, a position she held for eight years. Her first successful endeavors were to raise the money needed to build a clubhouse and then to buy a piano. These funds were raised by giving rummage sales and collecting dues from the members. The treasurer's report for 1906–1907 stated that monies were spent on the "the piano fund, mortgage, flowers for a sick friend, junior Red Cross, Girl Scouts, the student loan fund, and paint."

Blanche and her social acquaintances were under constant scrutiny and attention. At one reception that she hosted, a newspaper account described her as "most handsomely gowned in a black chantilly lace gown over white charmeuse with jewels and diamonds and a corsage of beautiful red roses."

The club met twice a month with objectives to "stimulate intellectual development; to promote unity and good fellowship among its members; to advance philanthropy and reformatory effort; and to aid in the civil betterment of the community." A discussion or presentation of educational and informative value usually took place during the meetings. Subjects included: The Panama Canal, Puccini Operas, Nevada Women Pioneers, A Mexican Journey, Education and Government in Mexico and Causes of Recent Revolution. Blanche, who was an accomplished vocalist, sometimes offered musical renditions at these programs.

In 1908, the club started becoming politically involved and petitioned the state legislators to recognize October 31 as Nevada Day. They joined the State Federation of Women's Clubs in 1910, a move that gave them a larger range of influence. At the 1913 state convention in Carson City, Blanche was chosen as a delegate to the national convention in Chicago. The

DATES OF BIRTH AND DEATH UNKNOWN CLUBWOMAN, HOSTESS, POLITICAL ACTIVIST, AND SOCIETY JOURNALIST women from Nevada took to that convention a plea to moviemakers to produce more educational films.

In 1914, after several years of research and hard work, Blanche was able to form the Montezuma Chapter of the Daughters of the American Revolution. In order to accomplish this, she had to find 12 women who could trace their lineages to a revolutionary patriot. Blanche was herself a direct descendant of Miles Standish and John Alden. This women's group also became politically active, and Blanche served as the state regent for the D.A.R.

In 1915, Blanche became the writer for the society page of the *Goldfield Tribune* and relinquished her role as president of the Women's Club. When Goldfield held the state Women's Convention in 1916, the topics of chief concern were "the injustice of our common property law toward women" and "women as citizen." Also addressed were such issues as public health, public sanitation, a "better baby" campaign and applying for an appropriation for an Indian school. Legislation against the whiskey and the subject of better roads were also discussed. Blanche held several lavish receptions that were described as the "delightful features of this convention."

As the population of Goldfield declined, the spirit of Blanche Sprague and her fellow club members did not. Through her social column she encouraged everyone to "do everything in our power to beautify the place." She noted, "if our ladies will work, perhaps our county commissioners, who already are doing so much, will tear down the unoccupied, unsightly tents and shacks that make our camp look so rugged and forlorn."

Even in 1920, when the population of Goldfield had dwindled to 1,500, there were still 40 members of the Goldfield Women's Club. Blanche became president of the club again in 1922. In 1923, her husband, Charles, was elected to the state senate, and she took on the duties and social responsibilities of a senator's wife.

In the male-dominated culture of the mining camp, Blanche and her comrades used their social, educational, and organizing abilities to create their own sphere of influence, which extended to include the well being of women and children everywhere. Blanche Sprague's involvement in her club gave her the deserved title of "A Diamond in the Rough."

Delphine Anderson Squires

Delphine Anderson Squires was born on January 8, 1868 in Portage City, Wisconsin, but would eventually have a great impact on Las Vegas, Nevada, through her memoirs, newspaper articles, and civic leadership. Delphine was known as a charming and hospitable hostess and tireless advocate for women and children. Her respect and love of the desert and the pioneering spirit of the people of Las Vegas were reflected in her desire to thoroughly chronicle her life there.

When she was a young woman, Delphine's family moved to Austin, Minnesota, where she became a close friend of a man named C.P. Squires, who was to have a great influence on the rest of her life. Delphine had prepared for a career as a music teacher and was awarded a contract with the Seattle public schools, but the Great Seattle Fire made her change her plans. She wrote to C.P. and told him that she was ready to get married. C.P. proposed to her in a letter, and they were married in August of 1899.

The panic of 1893 led C.P. to consider starting a venture in a new town that was to be established on the line that extended the San Pedro and Los Angeles Railroad to Salt Lake City. So,

1868—1961
NEWSPAPER COLUMNIST

he set off in 1905 for a little desert city known as Las Vegas.

Delphine moved to Las Vegas to join her husband on June 21, 1905. At the time she was living in Los Angeles with her children and had become quite attached to the educational and cultural advantages offered there. Years later, in a column for the *Las Vegas Age* newspaper, she explained, "But, there was 'Pop,' living in the terrible desert heat in very unsanitary surroundings trying to make a home for us in Nevada; so, we decided in favor of 'Pop' on the contention that we needed him and that he needed us more than the children needed culture."

They boarded the train to Las Vegas and did not look back. The next day, she raised the shade in her berth to witness the glory of an early morning sunrise on the desert. "I shall never forget the beauty of it! The great expanse of the desert, rimmed by the mysterious blue of the mountains..."

So began her new life, soon to be distinguished by her many contributions to the culture and spirit of Las Vegas. Her home became the center of hospitality in the new community, and she was always remembered as a "premier hostess." Fondly known as "Mom" and "Pop" Squires, Blanche and her husband also provided civic information and opinions with the newspaper they founded, the *Las Vegas Age*.

As a writer for the newspaper, "Mom" Squires provided readers with reflections on the history of Nevada. In one such column she looked back on what life was like for the early women who resided there. "Life was not 'one grand sweet song' in those early years in Las Vegas. Everything was done the 'hard way.' Housewives of that period, 50 years ago, were not lazy—in fact, they were a set of hard-working women." The summer heat was intense, and not a shade tree was in sight. Poorly ventilated tents were the norm. She recalled that there was no electricity and very few conveniences. Washing clothes and linens was a major chore.

The women of the town had founded the "Hostess Club" in 1905, and "Mom" was an active member. This organization of pioneer women let nothing keep them from holding their meetings. "Mom" fondly remembered that the houses were small and ill equipped for entertaining, but the women brought their own plates and silverware and came armed with scissors, needles, and thimbles to sew for the hostess. Content to sit on boxes, they exchanged friendly gossip and discussed the issues that were important to making the town a suitable place for bringing up children. The Hostess Club served as an informal Chamber of Commerce and became instrumental in lobbying for churches, schools, and the enforcement of sanitary laws.

Delphine also continued to expand the opportunities for Nevada women by active partici-

pation in organizations such as the Mesquite Club and Nevada State Federated Women's Club. She held a vital role in community leadership and established a branch of the Congress of Mothers in 1907. She was instrumental in the building of the Christ Church Episcopal and is credited as the founder of the Las Vegas Library.

Delphine sadly admitted to one problem: "Although I have loved Las Vegas from the first time I saw it, I soon discovered that with the coming of the hot weather I developed asthma." She was invited to spend time at the McFarland ranch in Indian Springs to see if the altitude might prove beneficial. She and her son Russell stayed in a little cottage there, and she had no more breathing problems. The Squires later bought a cabin at Deer Creek on Mt. Charleston. She spent many happy summers there with her family and friends.

"Mr. Squires and I have often been asked why we came to Nevada to make our home. I hesitate to admit that the pot of gold at the end of the rainbow was the only reason because if it were, then our quest has failed. I prefer to think that the pot of gold we were seeking contained something finer and more precious and that we found it in the beauty, peace, and contentment of our desert home, and the companionship of the many friends we have made and of the happiness they have brought us."

—*Jill Stovall*

171

Mary Bernice Stanford

Mary Bernice Stanford was born to William Franklin Baxter and Evalene Kealy Baxter in the Texas town of Lewisville, about thirty miles from Dallas. Mary Bernice was the couple's second but only surviving child.

Bernice, as she preferred being called, was taught to read by a cousin who was three years older and already in school. Bernice begged to be allowed to attend school but because she was too young, her father had to pay tuition for her the first year. She loved learning and progressed rapidly. She finished elementary school at age eleven with the highest average in the class. When Bernice graduated from high school, she was one of the class speakers and received an academic scholarship to North Texas State University. Bernice was a charter member of Kappa Delta Pi, an academic honor society, and a permanent member of the Bruce Honor Society.

Bernice's second teaching assignment was in Electra, Texas, where she met the handsome football coach Harvey Stanford. They were married on June 2, 1929, and eventually became the parents of four children—Jerry, Jo Ann, Monty,

1907—1994
TEACHER

and James—as well as eight grandchildren and four great grandchildren.

In 1936, the Stanford family moved to Las Vegas, where Harvey was hired by Las Vegas High School as a football coach. In 1941, Superintendent of Las Vegas Schools Maude Frazier hired Bernice as an English teacher for two periods a day. Las Vegas High School was the only high school in the county, and students were bussed in from Boulder City and other areas. Soon Bernice's teaching assignment became a full-time job, and she began a twenty-eight year career at Las Vegas High School. Among Bernice's former students is Richard Bryant, former Governor of Nevada.

Bernice taught Freshman English until 1954, when she became girls' counselor, a position she held until her retirement in 1970. She received her professional counselor's certification from UNLV, then known as Nevada Southern University.

In 1987, the city named a school after Bernice and her husband, an honor that Bernice felt was the perfect climax to their long teaching careers.

Bernice was a charter member of PEO Sisterhood and was a member of the First Baptist Church, where she was chairman of the Board of Christian Education.

Fifty-eight-year Las Vegas resident Bernice Stanford, 86, died on January 12, 1994, in North Las Vegas.

—*Jean Spiller*

Helen J. Stewart

Soon after Helen Jane was born to Hiram and Delia Gray Wiser in Springfield, Illinois, her father, a prospector, moved his family west, where Helen and her four siblings attended public school in Sacramento, California. She later attended Woodland College and, on April 6, 1873, married Archibald Stewart, a rancher and successful businessman of Scottish decent, who moved her to a ranch at Pony Springs, near Pioche, Nevada. On the ranch, Helen made friends with local Paiute women and gave birth to her first child, William James. Her husband then moved the family to Pioche, where he ran a butcher shop and continued to deal in cattle. Her next two children, Hiram Richard and Flora Eliza Jane (known always as "Tiza") were born in Pioche.

When a rancher that Archibald had lent money to defaulted on the loan, Archibald moved his family to the ranch that had been put up as collateral. It was here, in the Las Vegas Valley, that Helen's fourth child, Evaline La Vega, was born. The family's Las Vegas Ranch served as a way-station for travelers and also prospered by selling beef, vegetables, fruit, and wine to miners in the area.

1854–1926
TEACHER, HISTORIAN, POSTMISTRESS

When her husband was shot and killed on July 13, 1884, Helen was pregnant with her fifth child. She had the doors taken off the ranch house to build a coffin for her husband and was subpoenaed to testify at the murder trial. She inherited the ranch property from her husband and, on the advice of her attorney, applied for her widow's tax exemption under the name of Helen J. Stewart, the name that she always used legally from then on. Although the Lincoln Board of Equalization granted this exemption to her in the amount of $1,000, they also raised her taxed on the Las Vegas Ranch by $1,000.

Helen traveled to her parents' home in California for the birth of Archibald, Jr., while her father temporarily took over operation of the ranch. Although Helen knew nothing about the ranch business at the time, she eventually became an extremely proficient rancher and businesswoman. When she was unable to find a buyer for her ranch, Helen began purchasing adjacent land and by 1890 was the largest land-owner in Lincoln County, which at that time included present-day Clark County. In 1893 she was appointed the first postmaster of "Los" Vegas,

Nevada—spelled that way to avoid confusion with Las Vegas, New Mexico.

Because no formal schooling was available to her children, Helen hired an Oxford-educated tutor for the three younger ones. When this gentleman died, the children were sent to a boarding school in California. Helen would write to them about sitting in front of the ranch house and imagining a church steeple, tree-lined streets, schools, hotels, and all the components of a city. In 1902 Helen sold the ranch to a railroad company looking for a depot and watering source. While awaiting the construction of her new home near the ranch property, she moved temporarily to Los Angeles. That summer, she married Frank Roger Stewart, a man who had worked for her on the ranch since 1886. Helen required that her second husband sign a prenuptial agreement to ensure that all of her money and belongings would go to her children.

By the time Helen moved into her new home in Las Vegas, the city was beginning to grow quickly. Helen, who loved being around people, became an active part of the social, political, and business life of the community. She was instrumental in getting the first public school built so that parents would not have to send their children to California. She also helped found Christ Episcopal Church and was a charter member of the Mesquite Club. In 1916 she was the first woman elected to the Clark County School Board. Her request that she not be required to do the clerical work demanded by her assignment as "clerk" was upheld by the Nevada Attorney General. She also served on the jury for the first murder trial in Clark County where women were allowed to be jurors.

Helen was known as an authority on the history of women in Southern Nevada and helped organize a branch of the Nevada Historical Society in Las Vegas. As a prolific writer in her own journals, she encouraged women to record their stories and their histories. Helen's friendship with Paiute women led her to believe that the baskets they made told the stories of their lives. Over the years, she accumulated over 550 of them, considered one of the finest collections in the state. Her heirs eventually sold it to the Hardy House railroad chain.

Helen died of cancer in Las Vegas on March 6, 1926. Although she had been a very successful rancher and businesswoman, her death certificate listed her occupation as "historian." In a suiting epitaph, her friend Delphine Squires explained, "Her frail little body housed an indomitable will, a wonderful strength of purpose, and a courageous heart." She labeled her "The First Lady of Las Vegas."

—*Dorothy T. Bokelmann*

Mayme Virginia Clifton Stocker

Mayme Virginia Clifton Stocker was noted for possessing the first gambling license issued in Clark County. In 1920, on Mayme's 45th birthday, she and her sons opened the Northern Club, a hotel and card room on Fremont Street. The state of Nevada legalized gambling soon after, and the Stockers expanded the Northern Club to include all the popular games of chance. The Northern Club operated on Fremont Street until 1933.

Mayme Virginia Clifton Stocker was born in Reading, Pennsylvania, on September 5, 1875 to George and Anne May Clifton. She was the oldest of six children. Mayme's mother passed away when she was 12 and, since the burden of caring for her five siblings fell on her, all hope for her further education ceased.

It was about four years later, on December 26, 1891, that Mayme married Oscar W. Stocker, a railroad man. For thirteen years, Mayme and her husband remained in Reading, but progress and the World's Fair carried railroad man Oscar to St. Louis in 1904. The Stockers stayed in St. Louis for three and a half years. By that time, the family had grown to include three sons—Lester W., Clarence C., and

1875–1972
HOTEL AND CASINO
OWNER

Harold J. Mayme, Oscar, and their three sons moved to Los Angeles in mid 1907 and then in 1911 on to the bustling young city of Las Vegas, where Oscar was employed by the Los Angeles, San Pedro, and Salt Lake Railroad.

The Stockers were entranced by the goings-on and newness of Las Vegas. The family lived at first in railroad company housing but very soon after arriving in town they moved to 503 South Third Street. There, the feisty lady with the #1 Clark County Gaming License resided for 32 years.

Quite a gambler in her own right, Mayme loved to frequent the Fremont Street casinos. She retained ownership of the Northern Club for twenty-five years until, on her 70th birthday, she leased the property to Wilbur Clark, who in the '60s turned it into the well-known Monte Carlo Bar.

Mayme had a real zest for life and a special enthusiasm for air travel. She boasted of traveling over 400,000 miles by air. In 1927 she took her first flight over the Las Vegas Valley in an old plane held together mainly by bailing wire. She flew to Alaska, London, India, and various Scandinavian countries. Even though

her travels took Mayme away from Nevada for extended periods of time, she never forgot her genuine love for Las Vegas.

Mayme's myriad of interests may have played a large part in her longevity. She herself said, "I attribute my long life and good health to always being busy, never worrying about things." Among Mayme's interests were quilting, sewing, and crocheting, a skill taught to her when she was eight years old by her mother. Mayme's crocheting was so intricate that it was considered to be museum quality. She also took pride in turning out many of her own clothes on her sewing machine,

Mayme and her husband Oscar were married for almost 50 years. The blessed union was brought to an end with Oscar's death on September 10, 1941.

After the loss of her husband, Mayme became even more active in local organizations. She served three terms as president of the Auxiliary to the Brotherhood of Railroad Trainmen. Also, over the many years that she resided in Las Vegas, Mayme chaired and served on numerous committees and boards. She belonged to the National Society of the Daughters of the American Revolution, the Emblem Club of the Las Vegas Elks Lodge, and the Royal Neighbors in Las Vegas. Harold Stocker, one of her sons, was for a while the only living charter member of the Las Vegas Elks Lodge.

Mayme was also a member of the local Republican Club and always had a deep interest in politics. She died in 1972 at the age of 97 years of age.

—*Mary Gafford*

Idah Meacham Strobridge

Idah Meacham was an only child, born on June 9, 1855, to parents who were homesteading in Moraga Valley, California. While still a young, impressionable girl, Idah moved with her family to start a ranch in northern Nevada at Lassen Meadows, about halfway between Winnemucca and Lovelock. There, her father built the Humboldt House, a popular hotel and café that served as a rest stop for many of the travelers passing through Nevada. As she grew up, Idah came to know the wagon trains heading west, the new railroads that brought more homesteaders every year, Mexican vaqueros, Chinese placer miners, and Native Americans from the Paiute and Bannock tribes. From this eclectic childhood, Idah went on to pursue her formal education at the Mills Seminary in Oakland, California, graduating in 1883.

While in Oakland, Idah met and married Samuel Hooker (Whitmarsh) Strobridge of Auburn, California, the adopted son of James H. Strobridge. The young married couple moved back to Nevada and ranched on land that Idah's father had given them as a wedding gift. There followed a brief period of happiness before Idah's life was beset by a horrible series of tragedies, tragedies that would have broken the spirits of most women.

Her first-born son, Earl, died the day after his birth. Then came the devastating winter of 1888–1889, when the blizzards killed most of the family's herd of cattle and pneumonia took the lives of her husband and one other son. Idah was left with just one child, a son who died a year later. Within a short period of time, Idah had been stripped of everyone in her family except her parents. Later, in her book *The Lessons of the Desert*, she left behind a haunting description of the desert that must have come partly from this experience:

"Just a little flour, a piece of bacon, a handful of coffee, one's blankets, enough clothing for comfort—that is all. When one stops to think of it, it is astonishing to find how little one really needs, to live. It is only after you have been on a rough trip of weeks, when it was needful that you should debate well and long over not every pound, but literally every ounce of extra weight that you were to carry—casting aside all things but those that were vital to your absolute needs—that you came to

1855–1932
RANCHER, MINER, WRITER

178

realize how much useless stuff one goes through life a-burdened with."

Idah did not give up on life after her tragic losses; instead, she found solace in her work and in the vast, silent Nevada desert. In July 1895, a *Mining and Scientific Press* reporter found Idah hard at work on a "lost mine" claim:

"...persistent searches were made for the mine, but each time were abandoned until this spring when a cultured woman of the new age appeared in the person of Mrs. Ida M. Strobridge, in company with a young man lately employed on her father's ranch near Humboldt. She is a most remarkably bright woman, and will climb a precipitous cliff where the average man would not dare to venture. In addition to mining she looks after the business of her father's cattle ranch, and is quite a sportswoman and would probably carry off first prize in a shooting tournament, as she brings down her game every time. She wears a handsome brown denim costume, which she dons in climbing the very steep and rugged cliffs of the Humboldt Mountains. She has located five claims on the lode, laid out a new camp and named it after her father, 'Meacham,' and reorganized the district anew as the 'Humboldt'; she has four men to work and is superintending operations herself. She has also located the water and springs flowing over her claims, which are nine miles east of the Central Pacific Railroad, at the Humboldt House. She is the New Woman...Mrs. Strobridge is now engaged running a tunnel under the shaft where the vein is showing up finely, and if the present appearance is maintained, the New Woman will in due time be reckoned a millionairess, and all by her indomitable will and perseverance. She is now sacking ores for shipment."

She began writing at the age of 40, at first under the pseudonym "George W. Craiger." She eventually published three volumes, based mostly on her experiences and love of the desert. Editors of *Sagebrush Trilogy*, a compilation of Idah's writings, call her "Nevada's first woman of letters."

By May of 1901, Idah was finished with the ranching and mining phase of her life. She sold her property and moved to Los Angeles with her parents. Among her friends were authors like Mary Austin and men of letters like Charles Fletcher Lummis, publisher of the literary magazine *Land of Sunshine*, later renamed *Out West*.

Idah died on February 8, 1932, and is buried in Oakland's Mountain View cemetery next to her parents, husband, and sons.

—*Victoria Ford*

Laura May Tilden

1872–1928
LAWYER, SUFFRAGETTE

Laura May Tilden was born in Sacramento, California, on April 24, 1872, the fourth of six children. Her parents were Marcellus Crane Tilden and Elizabeth J. Ralston, both from Ohio. The U.S. Census for 1850 lists a 15-year-old Marcellus living with his parents, but by 1860 Marcellus was a Sacramento attorney, and by 1870 he was married to Elizabeth and had three children.

By June, 1880, the Tilden family had moved to Virginia City, Nevada. The 1880 Census lists nine-year-old Laura as being "at school" but also records the loss of Laura's mother and one of her older brothers. A cousin, A.M. Crane, has joined the household and is described as "keeping house."

Laura decided as a young woman to become an attorney like her father. There is no record of her having attended law school; Laura probably studied law in her father's law office, a common route to joining the profession in those days.

The *Virginia City Evening Chronicle* of July 24, 1893 credits Laura with obtaining the passage of a legislative statute the previous winter that gave women the same rights and privileges as males "so far as becoming attorneys is concerned." The article goes on to say that the women of Nevada owe her a debt of gratitude for this feat and that she is the first lady to be allowed to practice law in Nevada. Laura is reported as having passed a "creditable exam" and receiving "encomiums from the entire bench for the manner in which she had borne herself." Although she was Nevada's first female attorney, there is no available evidence that she actually practiced law in Nevada.

Her first victory in a California Superior Court was reported, however, in the *Virginia City Territorial Enterprise* of February 1, 1894, in a story originally published in the *Sacramento Bee*. She was said to be "young and rather pretty" and had "a clear, pleasing voice which was distinctly heard throughout the courtroom." Even though she had only recently "hung out her shingle," she addressed the court as though she had been accustomed to doing it every day. She defended a young boy who had been accused of burglary by his foster father by arguing that the boy had had no criminal intent and should be discharged. Both the district attorney and the judge agreed with her, and she won her case.

Capital Women: An Interpretive History of Women in Sacramento, 1850–1920, by Elaine Connolly and Diane Self, reports that the *Sacramento Bee* in 1895 described Laura Tilden as "Sacramento's woman lawyer" and that this implies that she was the only female in the city practicing law at that time. She was her father's law partner at the time, and Connolly and Self credit Laura's father with inspiring her interest in the law and in the women's suffrage movement. Marcellus Tilden had signed an equal suffrage petition that was circulated in Northern California in 1870. Mary Erickson, in *Women Lawyers' Male-Connectedness,* points out that women lawyers were typically mentored by husbands, fathers, or other men who were attorneys.

Connolly and Self report that Laura Tilden attended and spoke at a public meeting in the California Assembly chamber to give the "woman side of the woman suffrage question." They quote a sympathetic *Sacramento Bee* reporter as assuring readers that the suffragettes were not "panta-loonitics" or "bloomers" or "free lovers" or "dowdies." The reporter described Laura as beginning her speech "with a smile that could win a thousand votes" and went on to say that Laura was helping to pass around a woman suffrage petition that 19 out of every 20 women in Sacramento were signing.

Laura's father died on January 30, 1896. Laura married twice that we know of, first to Fred Ray in 1898 and then to Walter Curtis Wilson in 1908. At some time during those years she moved to Colorado and was practicing there by 1914. Laura Tilden Ray Wilson died in Montrose, Colorado, on May 31, 1928, at the age of 66.

—*Kathleen F. Noneman*

Kathryn L. Marbaker Tubb

Kathryn L. Marbaker was born near Stevensville in Bradford County, Pennsylvania, on November 15, 1886 to Edward Marbaker, Jr., and Almeda Wage, both born in 1847. Kathryn's middle name was either Luella or Lucille—her father called her by one name and her mother by the other. She was also known as Kittie or Kitty (spelling varies). Kittie's father was a farmer and had served in the Union Army during the Civil War. Edward and Almeda were married in about 1865, and by the time the 1880 census was taken the couple already had eight children. By 1900, Almeda and Edward Marbaker were divorced, and Almeda married a man named Russel Gibbs. Edward Marbaker also remarried in 1910 to a much younger woman named Lulu.

Kittie had at least some elementary education and was able to read and write. She does not appear to have been living at home with either parent by the time of the 1900 Census, when she was fourteen years old, and may have been at school or employed elsewhere. Family legend tells that at about the age of sixteen, Kittie left home and advertised herself in a Philadelphia newspaper as a mail-or-

1886–1957
RANCHER, PROPRIETOR
OF BOARDING HOUSE/
BROTHEL

der bride. Thirty-four-year-old Robert (Bob) M. Tubb (1868–1944) responded to the ad, and the couple was married around 1904.

It is not known where Kittie and Bob Tubb first settled. Their first two children, Leon (1905–1979) and Robert (1906–1980), were born in Crown King, Arizona Territory, where Bob had been running freight lines from Crown King to Las Vegas. On a layover in Las Vegas, Bob found a piece of property to the northwest that appealed to him, and the small family headed west in a covered wagon, arriving in the Ash Meadows, Nevada/Death Valley Junction, California, area about 1907.

Bob Tubb filed a homestead claim on the land between the mainline and the spur at Death Valley Junction (south of the present town) and built a saloon, grocery store, hotel, and brothel on the spot. Kittie ran the store, served in the saloon, cooked for the boarding house residents, and took care of the women in the brothel.

In 1908, Kittie took the TTRR to Los Angeles to give birth to their third son, George (1908–1962). By 1909, Bob had planted fruit trees and grain on their 340 acres at the Junction. He

ran a pipeline ten miles from Crystal Springs in Ash Meadows, Nevada to supply water to his crops. Unfortunately, the pipe broke that same year, and Bob was unable to fix it in time to save the crops. Later he was forced to abandon the pipeline altogether as it was illegal to transport water over the state line unless the water was free flowing.

The fourth Tubb boy, Danny (1909–1941), was born prematurely under a tree at the Junction. Bob and Kittie were living in a tent house near where the present-day Amargosa Opera House building now stands. The new baby was quite small, and Kittie is said to have kept him in a cigar box and fed him with an eyedropper.

Bob Tubb established the first school in Death Valley Junction in 1915. One report claims that when the new, young, single teacher arrived in the Junction to take up residence in the quarters offered by the Tubbs, Kittie sent her packing because she didn't belong in the rowdy brothel and saloon environment. By 1916, when Inyo County went "dry," Tubb had closed his saloon and brothel in the Junction and moved them over to Ash Meadows. He continued to hold a claim to his property at the Junction and still operated a business there until the borax company bought him out in around 1923. Kittie took up ranching in Ash Meadows and continued to ranch and farm there on and off until her death in 1957.

Kittie and Bob Tubb would eventually divorce and marry other people but continue to live in close proximity.

Kittie earned the nickname "Shotgun Kittie" because she never went anywhere without her shotgun—and she even carried it with her into the bars in Beatty, where no one dared to challenge her.

Kittie worked as a cook in various hotels and cafes from Death Valley Junction to Beatty, Nevada. She also raised horses on her ranch at Ash Meadows. In her later years, she became something of a tourist attraction since visitors to the nearby brothel or the tourists from Death Valley Junction would stop and talk with her as she sat on her front porch.

Besides having a violent temper, Kittie was reported to be a very observant and vigilant. She also had her own system of medical remedies that included liberal use of topical kerosene for wounds and urine for superficial skin conditions.

The Tubb home and family heirlooms were lost to a fire in the early 1970s. Little survived beyond a few old photographs and, of course, plenty of legends. The National Park Service finally purchased the Tubb property in 1997 as part of the newly created Ash Meadows Wildlife Refuge.

—*Janet E. White*

Gue Gim Wah

Gue Gim Der was born in 1900 in Lin Lun Li, between Hong Kong and Guangzhou. By 1912, her father was a businessman in San Francisco's Chinatown, and he returned to China to bring his family, including Gue Gim's stepmother and four other siblings, to America. The family sailed to California by way of Hong Kong and Honolulu. Gue Gim remembered being very ill from medication taken for worms (a requirement for all immigrating peoples), and she found the experience at Angel Island unpleasant. She was questioned for two days by officials and was required to be locked up in jail-like conditions for five days on the island.

Gue Gim stayed for four years in San Francisco, a time she found not as pleasant as she had hoped. She later recalled, "I no like San Francisco. Dirty city. Horses make manure on the street. Always smell. [I like] Hong Kong better. No horses. Use rickshaw, no dirty up streets." She worked in her father's store and, as the eldest female child, helped her stepmother with the growing family.

As a girl in the new city, Gue Gim had two approved activities outside the home. One was

Chinese language school, and the other was church. Her father, reasoning that English was largely unnecessary to a young well-bred Chinese girl and that well-to-do Chinese men preferred traditional Chinese wives, sent Gue Gim to a private Chinese language school rather than an American public school. But her second outside activity, the Methodist church, helped her acculturate herself to America. The Sunday school classes were taught in English, and some of her fellow students were Caucasian. Her father's conversion to Christianity, a decision that paved the way for Gue Gim's later acceptance into the community of Prince, Nevada, meant that his family were not thought of as "those heathen Chinese" at a time when anti-Chinese sentiment ran fairly high.

At the age of fifteen or sixteen Gue Gim was married to Tom Fook Wah, an American-Chinese who walked into her father's store, saw her, and asked for her hand in marriage on the spot. Although Tom had been born in America, he lived his first 21 years in China after his parents died. Returning to the United States in 1892, Tom was "re-admitted' to the country (after a

great deal of difficulty) and moved to Marysville, California, with his uncle, where he cooked for an American family. Tom had heard about a new mining boom town in Nevada and decided to try his luck there. However, he didn't know that Nevada was primarily a hard rock, not a placer, mining state. Hard rock mining required a great deal of capital, which Tom did not have, and he faced some difficult times before becoming, once again, a cook. By 1915, he had begun to settle down and felt it was time to find a wife.

Visiting San Francisco before a long-planned trip to China to find a bride, Tom saw his bride-to-be in her father's store. At 15, Gue Gim was not enthusiastic about marrying a man who was so much older (28), but being a dutiful daughter, she obeyed her father's directive. The couple had a traditional Chinese wedding with two religious ceremonies—Buddhist and Christian—during the event.

Following the wedding, the couple went to Prince, Nevada, where Gue Gim's life began anew. She was welcomed into the community by the mine supervisor and his wife, and Gue Gim attended a party in her honor wearing her traditional Chinese long gown. Tom taught her the English expression, "You come again," so that she could encourage the guests to come visit them in their home. Gue Gim began to learn English from various progressive women's groups that advocated the education of women. She also attended the local Prince School, where she was a popular student despite the age difference between her and the children. Her attendance at the school sparked interest in a cultural exchange; one evening, parents and friends were invited to attend a special program called "A Trip to Asia." Gue Gim made many friends among the Caucasian community in Nevada during her life there and served as a positive example for women of all backgrounds.

—*Kathleen Thompson*

Anna B. Mudd Warren

Anna Mudd was born at Pilot Hill in El Dorado County, California, on September 21, 1863. She was the daughter of George B. Mudd and Wilhelmina Marshall Mudd. The family moved to Gold Hill, Nevada, in 1872, when Anna was nine years old. Her father worked in the mines of the Comstock until he lost his life during a fire in the Crown Point Mine in 1873. Anna graduated from the Gold Hill public schools in 1881 and became a teacher in Greenfield, Nevada (later named Yerington). She taught primary and grammar grades for pupils aged six to twenty. In 1885, Anna accepted a job as a teacher in Virginia City, and it was there that she met Charles Warren, a Virginia City businessman from Massachusetts. Anna and Charles were married in 1887, but four years later Charles died, leaving Anna with two small children.

After her husband's death, Anna went to work at the law offices of C.E. Mack. She studied typing and stenography to become a court reporter. In 1895, Anna transferred to the law office of W.E.F. Deal, where she continued court reporting while studying law in her free time. By 1899

1863–1944
TEACHER, ATTORNEY,
COURT REPORTER

Anna was enrolled as the second female member of the Nevada State Bar. Once she decided to settle in Reno in 1903, Anna moved her home from Virginia City to Island Avenue in Reno—literally. The house was taken down over the old road in sections and reassembled in Reno.

Anna joined a successful practice in Reno, and in 1907 the *Nevada State Journal* stated that she "...appeared in Judge Orr's court, not the initial entrance of a female barrister in a Reno courtroom.... she is now in full charge of all probate matters for Mack & Shoup. Before admission she was a court reporter for several years."

The *Carson City Daily Appeal*, July 27, 1910, reported: "Nevada's only woman lawyer, Anna Warren, has been quite successful, although she is not engaged in the practice of her profession regularly at this time. She won a case against Nevada Consolidated Mining and Milling of Olinghouse Canyon. She appeared for Richard Kirman, Reno's former mayor."

In 1913, Anna was appointed to the office of U.S. Commissioner, a position she held the rest of her life. She was a member of the American Bar Association, the Nevada State Bar, and the

Washoe County Bar. Sometime during her law career in Reno, Anna opened a button shop on West First Street. This became a much needed diversion from routine office work. She later moved the shop into her own home.

Warren was a president of the Rebekah Assembly and the Professional Women's Club, as well as being active in the Order of the Eastern Star. She was first a member of Esther No. 3 in Carson City, demitting to become a charter member of Argenta Chapter No.7, later demitting to take an active part as a member of Adah Chapter No. 4. Anna Warren was Worthy Grand Matron during the years 1905–1907. Under her wise guidance, the chapters were incorporated into a Grand Chapter, with the first meeting being held on September 19, 1905. The officers formed by-laws, a constitution, and all rules and regulations. Anna and her officers are given credit for the present system followed in the Order of the Eastern Star.

Anna was active in the Nevada League of Women Voters in the early years following its founding in 1919 at a meeting in Reno conducted by national suffrage leader Carrie Chapman Catt. In 1923, she chaired the League's Committee on Uniform Laws and worked with Sadie Hurst (Nevada's first Assemblywoman) to compile a "Summary of Laws Concerning Women & Children in Nevada."

Anna died in Reno on July 31, 1944, still held in high regard by friends, coworkers, and women's club members for the outstanding caliber of her work in the community.

—*Sandra Young*

Hannah Reese Welde

1879–1974
MIDWIFE

The story of Hannah Reese Welde tells much about the lives of early pioneer women in White Pine County, of their joys and sorrows, of the hardships they accepted and overcame. Her story also spans to a great extent the history of mining in the county.

Hannah Reese was born in the small mining town of Frisco in eastern Utah on December 16. 1879. She attended grade school in the farming community of Stockton, just south of Tooele, Utah, and married Jack Welde, who worked in the nearby mines. While in Utah, the Weldes had four daughters: Marjorie, Anne, Stella, and Becky.

In 1906, Jack Welde left his family in Utah to work in Nevada. This was the year that the Nevada Northern Railway Company completed its rail line from Cobre to Ely, thus making the mining of copper in White Pine County profitable. Subsequently, the Guggenheims of New York gained controlling interest in the railway, the mines of Nevada Consolidated Copper Company at Ruth and Copper Flat, and the W.N. McGill Ranch with its water rights. It was the opening of the mill and smelter and the promise of higher wages that drew Jack to Nevada. He became a powder crew foreman working on the tunnels that would connect the railroad in Ely to the mines in Kimberly and Ruth and to the site of the mill and smelter. One day, while Jack was checking the dynamite, it exploded, and he lost a leg. He was cared for in the Ely Hospital and convalesced for about a year in the tent hospital in McGill. Jack was then fitted with a wooden leg and assigned to work at the smelter.

In 1907, Jack brought his family from Utah to McGill. It was common in western mining towns that the first people to arrive lived either in rickety shacks or in tents. The Weldes lived in a tent without indoor water or plumbing. Wind chill temperatures could reach as low as 60 degrees below zero when the winter winds screamed down Steptoe Valley.

The Welde's baby boy, Johnny, died at nine months of age, but in McGill, Hannah gave birth to two healthy girls: Bessie and Madeline. Eventually, the family moved into a McGill house known as the "Katzenjammer house."

In spite of primitive and inhospitable living conditions, the early residents of McGill created a close-knit community by making their own entertainment, offering help to each other when it was needed, and forming long-lasting friendships. The W.N. McGill family home, now owned by Nevada Consolidated, provided a beautiful backdrop for many of the town's celebrations: Labor Day, July 4th, and Mormon Pioneer Day on July 24th. On these oc-

casions, a pavilion for dancing was built. Float parades, foot and horse races, drilling contests, "badger fights," baseball games, barbeques, and a grand ball filled the day. People from the area, including the Weldes, sometimes traveled to the Mormon settlement of Lund to celebrate Pioneer Day. This 36-mile trip took two days by horse, buggy, or wagon.

The worldwide influenza epidemic of 1918 closed many of the district's schools, bars, churches, and movie theaters. Hannah lost an aunt in that epidemic. Hardly a family was left unaffected. Also in 1918, the Weldes moved to a brand-new company house on Third Street. McGill had a population of about 2,850 by this time and was becoming a well-kept company town with streets, sidewalks, and curbing. The mining company owned its own power plant, dairy, water system, emergency hospital, and commissary. A grammar school and three churches were also established. Numerous social and fraternal organizations flourished. The Welde girls frequented the McGill clubhouse with its gym, bowling alley, pool tables, swimming pool, dance/recreation hall, library, and tennis court. In winter, sledding and ice skating were popular forms of entertainment.

A big influence on the development of the town was the presence of John C. (Jack) Kinnear, Sr., considered by some to be the "benevolent dictator" of the mining company. An engineering graduate of M.I.T., Kinnear was general manager of NCCC and saw to it that the company's workers and their families had necessities, health care, and recreation. McGill could have gone the way of other "boom to bust" towns when the gigantic mill burned to the ground in 1922. But another larger-than-life presence, D.C. Jackling, the "boss" from Salt Lake City, sent a telegraph message: "Rebuild it." The mill rose again, bigger and better, rebuilt in a record 523 days and giving stability to the district for the next 50 years.

In 1923, Jack Welde died of cancer, leaving Hannah to raise her large family alone. Company policy was that a widow had to move from her company-owned house upon the death of her employee spouse. However, Mr. Kinnear made an exception for Hannah. She became a practical nurse and midwife, working with Drs. O. Hovendon and Noah Smernoff on confinement cases. She also provided child care for the Kinnears and others in town. She continued this type of work until about 1945 and remained active in the Community Methodist Church, Wesleyans, and Rebekahs Lodge until her death in 1974 at age 95.

—*Doris Drummond*

Margaret M. Wheat

Margaret "Peg" Marean was born to Stanley and Ruth Marean in Fallon, Nevada, in 1908. Peg was the couple's middle child. She received her education in the Fallon public schools and at the University of Nevada–Reno. After completing two years of college, where she majored in geology, Peg left school to marry William Hatton of Tonopah. William's mother did not support the marriage, because it interrupted her son's education. Peg and William lived in the Fallon area, where Peg gave birth to four children: Bill, Jack, Sylvia, and Don. The Hattons were divorced in 1937 after the birth of the last child.

Not long after her divorce, Peg married Wendel Wheat, whom she met while he was with the Civilian Conservation Corps. They stayed in the Fallon area, buying a place on the Carson River. Wendel was something of a mountain man, and he introduced Peg to a broader view of the Great Basin as they wandered the desert together. It was during this time that she developed her interest in caves, fossils, and Native American culture.

1908–1988
ANTHROPOLOGIST,
GEOLOGIST, AUTHOR

The Wheats were always short of money, so Peg hired out to do odd jobs. Because she frequently was gone from home, many of the Wheat household chores were left to her daughter Sylvia, who, by the age of nine, was largely responsible for the care of her brothers. Peg worked for the telephone company during World War II and also had a job housesitting at Lake Tahoe for a year or so. Once, she took a job as a nanny in Los Angeles so that she could spend time at the Southwest Museum there. As a self-taught person, unusual jobs, such as being a cook for persons at an archeological dig, allowed Peg to be close to experts in various scientific fields and to enrich her enquiring mind.

For twenty years, starting in 1940s, most of Peg's life work was devoted to recording the traditional arts and sacred beliefs of the northern Nevada Paiute tribes. Using only a crude wire recorder and a box camera, Peg was able to elicit honest and open responses from the tribal elders through her relaxed interviewing style. Even though Peg was well informed about the Paiutes from reading and was able to ask pertinent questions, she never dominated the dialogues.

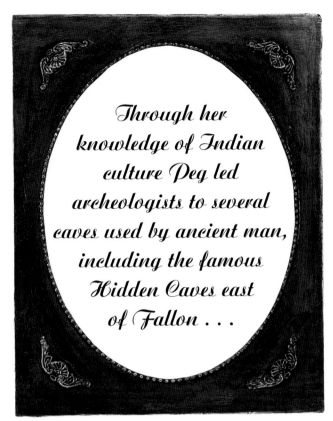

Through her knowledge of Indian culture Peg led archeologists to several caves used by ancient man, including the famous Hidden Caves east of Fallon . . .

Transcripts reveal that she was always respectful and sensitive during a conversation.

One of her important Paiute contacts was Wuzzie George. Wuzzie George and her husband Jimmie shared Peg's passion for preserving their culture. They showed her how the Paiute people built houses and boats from tules and cattails, how they wove baskets, and how they gathered and processed pine nuts. Peg's 1967 book, *Survival Art of the Primitive Paiutes*, stands as the definitive record of their ingenious knack for eking out an existence from the limited resources of the dry Great Basin.

Through her knowledge of Indian culture Peg led archeologists to several caves used by ancient man, including the famous Hidden Caves east of Fallon, which has now been set aside by the Bureau of Land Management for research and public tours. While pursuing her anthropological studies, Peg persuaded paleontologists from the University of California–Berkeley to excavate skeletons of ichthyosaurs in Nevada, and she served as a member of the Nevada Parks Commission appointed by Governor Sawyer, where she was instrumental in convincing the state to acquire and preserve the area known as the Berlin-Ichthyosaur Park.

Peg assisted in numerous other such projects as well. One of them, in Nevada State Museum's Tule Springs dig, established evidence of a Paleo-Indian culture dating back more than 11,000 years. Recognized as a self-taught geologist and anthropologist, Peg's fieldwork experiences ranged from working for the U.S. Geological Survey to protecting important cave sites from vandals. The Nevada State Museum hired her for archaeological fieldwork. She also worked on water resource projects for the Desert Research Institute.

At the first annual Ladies of the Press luncheon in 1969, the Reno Professional Club and the Nevada Library Association honored Peg as an outstanding Nevada woman. Although Peg had dropped out of the University of Nevada–Reno as a young woman, she lectured there frequently in her later years. In 1980, the university awarded her an honorary Doctor of Science degree.

Margaret Wheat resided in Fallon until her death in 1988. In 1991 she was remembered by the Rancho San Rafael Botanical Plant Society with the planting of a Pinion Pine in her honor. About sixty of her friends and family were present at the ceremony.

—*Sally Wilkins*

Jeanne Elizabeth Wier

Jeanne Elizabeth Wier was born in Iowa to Adolphus William and Elizabeth Greenside Wier. Jeanne had one sister named Eva and was educated in the public schools of Iowa and at the Iowa State Teacher's College, from which she graduated in 1893. As a teacher, Jeanne worked in public schools in Iowa and the western United States from 1889 to 1895. She became assistant principal of the Hepner High School in Oregon for two years and during her summer vacations studied at Stanford University, where in 1901 she graduated with a B.A. and where she later pursued a master's degree.

In 1897, Jeanne came to Nevada to study the Washoe Indians, who were believed at the time to be a dying race. A friend from Stanford urged her in 1899 to come and join the history faculty at the University of Nevada–Reno. Jeanne promptly established herself on the campus and soon became a popular member of the teaching staff. By 1907, she was the head of her department and was deeply involved in the study of Nevada's history.

1870–1950
HISTORIAN, PROFESSOR, RESEARCHER, WRITER

At the time of her arrival in the state, it was thought by historians that the frontier era in Nevada was coming to an end without much documentation or records of the milestones of the state's first century. But Jeanne was a woman of force and energy. She traveled all over the state by horse, car, and train to gather newspapers, relics, and manuscripts from Nevadans. In her diary of 1908 she wrote that she "would collect anything that in any way would throw light upon the history of Nevada from its earliest day to the present." Items of no importance to others were priceless to her. One of the problems she faced was the apparent disinterest of Nevadans in their history. However, she persevered in her pursuit of these objects of historical interest and gradually garnered attention from Nevada's citizens.

Jeanne was one of the founders of the Nevada Historical Society in 1904 and served as its first secretary. She took on the task of supervising the publication of the society's annual historical papers and of soliciting needed biennial appropriations from the legislature. Largely due to her efforts, the state legislature made the society an official state institution in 1907. Jeanne

did not receive any monetary compensation for these labors but did it out of her duty to the state's history. In January 1946, Dr. Jeanne Wier was honored by both houses of the Nevada legislature for her long service to the state. In 1968, the historical society finally acquired a permanent home on the campus of UNR. Many of the papers and artifacts from pioneer days in Nevada owned by the society are there because of Jeanne's unceasing hard work. Students and researchers have a priceless source of material available to them.

Jeanne wrote extensively and contributed valuable research to the *Encyclopedia Britannica*, the *World Encyclopedia*, the *Dictionary of American Biography*, and the *Dictionary of American History*. She also contributed a chapter to the book, *Rocky Mountain Politics*. In 1941, Jeanne received an honorary Doctor of Law degree from the University.

Jeanne served as vice-president of the Pacific Coast branch of the American Historical Society in 1914–1915 and announced the society's first women's suffragette meeting, which included Carrie Chapman Catt, pioneer suffragist. Jeanne continued to take an active part in the women's movement for several years thereafter. The records give the impression that she did not have close relationships with either men or other women, and Jeanne seems to have usually traveled and lived alone. In her later years, she developed a heart condition from which she finally succumbed on April 13, 1950, at the age of 80.

—*Dorothy T. Bokelmann*

Sophie Ernst Williams

Sophie Ernst Williams was born in Dubuque, Iowa, but came west with her family when she was 14 to join her brother, George Ernst, who operated a stage station at Twin Springs, Nye County, Nevada.

In 1870, Sophie married Joseph Thomas Williams, a young miner who had made a fortune in Virginia City and who was developing a mine in Nye County's Revielle Mining District, an area rich with gold, silver, copper, and lead. Discovered by "Indian Jim" in 1866, the district eventually produced over 1.5 million dollars for Joseph and other investors. Joseph Williams later served in the Nevada state government, spending six years in the legislature and senate during the early 1900s. He was the descendant of a southern family whose ancestors fought with distinction in the Revolutionary War.

Shortly after their marriage, Sophie and Joseph settled in Hot Creek, Nevada, to begin ranching. Hot Creek had flourished in the late 1860s after the discovery of silver, but by the early 1870s, it was a town in decline and never managed to recapture its earlier success. Nevertheless, Sophie and Joseph made it home for the rest of their lives.

1842–1927
RANCHER, EDUCATOR, POLITICAL ACTIVIST

Despite the town's dwindling population (from 300 in the 1860s to 25 in the 1880s), Joseph paid $6000 to build a hotel in 1875. In 1878, he built a larger hotel that boasted both a dance hall and bath-house. Finally, in 1908, he built another hotel; like the first two, it was constructed of stone, a common building material in the Hot Creek area.

Joseph continued his mining interests, but Sophie decided to start her own brand with four cows that her husband had given her. By buying more heifers, she was eventually able to build up a large herd. Sophie also bought her brother's land, an action that greatly enlarged the scope of her ranching activities.

When there were cattle to be sold, Sophie drove many miles in a horse and buggy to collect the money. All money from cattle sales was set aside for the education of her children. The Hot Creek Ranch School went through the eighth grade only and was able to stay open because Sophie bought the desks and books and boarded the school teacher without compensation.

Pioneer women faced loneliness, fear of Indian raids, and the absence of doctors in times

When her husband was away on long trips, she would put all her children to sleep on the floor . . . She would arm her sister with a broom and herself with a fireplace poker.

of sickness, but they were free from many of the dangers that threatened city women. Sophie was known to carry a gold belt with never less than $500 and sometimes with thousands in it, but on her long, isolated rides she was never robbed or threatened.

Sophie never learned to shoot a gun, but she was fearless in the face of danger. When her husband was away on long trips, she would put all her children to sleep on the floor of one bedroom and wedge a bureau against the door. She would arm her sister with a broom and herself with a fireplace poker.

Once when a squaw ran away from her tribe rather than be burned on her husband's funeral pyre—a custom of the Shoshone at the time—Sophie hid the squaw in her cellar for several days, risking her own life in the process. Indians came looking for the squaw and became angry when they didn't find her. Sophie assuaged their anger by giving them pancakes and syrup. When the disgruntled braves were finally forced to burn the dead warrior, the squaw came out of hiding and returned to her tribe.

Both Sophie and Joseph Williams believed that women should be financially independent. Sophie not only had her own cattle, land, and bank accounts, she and her daughter, Elizabeth Williams Barndt, also acquired and sold mining claims in their own names.

Sophie took an active interest in politics. Even before women could vote, she engaged in vigorous campaigns for the candidates of her choice. All of Nevada's early governors were her friends. No gossip was ever heard at her table; the conversation concerned topics dealing with the welfare of the state. She prided herself on the fact that no one, from the governor of Nevada to the tramp passing on the road, left the Hot Creek Ranch hungry.

Sophie was widowed in 1910, but she continued to pursue her educational and ranching interests. In 1923, Governor Scrugham recognized Sophie's dedication to education by appointing her a regent of the University of Nevada. She was to fill out the term of Miles E. North, with an appointment running from 1923–29. However, Sophie died in 1927. Honored and respected by all, she was buried in the family plot at her beloved Hot Creek Ranch, near her husband Joseph.

—*Fran Haraway*

Frances Williamson

The lady who was to become one of Nevada's leading women's suffrage activists was born Frances Slaven in Canada in 1842. Little is know about her early years, but, in 1863, it was as an independent, educated woman that Frances arrived in Austin, Nevada, where she first worked as a teacher and later (by 1865) as a school principal.

Frances married John R. Williamson, a prominent member of Austin society, on June 28, 1863. The Williamsons eventually had six children, but Frances always continued to serve as principal and teacher in the Austin school. She also took an active part in community projects. John was superintendent of schools, ran his own mercantile business, and was active in state politics.

Tragedy struck the family in the 1870s. Four of the Williamson children died from various diseases in 1876 and 1877. (A fifth child, John Jr., would die in Carson City in 1891, while his father was representing Lander County in the state senate.) In spite of these setbacks, Frances continued to teach, to write (she displayed a collection of her books at the 1893 World's Fair), and to be active in Austin society.

1842–1919
TEACHER, PRINCIPAL, JOURNALIST, WOMEN'S RIGHTS ACTIVIST

While Frances found a way through her tragedies, her husband did not. On Saturday, April 28, 1894, he shot and killed himself.

John Williamson's suicide resulted in Frances's involvement in the women's suffrage movement. In June 1894, Frances put the mercantile store up for sale, and on November 10, 1904, she, along with a Mrs. Lund and a Mrs. Weller, organized an equal suffrage meeting at the Austin courthouse. About 125 people—both men and women—attended this meeting and heard Frances Williamson speak about the organization of the movement and laud the careers of Lucy Stone, Harriet Beecher Stowe, and Susan B. Anthony. By the end of the meeting, Frances, who had been acting as temporary chair, was elected corresponding secretary of the newly formed Lucy Stone Non-Partisan Equal Suffrage League— Nevada's first specific equal suffrage organization.

The league was formed "expressly to secure the political enfranchisement of the women in the state of Nevada and to study the duties of citizenship." Because this campaign was non-partisan, Frances and her supporters had the backing of no specific political party, so they

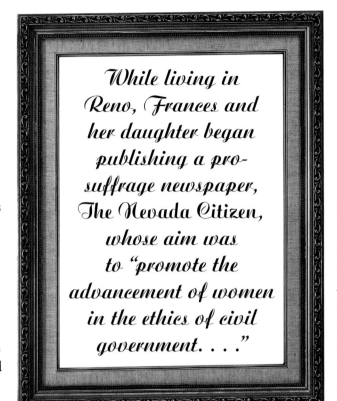

While living in Reno, Frances and her daughter began publishing a pro-suffrage newspaper, The Nevada Citizen, whose aim was to "promote the advancement of women in the ethics of civil government. . . ."

could cross party lines with their message and thus gain wide support.

By April 1895, one year after John's suicide, the suffrage league had disbanded. However, Frances had spent this time writing letters to several newspapers and had become known throughout the state as an equal suffrage advocate. Her work and the work of like-minded individuals led to the passage of a suffrage resolution in both the Nevada assembly and senate in February 1895.

The first state Equal Suffrage Association convention was held in Reno on October 29 and 30, 1895. The event had been preceded in May by a suffrage meeting at which Susan B. Anthony and Anna Howard Shaw were guests. Frances Williamson was a speaker at that first meeting, and, at the state convention, she was elected president of the State Equal Suffrage Association, an adjunct to the National Equal Suffrage Association. Her duties consisted of chairing the legislative work committee and canvassing the state for support. She visited every town accessible by stage or rail, and she helped organize many local suffrage organizations.

During the next two years, Frances traveled continuously throughout the state. She also attended a national convention in Washington, DC, where she testified before a U.S. Senate committee that was considering an equal suf-

frage amendment. In 1896, she chaired the second convention of the State Equal Suffrage Association, which was held in Reno where Frances and her remaining child, Mary Laura, then lived. In spite of unending efforts of Frances and her colleagues, their suffrage resolution did not pass the Nevada legislature in the 1896 session.

While living in Reno, Frances and her daughter began publishing a pro-suffrage newspaper, *The Nevada Citizen*, whose aim was to "promote the advancement of women in the ethics of civil government...." Published through August 1898, it proved to be a valuable resource for the Nevada suffrage movement.

On October 30, 1897, the State Equal Suffrage Association held its third convention, this time in Carson City. Frances addressed the assembly, but soon after the meeting, Frances and Mary Laura left Nevada for Washington, DC, where Frances worked in the Women's Press Bureau and Mary Laura enrolled in Washington Law College.

She died at her Oakland home on December 21, 1919, the same year that the Equal Suffrage Amendment was passed by Congress and sent to the states for ratification.

—*Fran Haraway*

Bird May Wilson

Bird May Wilson was born in Sandoval, Marion County, Illinois, on May 20, 1865. Bird's father was Hazen Wilson, a direct descendant of Revolutionary War officers, and her mother was Susan Dean. The U.S. Census records that in 1860 Hazen Wilson, then 35, was still living on the family farm with his wife Susan, 25. The household was headed by Hazen's mother Ada Wilson.

Bird Wilson studied court reporting in Chicago, which reportedly had more women lawyers than any other city in the world, before embarking for San Francisco, where she became private secretary to Judge William W. Morrow.

Bird attended Hastings Law School while she was working for Judge Morrow and graduated from the school with "high honors." The *Chicago Legal News* of June 6, 1903, picking up an article from the May 19, 1903 *San Francisco Chronicle*, reported that Judge Morrow had moved the Ninth Circuit Court of Appeals to admit Bird to practice before it, and that she was the first woman on the Pacific Coast to win that distinguished honor. She had previously been admitted to practice before the United States District Court on the motion of United States Attorney Marshall B. Woodworth.

In an interview, Bird Wilson stated that she wanted to actively practice her profession but that she would continue to work for Judge Morrow for a time. She was also interested in educating women about their rights under the law. Bird stated that she had previously written about legal topics and wanted to compile a volume about rights that would give women and girls some elementary knowledge of the subject. She is quoted as saying: "There is a lamentable lack of knowledge among women as to their status and rights under the law, and I hope I may be enabled in some way to make this less."

She moved to Nevada after the big San Francisco earthquake and was licensed to practice on June 28, 1906, just the seventh woman to be admitted to the profession in Nevada. Bird was just 41 years old when she began practice in Manhattan, Nevada, where she did general civil law and mining and contract law. Less than six months after she moved to Nevada, an article in the *Tonopah Bonanza* of September 18, 1906 was describing her in glowing terms:

1865–1946
COURT REPORTER, SECRETARY, STOCK BROKER, MINE OWNER

"Miss B.M. Wilson, the prominent lady broker and attorney of Manhattan passed through this city Friday, en route for a two weeks trip to San Francisco. She reports everything booming in Manhattan and predicts a still greater increase in the activity there. Miss Wilson is heavily interested in the Happy Hooligan and states that the giving of a contract for the sinking of a shaft on the ledge running through that claim has been attended with the happiest results, ore of a very high grade having been taken out, and there being every sign of permanence."

On May 19, an earlier edition of the *Tonopah Bonanza* was enthusiastic about Bird's arrival in town and told of her plans to set up a mining brokerage business in conjunction with her legal work in her office on Erie Street. It told of her belief in the greater opportunities and wider horizon to be found in a promising, live mining camp like Manhattan. She predicted that San Franciscans were looking to the mines to give them a "speedy recovery on investments." Bird prospered in Nevada and became a stockbroker, the owner of a ranch in Indian Springs, and holder of mining interests in Round Mountain, Tonopah, and Goldfield. The *Bonanza* of October 18, 1906, reported that Bird had won a divorce case on the grounds of "failure to provide" for her client. Less than three years later, in January 1909, she moved her law practice to Goldfield.

In Goldfield Bird became a charter member of the Montezuma chapter of the Daughter's of the American Revolution. Her interest in suffrage and the plight of women, led Bird to become a member of the Goldfield Women's Club, which joined the Federation of Women's Clubs in 1910. She worked toward the establishment of a public library and a watering trough for thirsty dogs. She also supported a congressional bill to outlaw the slaughter of birds for hat plumage and opposed a bill to license draw poker. She participated in bringing enrichment programs to Goldfield and gave many cultural programs, including one on Japanese art and decoration and one in which she recited the poems of Edward Markham. Bird served as vice-president of the State Federation of Women's Clubs and as their lobbyist at the legislature in Carson City. Bird also became the first woman to serve on the examining board of the Nevada State Bar.

In both the 1913 and the 1915 Nevada state legislatures, Bird lobbied for the establishment of industrial schools for delinquent children, for married women to have equal rights with their husbands, for community property rules, and for easier divorce laws. She favored joint guardianship of children and was for anti-gaming legislation and public kindergartens.

Bird Wilson died in Alameda County, California, on January 27, 1946, at the age of 80.

—*Kathleen F. Noneman*

Margaret Arnoldus Windous

Margaret Christina was born to Hans Jacob and Inger Sophia Arnoldus in Moroni, Utah, in 1870. Both of her parents were Danish immigrants and converts to the Mormon church. As a child, Margaret's life centered around her family's farm, and she worked long hard hours in the fields with her father. She received only a limited education in the Moroni schools.

At age eighteen, Margaret married Thomas Christian Windous. Thomas had spent his early childhood in the desert herding sheep with his father. As a young man he worked for the "wealthy" Arnoldus family, which is how he met Margaret. The young couple spent nine years in Moroni, during which time they had six children. In 1896, they moved to Manti, where Thomas worked on the Manti LDS Temple. Three years later, the Windouses were among several young couples who volunteered to go to eastern Nevada to colonize the three LDS church-owned ranches in the White River Valley. They were also to establish wards for the church in Preston, Nevada. The Windous family made the difficult trip by covered wagon in eighteen days. When Margaret got out of the wagon and

1870–1958
MIDWIFE, NURSE

surveyed the never ending desolate sagebrush valley with the majestic White Pine Mountains to the west and the Egan Range on the east, she knew life here would be a challenge. But she and the other pioneer women in this small Mormon community bravely accepted this challenge.

A year later, the Windouses moved to the Moon River Ranch, where Tom took charge of the mail route between Sunnyside and Fryberg. For Margaret, the two years they spent here were a time of loneliness, isolation, poor health, and sadness due to the death of her sister and because her daughter had to spend the winter with Grandmother Arnoldus in Salt Lake City. Neighbors who might have eased her grief were few and far between.

Upon returning to Preston, Margaret spoke with church leaders about the great need for medical care in Preston and the outlying ranches. There were accidents, illnesses, and women were without care during childbirth. Many mothers and babies died. There were no telephones, no automobiles, and the nearest doctor was an impossible 35 miles away. In 1912, when the LDS church requested that at least one Relief Society member from each ward be sent to Salt Lake City for obstetrics training, Margaret was chosen. She had eight children by now, and she took four with her to Salt Lake and left four at home with her husband. In Salt Lake, Margaret was trained by Dr. Ramona B. Pratt in general nursing and obstetrics. In spite of her limited education, Margaret finished her medical courses but soon learned that neither Utah nor Nevada issued midwifery certificates. Not one to give up easily, she went before a board of doctors, took a difficult test, and was given permission to practice as a nurse. Later, she received an official nursing certificate from the Chautauqua School of Nursing.

In forty-two years of working in the Preston/ Lund area, Margaret delivered over 1,000 and never lost a mother. She relied on her excellent training from Dr. Pratt, her will and determination, and her strong religious convictions and faith to get her through the many difficult circumstances she confronted. She was called on night or day to make lonely journeys to the region's scattered ranches during cold winter blizzards or dusty summer heat. She depended on her faithful horse Doll, her black buggy, and her little dog to take her where she was needed and to get her home safely. Sometimes she was gone from her home for four or five weeks at a time, since midwives often stayed to care for the families of their patients, doing cooking, laundry, house-

work, or whatever was needed.

By 1914, Margaret and Tom had two more children, making a total of ten. In addition to her nursing duties, Margaret was a devoted worker in the LDS church, the Relief Society, and the Primary Association. With three other women, she raised money to build the Relief Society Hall in Preston by holding bazaars and asking for donations of, work and money.

Telephone service came to the White River Valley in 1914, greatly helping Margaret in her medical practice. By 1916, Tom had built a new house with extra rooms to provide for her growing maternity practice. During the deadly influenza epidemic of 1918, Margaret had over 200 patients but lost only one newborn baby. She received little or no pay for her work and must have seemed like an angel of mercy. When Thomas Windous died in 1923, Margaret continued her work in the White River Valley for several years and then moved to Ely with her son Dell. She took over nursing duties at the White Pine General Hospital in 1927. From there, Margaret went to Ely, where a new brick house was built and named the Windous Maternity Home. Margaret never turned away anyone. Her selfless devotion to those in need, her unlimited hospitality, and her cheerfulness were known throughout the state.

—*Doris Drummond*

Hazel Bell Wines

Hazel Bell Wines was born in Paradise Valley, Humboldt County, Nevada, to William John Bell and Freely Clementine Choate, who resided in the nearby mining town of Silver City. Freely's family lived in Paradise Valley, so she had gone there for Hazel's birth.

Eventually the Bell family moved to Winnemucca, where William had made considerable money on gold and silver from the Buckskin Mine in north Humboldt County. Later, Hazel's father added a saloon to his various Winnemucca holdings.

Hazel graduated from Humboldt County High School in 1902 and went on to the California State Normal School in San Jose, California, graduating on June 23, 1904. She then received her Nevada Teacher's Certificate on September 16, 1904.

The young teacher first went to the small mining camp of Kennedy. After a year there, Hazel moved to Ruby Valley in Elko County, where she taught for the next two years. Like many teachers before and since, she found maintaining order in the classroom a trying experience. She often recounted the story of "one angry valley rancher who even came

1885–1949
TEACHER, POLITICIAN

calling with his rifle after I disciplined his six-foot son." Once the rancher saw the petite but determined young lady before him, he backed down.

It was during this period that Hazel met Stanley L. Wines, who owned the stage line between Halleck and Ruby Valley. He also served as Justice of the Peace for the area. Hazel and Stanley were married on June 22, 1907, in Winnemucca at the home of the bride's parents.

Hazel returned to Winnemucca for the birth of her first two daughters, Margane and Marian. Her son, S. Vernon, was born in Halleck. Daughters Merle and Genevieve were later born in Ruby Valley.

Busy raising five children, Hazel nevertheless made time for the interests she loved, including china painting, watercolors, and fishing. She also learned the art of politics as she followed the political career of her father, who served in the Nevada state senate from 1907 to 1915.

From 1920 until the Depression, Stanley and Hazel divided family life between Salt Lake City, Utah, and northeastern Nevada's Buckskin Mine. Stanley built an apartment house in Salt Lake called "Bell-Wines" on First South between Fifth and Sixth East.

After wintering in Salt Lake City, the family moved to the Buckskin Mine each summer. There the children could ride horses or climb to the top of Buckskin Mountain, where one can stand and see as far as Oregon, Idaho, and California. Sometimes, Hazel sent her children to take food to the Basque sheep herders working below.

Once, the children trapped a groundhog and took it home for the winter to Salt Lake City. Since the groundhog could not be tamed, they could never let it out of the cage. It even bit the finger of the postman who tried to pet it. The next summer, they returned the groundhog to Buckskin. It never looked back after being let out of the cage.

During the Depression the Wines lost the apartment house. The family moved to Reno, where Stanley Wines became a construction contractor. Hazel Wines cared for the children and made time to organize "The Native Daughters." This group of Reno women made it their business to preserve Nevada's historical papers and properties. She also supported her father's many political activities.

Hazel's father "Johnny" Bell was a Democrat who attended many of the National Democratic Conventions. He was a close friend of Senator Pat McCarran, another good Irish Catholic and Democrat. Bell wanted the senator to appoint Hazel postmaster of Humboldt County in Winnemucca. In 1933 the family even moved to Winnemucca in anticipation. When Hazel did not get the appointment, Bell began calling the Senator McCarran "that shanty Irishman" instead of "Pat."

Striking out on her own politically, Hazel ran for the Humboldt County Assembly seat in 1934. She loved the campaigning. Taking one of her children with her, she went to every ranch in the area. She won the election and served one term in the legislature, introducing six bills, one of which passed both houses of the legislature. Although is was vetoed by Governor Griswold, her Nevada Historical Bill would have provided for an appropriation of $15,000 to restore to the Nevada Museum and Historical Library, the relics, documents, and pictures which had originally been collected by the Nevada Historical Society. Her efforts drew attention to the fact that these historical treasures were gathering dust in Reno's State Building.

Hazel Bell Wines passed away in San Francisco, California, in April of 1949. She asked that the date of her passing not be recorded.
—*Jane Ellsworth Olive*

Sarah Winnemucca

Sarah Winnemucca's birth coincided with the beginning of an era of dramatic historical changes for her people, the Paiute, changes in which she would play an important and often thankless role. She worked throughout her life to defend the rights of the Paiute and to foster communication and understanding between her people and the white people.

Sarah was born into the Northern Paiute tribe in 1844 and given the name Thocmetony, which means "shell flower." At the time of her birth, Northern Paiutes and Washoes were the sole inhabitants of the land that is now western Nevada. Sarah's grandfather was chief of the entire Paiute nation, and was camped near Humboldt Lake with a small portion of his tribe when a party traveling eastward from California was seen coming. Chief Truckee, welcomed the arrival of his "white brothers." However, Sarah's father, Chief Winnemucca, did not trust the white people and cautioned his own people to keep their distance. These opposite viewpoints became a symbol of Sarah's life, which was spent trying to translate the two cultures to each other.

1844–1891
LECTURER, ACTIVIST,
SCHOOL ORGANIZER,
AUTHOR

Sarah was first introduced to white people at age six when her grandfather insisted she go with him to California. She was initially frightened but ended up liking such luxuries as beds, chairs, brightly colored dishes, and the food she was served. When she was 13, Sarah's grandfather arranged for Sarah and her sister to become members of Major Ormsby's household at Mormon Station, now Genoa, Nevada. By the time she was 14, Sarah had learned five languages: three Indian dialects, English, and Spanish.

Sarah's final foray into the increasingly dominant white culture occurred at age 16, when she fulfilled her grandfather's deathbed request that she and her sister Elma be educated in a convent school at San Jose, California. The two girls were never officially admitted to the school, but during their few weeks there, Sarah continued to acquire more knowledge and experience with the new culture.

As Sarah reached maturity, the white emigration west continued to encroach on Paiute territory, and eventually, whites insisted on moving all Paiutes onto reservations—first the Pyramid Lake Reservation in Nevada, then the Malheur Indian Reservation in

Oregon, and finally to Yakima, Washington. The days of hunting and gathering freely had ended for her tribe. In 1871, at the age of 27, Sarah began working as an interpreter for the Bureau of Indian Affairs at Fort McDermitt on the Oregon border. During this time, she married Lt. E.C. Bartlett but left him within a year because of his intemperance. She later married an Indian husband but left him as well because he abused her.

In 1872, Sarah was with her people on the Malheur Reservation in Oregon. The Indian Agent in charge, Samuel Parrish, treated everyone fairly, but he was replaced with a less reliable agent. As problems mounted on the reservation, Sarah prepared to travel to Washington, DC, to speak out on behalf of her people, a trip that was interrupted while she aided U.S. troops in the Bannock War of 1878 as an interpreter and scout. She even saved her father, whose lodge had been surrounded by hostile Indians, by traveling over 200 miles in 48 hours without sleep over treacherous Idaho terrain.

In January, 1880, Sarah pleaded the Indian's cause in Washington, DC, before Secretary of the Interior Carl Schurz and President Rutherford B. Hayes. Eventually, she did receive promises of improvements for her people, but they were later broken by the government. Despite her advocacy for her people, the broken promises caused them to distrust Sarah. Still, she dedicated the remainder of her life to her work, giving more than 400 speeches to gain support for the Paiutes. Many of her speeches were given on the East Coast through the support of Elizabeth Peabody and Mary Peabody Mann.

She also was dedicated to teaching school to Paiute children and opened a school for Indian children called Peabody's Institute near Lovelock, Nevada. When her husband at that time, Lt. L.H. Hopkins, died of tuberculosis, Sarah closed the school and moved to Montana to spend her last days with her sister Elma. She died there of tuberculosis at the age of 47.

"Sarah Winnemucca will always be remembered as a dedicated Native American woman who belonged to two cultures. With one foot in the Indian Nation and the other in the white man's world, she sped across the plains like a blazing arrow only to fall short of her target. Although the Princess was recognized throughout the land as the passionate voice of the Paiute Indians, she was treated with indifference by the United States Government. Disillusioned and betrayed, Sarah died before she completed her, mission, believing herself to be a failure (Seagraves, *High Spirited Women of the West*).

Life Among the Paiutes is Sarah Winnemucca's powerful tribute to the cultures of both Native Americans and whites. It appeared in 1883, the first book ever published that was written by a Native American woman. Posthumously, she was awarded the Nevada Writers Hall of Fame Award for her book from the Friends of the Library, University of Nevada–Reno. In 1994, an elementary school in Washoe County School District was named in her honor.

—*Victoria Ford and Janet E. White*

Josie Alma Woods

Josie Alma Woods was born in Clyde, Texas, but by the early 1900s had arrived in Nevada, where she spent five years riding a circuit between mining towns in a horse-drawn buckboard, assisting her business partner Dr. Mabel Young in her dentistry practice.

Around this time, Josie purchased 40 head of cattle at an estate auction and also acquired a former stagecoach and Pony Express station located between Eureka and Austin, which she named "The Willows." Despite having no previous ranching experience, Josie soon became known as an expert judge of cattle, and she transformed the 320-acre homestead into a successful cattle ranch that encompassed 1,200 square miles by the time it was sold in 1954. Dr. Young shared both the ranch's log cabin home and a house in Eureka with Josie.

In her book *Here is Our Valley*, Molly Flagg Knudtsen described her as having an unerring eye for quality livestock:

"In the years that she lived in the neighborhood, Grass Valley sold registered Hereford range bulls. Many of the neighboring ranchers bought them from us. It was

1889–1983
POLITICIAN, RANCHER

Dick Magee's practice to bring in all the calves he had for sale and let the rancher take his pick.

With the exception of an old Indian called Frank Rogers, who lived in Smoky Valley, Josie Woods was the best judge of anyone who bought our bulls. Not only could she select the top individuals from the herd, but once she bought them, she knew how to take care of them and use them to the best advantage."

She lived—first with her partner, a lady dentist, and later alone—in a little log cabin which reminded me of the gingerbread house in the fairy tale. Every nook and cranny was crammed with objects she had accumulated in the course of her life. Dried flowers and grasses sprouted from purple bottles, and ox shoes and rock specimens were displayed in a tangled jumble that would have driven an interior decorator crazy.

One day a man came walking up the winding dirt track from the highway (now Highway 50, known then as the Lincoln Highway) and asked Miss Woods if he could do some chores to pay for a meal and a night's lodging in her barn. The man's name was Campbell. Twenty years later he was still working for Miss Woods. Josie valued him highly. When she retired, Campbell was financially able to retire, too.

Josie joined the state and national livestock associations and was a director and vice-president of the Eureka Farm Bureau. According to a biography of Josie published in 1975 by Mary Ellen Glass, it was in the summer of 1940 that she first filed as an Independent candidate and ran for the short-term county commissioner's post, receiving less than 25% of the vote that year against a Republican and another Independent—both men.

In 1942, with renewed determination and the lessons learned in 1940 as her guide, she filed for the state assembly on the Republican ticket. She conducted a personal campaign, spending no money for advertising in the local newspaper. She won the election, receiving more than 60% of the vote and achieving the distinction of being the first woman elected to the state legislature in Eureka County. She took her seat in the 1943 legislature along with one other woman, Democrat Mary Sharp of Nye County.

Josie was re-elected in 1944, becoming only the second woman in Nevada legislative history to achieve a second term. She served on committees dealing with agriculture, banks and banking, counties and county boundaries, livestock, and state publicity. In the 1945 session there were two additional women in the Assembly: Martha Woolridge of Nye County and Edna Montrose of Mineral County.

Josie introduced no legislation in either session, made one recorded speech, and generally voted with the majority. She ran for a third term in 1945 but lost to a veteran who had just returned from the war, Lester Bisoni. According to Glass, Josie herself believed she had been used in a political "deal." The incumbent state senator, she said, planned to run for reelection himself and she was originally determined to challenge him. The senator visited her, promising the local political organization's support for another term in the assembly if she would give up her desire to run for the state senate. She agreed but lost her election, and the 1947 Nevada legislature convened with no women lawmakers.

Back home in Eureka, Josie became active in the Business and Professional Women's Club, serving as legislative chairman and then president.

Josie Woods sold The Willows in December 1954 and spent her last years traveling or living in retirement in Arizona. In her later years, Josie wanted to write the story of her life, but being by her own admission "not a writer," she hired a professional to pen the book for her. The ghost writer sold her memoirs to a studio in Hollywood without Josie's permission, and the result was a motion picture: *The Ballad of Josie*, starring Doris Day in the leading role.

Josie Alma Woods died on February 18, 1983.

—*Jean Ford*

Bibliography

EVA ADAMS

Hopkins, A.D. *The First 100 Persons Who Shaped Southern Nevada.* Las Vegas, NV: Huntington Press, 1999.

Eva Adams. Obituary. *Nevada State Journal*, August 26, 1991.

"Eva B. Adams: Windows on Washington—Nevada Education—The U.S. Senate, The U.S. Mint." Oral History Program, University of Nevada. Interviewer: Mary Ellen Glass, 1982.

Great American Women—Nevada. www.epics.ecn.purdue.edu

A Guide to the Papers of Eva Bertrand Adams. University of Nevada Special Collections.

"Staff Report." *Nevada State Journal*, August 25, 1991.

EDNA C. BAKER

California Death Index, 1940–1997.

"Funeral for First UN Woman Regent," *Carson Appeal*, July 15, 1957.

Glass, Mary Ellen. "First Woman Elected in Nevada: The Election of 1916." This Was Nevada, No. 157. *Nevada State Journal*, April 30, 1978, p. 61.

"Mrs. Edna C. Baker." *Nevada Newsletter and Advertiser.* December 2, 1916, p. 7.

Nevada State Journal, various years.

Reno Evening Gazette, various years.

Sparks Tribune, various years.

United States Federal Census, 1880, 1900, 1910, 1920, 1930.

RUTH BALL

"Henderson Recreation Board Gives Appreciation Award." *Henderson Home News*, June 18, 1964.

"Pioneer Resident Ruth Ball Passes Away." *Henderson Home News*, March 4, 1974.

CLARA ISABELLE SMITH BEATTY

"Clara Beatty, 77, Dies." *Reno Evening Gazette*, October 26, 1967, p. 10.

"College Women are Forming a Suffrage League." *University of Nevada-Reno Sagebrush.* April 23, 1912.

"Dedication to the Memory of Clara Beatty." *Nevada Historical Quarterly*, Winter, 1967. Vol X, no.4.

Who's Who in the West. Chicago, IL: Marquis Who's Who, 1956.

CLARA BOW BELL

"Boyhood on the Walking Box." *The Nevadan*, October 6, 1974.

The Modern Period. New York: Howard Press, 1980.

Proctor , Carolyn Hamilton. "From "It" Girl to Nevada Woman—The Story of Clara Bow." *Nevada Woman*, November/December 1995.

LAURA WEBB BELL

Bell, Laura Webb. *Buckskin.* Unpublished memoir, edited by Norman Bell.

Segerblom, Gene. Reminiscences about her aunt, Laura Webb Bell. Boulder City, NV, 2001.

MINNIE NICHOLS BLAIR

Blair, Minnie. "Days Remembered of Folsom & Placerville, California: Banking and Farming in Goldfield, Tonopah, and Fallon, Nevada." Oral History Project, University of Nevada, Reno, 1966–67.

Blair, Minnie P. Papers, 1914; 1947; 1961–70. University of Nevada Special Collections.

KITTIE BONNER

Distinguished Nevadans, Commencement Exercises, University of Nevada–Reno, May 14, 1977.

Doughty, Nanelia S. "Kittie Bonner and the Comical Town." *The Nevadan*, October 8, 1972.

Miles, Evelyn Madsen. "A Teacher's Perspective of Austin, Nevada: 1932–1936." Oral history conducted by Nancy Myers, Oral History Program, University of Nevada, Reno. c1983.

"Services are Held for Kittie Wells Bonner." *Reese River Reveille*, Vol. 121, No. 6, February 7, 1985

MILDRED BRAY

Couch, Ellen M., retired teacher and former State Superintendent of School Lunch Programs. Interview, 1993.

"Educator Mildred Bray Died, 83." *Nevada Appeal*, October 24, 1975;

Houghton, Joan S., distinguished Carson City community volunteer. Interview, 1993.

Inside Nevada Schools: A Challenge for the Future. Carson City, NV: Nevada State Retired Teachers Association; 1976.

"Two Prominent Nevadans to be Honored Saturday." *Nevada Appeal*, June 5, 1969.

Women Who Made Their Mark. Delta Kappa Gamma, Nu Chapter, Research Committee; 1981–82.

IDA BROWDER
Interviews
Garrett, Elton. Interview with Dennis McBride. Hoover Dam Oral History Series. Boulder City, Nevada, November 10–11, 1986.

Godbey, Erma O. Interview with Dennis McBride. Hoover Dam Oral History Series. Boulder City, Nevada, November 7–8, 1986.

Jenne, Floyd. Interview with Dennis McBride. Hoover Dam Oral History Series. Boulder City, Nevada, November 20, 1986.

Morrison, Lillian. Interview with Dennis McBride. Hoover Dam Oral History Series. Boulder City, Nevada, November 14, 1986.

Boulder City News Articles
"Another New Store for Lease Soon on Nevada Highway." *Boulder City News*, December 8, 1948.

"Beautiful Boulder City Home of the Week." *Boulder City News,* October 6, 1960.

"City's First Business Lady is Heart Victim." *Boulder City News*, January 19, 1961.

"Thomas Hancock, Pioneer, Passes Away in California." *Boulder City News*, January 22, 1952.

Las Vegas Age Articles
"Browder Café to be Enlarged," *Las Vegas Age*, April 20, 1932.

"To Open Lunchroom." *Las Vegas Age*, December 6, 1931.

"Young Son of Mrs. Browder is Dead." *Las Vegas Age*, June 26, 1932.

Las Vegas Review Articles
"Boulder Briefs." *Las Vegas Review-Journal*, December 12, 1931.

"Browder's Café Shifts Managers." *Las Vegas Review-Journal*, June 18, 1937.

"Honoring Mrs. Ida Browder." *Las Vegas Review-Journal*, January 12, 1940.

"Marbus Browder Dies in Salt Lake." *Las Vegas Review-Journal*, June 24, 1932.

"Marriage of Ida Browder Revealed." *Las Vegas Review-Journal*, June 30, 1937.

"Mrs. Browder Weds in Yuma Recently." *Las Vegas Review-Journal*, August 14, 1933.

"Mrs. Browder will Feed 'em Soon." *Las Vegas Review-Journal*, December 3, 1931.

"Mrs. Ida Browder Opens Lunchroom." *Las Vegas Review-Journal*, December 28, 1931.

"Parents to Meet with Teachers to Discuss B.C. School House Problem." *Las Vegas Review-Journal*, December 29, 1931.

"Sixteen Leases, Mostly for Business Establishments, Signed by U.S. Officials and Permit Holders." *Las Vegas Review-Journal*, November 2, 1931

"Two Downtown Stores Being Built Now in B.C." *Las Vegas Review-Journal*, November 10, 1931.

"VFW Installs Head." *Las Vegas Review-Journal*, March 4, 1937.

JULIA BULETTE
Brown, Dee. *The Gentle Tamers: Women of the Old Wild West.* Lincoln and London: University of Nebraska Press, 1958

McDonald, Douglas. *The Legend of Julia Bulette and the Red Light Ladies of Nevada.* Las Vegas: Nevada Publications, 1980, 1983

FELICE COHN
Cohn, Felice. "Women of Nevada Interested in Politics." In Max Benheim, *Women of the West.* Los Angeles: Publisher's Press, 1928

Felice Cohn Papers, 1884–1961, Nevada Historical Society, Reno

White, Janet, Unpublished research paper, 1995, 1996.

ELIZA COOK
Bergevin, Luette Dressler, Cook's great-niece. Several personal interviews with author, 2001.

The Carson Valley Connection. "The Saga of Nevada Women's Suffrage," script from "Historic Dramatic

Presentation," April 26, 1996.

Cook, Eliza. "Outline of My Life." A one-page document written just prior to her death.

Cooper Medical College. *Annual announcement, session of 1884.*

Genoa Courier. Article. December 21, 1894.

Hansen, Janice, Cook's great-great-niece. Several personal interviews with author, 1998.

Henningsen, Mary. Article. *Nevada State Journal*, June 9, 1946.

Reno Gazette. Article, October 31, 1895

BEDA BRENNECKE CORNWALL

Beda Cornwall Obituary. *Las Vegas Review-Journal*, June 16, 1994.

Beda Cornwall papers, 1941–1974. Special Collections, University of Nevada, Las Vegas.

Kepper, Anna Dean, compiler. *Las Vegas Public Libraries: An Exhibit*, a booklet printed and distributed by University of Nevada, Las Vegas Special Collections, 1978.

HILDA M. COVEY

Construction Notebook, vol XLIX, No 41.

Construction Notebook, vol XXX No 50, December 10, 1982.

Interviews with Paula R. Lawson, Fall of 2001.

Personal memorabilia of daughter Paula R. Lawson

MARTHA CRAGUN COX

Cox, Martha Cragun. *Face Toward Zion.*

The Desert Echo. Article. June 4, 1992, p. 7

Hafner, Arabell Lee. *100 Years on the Muddy.* Springville, UT: Art City, 1967.

History of Clark Country School District, Harvey Dondero.

Interviews with Charlene Cox Cruze.

CLARA DUNHAM CROWELL

Earl, Philip I. "This Lady Was a Sheriff." *Reno Gazette Journal*, April 12. 1987

McDonald, Craig, "Nevada's First Woman Sheriff." *Nevada Magazine*, January-February, 1981

Parker, Stanley W., ed. *Nevada Towns and Tales, Volume I—North.* Las Vegas: Nevada Publications, 1981.

DAT-SO-LA-LEE

Burton , Henrietta K., "A Study of the Methods Used To Conserve the Art of the Washoe Indian Basketry." Unpublished manuscript. May 1932.

Chase, Don M., Carl Purdy, & Clara McNaughton. *Basket-Maker Artists.* Sebastopol, CA, 1977.

Cohn, Abraham. Papers. Nevada Historical Society, Reno .

Codohas, Martin. "Dat-So-La-Lee and the Degikup." *Halcyon, A Journal of the Humanities,* 1982.

Codohas, Marvin. "Washoe Basketry." *American Indian Basketry Magazine*, July 2, 1983.

Hickson, Jane Green. *Dat-So-La-Lee, Queen of the Washoe Basketmakers.* Popular Series #3. Nevada State Museum, December 1967.

Kern, Norval C., Jr. *A Presentation of Sculpture: A Synthesis of a Design Alphabet Derived From The Art Forms Of A Primitive People.* New York: New York University, 1969.

Mack, Effie Mona. "Dat-So-La-Lee, World-Renowned Washoe Basket Weaver." *Nevada Magazine*, February-March 1946.

McNaughton, Clara. " Native Indian Basketry." *The New West*, October 1912.

Obituary. *Carson City Daily Appeal*, January 29, 1934.

"Scrapbook." Number 194-G-22. Nevada State Museum. Carson City, Nevada.

NELLIE MIGHELS DAVIS

Daily Morning Appeal, Carson City, February 18, 1878.

Daily Morning Appeal, March 18, 1897.

Davis, Sam. *History of Nevada, Vol. I and II.* Reno, NV: Elms Publishing, 1913.

Davis, Sam Post, Papers, 1865–1960, and Microfilm, Special Collections, University of Nevada, Reno.

Dolan, William. Oral interview with "Pages from the Past" editor. October 2, 1996.

Doten, Alfred, *The Journals of Alfred Doten.* Reno: University of Nevada Press, 1973.

Gardner, Paul K. *History of the Leisure Hour Club, 1896–1969*. Manuscript. Carson City, Nevada.

Historical Society Papers, 1917–1920. Reno, NV: A. Carlisle, 1920.

Kintop, Jeffrey M., and Guy L. Rocha. *The Earps' Last Frontier*. Reno, NV: Great Basin Press, 1989.

Letters from Henry R. Mighels to Nellie Verrill (Mighels) 1830–1879, Special Collections, University of Nevada, Reno.

Mighels, Henry Rust, III. "Reflections of Carson City" Oral interview with Barbara K. Zernickow.

Morning Appeal, February 10, 1897.

Stoddard, Sylvia Crowell. *Sam Knew Them When*. Reno, NV: Great Basin Press, 1996.

CLARABELLE HANLEY DECKER

Andress, Donna. "I Remember Mama." *Nevada Woman*, May/June 1996.

Clark County School District school dedication file

Coakley, Dee. "Clark County Schools and the People Behind Their Names: No. 6, Clarabelle Decker." *Las Vegas Sun Magazine*, May 6, 1982.

"Dedication and Open House" Program, Jaunary 16, 1978, Clarabelle Decker Elementary School.

Letter from Donna Anders to Helen Cannon, Trustee.

Letters to Harvey Dondero re: recommendations to the name a school in honor of Clarabelle Hanley Decker.

"LV Teacher Dies." *Las Vegas Sun*, November 11, 1984.

Tretreault, Steve. "Decker Began School Library System." *Las Vegas Review-Journal*, February 24, 1984.

Waller, Andrea. "Honored at 'Her' School." *Valley Times*, January 17, 1978.

HAZEL BAKER DENTON

Hazel Denton papers, 1887–1957, Special Collections, University of Nevada, Las Vegas.

Obituary. *Reno Evening Gazette*, February 1, 1962.

Scrugham, James A. *Nevada: A Narrative of the Conquest of the Frontier Land*. American Historical Society, 1935.

Vincent, Bill. "The Dentons and Lincoln County." *Nevadan*, May 1, 1977.

MARY STODDARD DOTEN

Bremer, Lynn. "Mary Stoddard Doten." Available from http://www.unr.edu/sb204/nwhp/doten.htm

Haskins, Debbie. *Mary Stoddard Doten*. Unpublished manuscript, 1996.

ANNA NEDDENRIEP DRESSLER

Interview with Luetta Dressler Bergevin, Anna's daughter, 1997.

Neddenriep Family Scrapbook, Privately held.

EDNA CRAUCH TRUNNELL EDDY

Personal Edna Eddy Effects

Her original "Visitor's Book" containing sketches, photos, and letters.

Nevada Chauffeurs' License, January 21, 1876, with picture of Edna.

Letter, 10-5-1916, to George Kitzmeyer, Secretary, Nevada State Board of Embalmers, Carson City, NV.

"Pilot's Flight Log," License No. S561839, 2-16-43 to 9-14-44.

Humboldt County Recorder. Documentation of real estate purchases and sales.

Other Sources

Lovelock Review-Miner, Lovelock, NV, July 26, 1918.

Kitzmeyer, George E. Original letter, 10-6-16, to Edna T. Eddy.

McEachern, Gloria. (Edna's granddaughter) Personal Interview, June 3, 1996.

Reed, Waller. *A County Political Directory for Nevada*. State of Nevada.

Scrugham, James A. *Nevada: A Narrative of the Conquest of the Frontier Land*. American Historical Society, 1935.

Supreme Court of the State of Nevada, Reports of Cases, Vol. XL, January Term, 1917. Edna T. Eddy, Petitioner v. The State Board of Embalmers, Respondent

Trunnell Obituary. *Nevada State Journal*, August 27, 1946.

Trunnell Obituary. *Lovelock Review-Miner*, Lovelock, NV, August 29, 1946.

Who's Who in Nevada. Biographical Dictionary of Men and Women Who Are Building a State. Vol 1, 1931–1932.

Reno, NV: Who's Who Publishing.

"Woman Embalmer Demands License." *Humboldt Star*, Winnemucca, NV, January 22, 1917.

Worsham College of Mortuary Science. Letter dated September 23, 1999, addressed to author.

CHARLOTTE ROWBERRY ELLSWORTH

Taped interviews with Charlotte R. Ellsworth, family records, interviews with Mrs. Angie Kaye, Mrs. Linda Love Lee, and Mrs. Cec Kier.

RUTH MARY COOPER FERRON

Blackman, Isabell Slavin, "Ruth Cooper Ferron, President 1922–1923," *Biographies of Past Presidents of Mesquite, 1911-1967*. Las Vegas, NV: (n.p.), 1967.

Cahlan, Florence Lee Jones, Transcript of speech given at the Las Vegas Rotary Club's 50th anniversary, with notes by Barbara Ferron Doyle. William E. Ferron Family Papers, 1973, 1-7. University of Nevada, Las Vegas.

Doyle, Barbara Ferron, "Ruth Mary Cooper Ferron." Biography transcript. William E. Ferron Family Papers, 1974. 1-9. University of Nevada, Las Vegas.

Ferron, Ruth C. Transcript of speech presented at Mesquite Club, April 9, 1976. William E. Ferron Family Papers. 1-4. University of Nevada, Las Vegas.

Jones, Florence Lee. "Vegas Druggist, Wife Helped Build a Dream." *Las Vegas Review-Journal*, April 9, 1963. 6–7.

ANNA MARIZA FITCH

Raymond, Elizabeth, & Eric N. Moody. *"An Able Romancist of the Ineffable School": Anna M. Fitch, Early Western Writer*. Las Vegas, NV: Nevada Historical Society, n.d.

IMOGENE (JEAN) EVELYN YOUNG FORD

Jean Ford: A Nevada Woman Leads the Way. University of Nevada Oral History Program, Reno, Nevada, 1998.

KATIE CHRISTY FRAZIER

Frazier, Katie. *That Was Happy Life: A Paiute Woman Remembers*. Videotape.

Macias, Sandra. Interview with Katie Frazier. *Reno-Gazette Journal*, February 9, 1986.

MAUDE FRAZIER

Green, Michael. "Happy Mother's Day, Las Vegas: Remembering the Founding Mothers." *Las Vegas Weekly*, May 10, 1995.

"LV Pioneer Miss Frazier Dies at 82," *Las Vegas Review-Journal*, June 21, 1963.

Schank, Pat. "Good LV schools are Frazier's Memorial." Nevadan, May 23, 1982.

Schank, Pat. "Maude Frazier: Schoolmarm of Nevada." *Nevadan*, May 16, 1982.

MARY FREEMAN

A Desert of Change: Mary Freeman, Photographer. Churchill County, NV: Churchill County Museum Association, 1994.

FRANCES GERTRUDE FRIEDHOFF

Curran, Evalin, comp. *History of the Order of the Eastern Star*. State of Nevada, 1949.

Nevada State Journal, March 17, 1935.

Nevada State Journal, May 9, 1954.

Obituary. *Nevada State Journal*, March 9, 1958.

DR. MARY HILL FULSTONE

Chicester, Elsie F. "Dr. Mary Fulstone." Unpublished pamphlet, 1984.

DeCristoforo, Rose Anne. "Dr. Mary." *Nevada Magazine*, December 1982.

Fulstone, David. Personal interview. March 12, 1995.

Fulstone, Dr. Mary. *Recollections of a Country Doctor in Smith, Nevada*. Reno: University of Nevada Oral History Project, 1980.

LAURA KITCHEN GARVIN
Garvin, Laura "What it was Like to Grow Up." *Nevadan*, February 6, 1977.
Oral interview with Don & Laura Garvin by Michael Martocci.

WUZZIE GEORGE
Fowler, Catherine. "Tule Technology: Northern Paiute Uses of Marsh Resources in Western Nevada."
Smithsonian Folklife Studies, Number 6, 1990.
Wheat, Margaret. *Survival Arts of the Primitive Paiutes*. Reno: University of Nevada Press, 1967.

MARY LOUISE GRANTZ
Zanjani, Sally. *A Mine of Her Own: Women Prospectors in the American West, 1850-1950*. Lincoln: University of
Nebraska Press, 1997.

DORIS VIRGINIA HANCOCK
Bouton, Ken. Retirement article. *Las Vegas Sun*, May 16, 1963.
Clark County School District Dedication File.
Hamann, Joy. Retirement article. *Las Vegas Review-Journal*, May 16, 1963.
Hancock, Doris V. Autobiographical sketch. Self-Published.
Whitten, Christine. Interview. Chapter P, PEO.

GRACE HAYES
The material for this biography was extracted from the Nevada Women's Archives files located in the Special
Collections Department of the Lied Library at UNLV. The donated collection number is 86-75 and
includes newspaper clippings, personal memorabilia, photos, legal documents and correspondence.

FRANCES GORE HAZLETT
Randall, Dixie. Scrapbooks from granddaughter.
Tennant, Laura. *Reflections*. Lyon County, NV: n.p., 1991.

SARAH DOTSON HURST
American Mother's Committee. *Mothers of Achievement in American History, 1776–1976*. Rutland, VT: Tuttle
Co., 1976.
Bennett, Dana R. "Leading Ladies." *Nevada Magazine*, March/April 1995.
Carson City Daily Appeal, February 6,7, 1920.
Elko Daily Free Press, December 11, 1918.
Glass, Mary Ellen. "Nevada's Lady Lawmakers: The First Half-Century." *Nevada Public
Affair Review*, October 1975.
United States Census 1920. Latter-Day Saints Family History Center, Reno, NV.
Watson, Anna Ernst. *Into Their Own: Nevada Women Emerging Into Public Life*. Nevada Humanities
Committee, n.d.

THELMA BROWN IRELAND
Fleming, Jack. *Copper Times*. Seattle, WA: Murray Publishing, 1987.
Notes from Bill and Jeanne Ireland, June 2002.
Nelson, Agnes. "Yesterday." *Nevadan*, November 3, 1985.

THERESA SMOKEY JACKSON
Carey-Sage, Darla. *The Life History of a Contemporary Washoe Woman*. n.p., 1995.
Notes written by the Chairman of the Washoe Tribe.
Women's History Remembering Project, Carson Valley Historical Society, February 2000.

LUBERTHA MILLER JOHNSON
Burkhart, Joan. "Las Vegan Recalls Role in Local Civil Rights Efforts." *Las Vegas Review-Journal*, February 9,
1989.
Knight, Sarann. "The Lubertha M. Johnson Story." Alpha Rho Chapter, Gamma Phi Delta Sorority, Inc.
Papers. November 1978.
McClure, Florence. "A Time to Weep . . . But Also Rejoice." *Mentor*, February 1996.

BERTHA C. KNEMEYER

Geuder, Patricia. *Pioneer Women of Nevada*. Carson City: American Association of University Women-Delta Kappa Gamma, 1976.

MOLLY FLAGG KNUDTSEN

Clifton, Guy. "Sagebrush Almanac" *Reno Gazette-Journal*, July 29, 2001.

Fowler, Don. *The Maverick Spirit: Building the New Nevada*.

Davies, Richard O., Ed. Reno: University of Nevada Press, 1999.

Hillinger, Charles. "Socialite-Turned-Cowboy Acts, Gold Mine Bought—to Save Nevada Castle." *Los Angeles Times*, April 21, 1971.

Tonopah Times Bonanza. May 25, 1973.

THERESE LAXALT

Laxalt, Robert. *Sweet Promised Land*. New York: Harper & Row, 1957.

Nylen, Robert. *Kit Carson Trail Inventory*. Carson City: n.p., 1995.

Nevada Appeal, March 23, 1967.

Obituary. *Nevada Appeal*, May 11, 1978.

Reno Evening Gazette, November 19, 1971.

MOYA OLSEN LEAR

"Gibbons Mourns the Passing of Moya Lear." Available at house.gov/gibbons/press01/pr/moyalear

"Moya Lear Passes." Available at aafo.com/libraryhistory/moya_lear

"Wings over Kansas: Aviation Profiles." Available at wingsoverkansas.com/archives/profiles2202

JESSIE CALLAHAN MAHONEY

Eureka Memories. Eureka, NV: Eureka County History Project, 1993.

Biographical sketch by Jean Ford, primarily from an oral history by Aileen Mahoney Schlager.

Knudtsen, Molly Flagg. "The Callahan House: Grass Valley, Nevada."

Northeastern Nevada Historical Society Quarterly, 93.

Patterson, Edna, Louise A. Ulph, & Victor Goodwin. *Nevada's Northeast Frontier*. Sparks, NV: Western Printing and Publishing, 1969.

LILLIAN MALCOLM

Tonopah Bonanza, Nov. 2, 1907.

Zanjani, Sally. *A Mine of Her Own: Women Prospectors in the American West, 1850-1950*. Lincoln: University of Nebraska Press, 1997.

ANNE HENRIETTA MARTIN

Howard, Anne B. *The Long Campaign: A Biography of Anne Martin*. Reno: University of Nevada Press, 1985.

Martin, Anne; Basso, Dave, comp. *Anne Martin, Pioneer Nevada Feminist: Selected Writings*. Sparks, NV: Falcon Press, 1986.

Rocha, Guy. "Who was the First Woman to Run for the U.S. Congress?" Nevada State Archives, Historical Myth a Month, Myth #47.

Stanley Paher, ed. *Nevada: Official Bicentennial Book*. Las Vegas, NV: Nevada Publications, 1976.

MILA TUPPER MAYNARD

Tucker, Cynthia Grant. *Prophetic Sisterhood: Liberal Women Ministers of the Frontier, 1880–1930*. Bloomington: Indiana University Press, 1994.

JEAN SYBIL McELRATH

"Death Claims Jean McElrath." *Nevada State Journal*, October 7, 1967.

Howard, Ruth. "A Christmas Inspiration." *Nevada Business Woman*, December 1965.

"Last Rites Held in Elko Tuesday for Jean McElrath." *Wells Progress*, October 13, 1967.

Lerude, Warren. "Story Behind Book is One of Courage." *Reno Gazette Journal*, October 30, 1964.

McElrath, Jean. Personal Diaries and Journals, 1935–1967.

Pengelly, Eugene, Mayor. Official Proclamation. City of Wells, March 29, 1962.

"Sad News for Folks." *Folks*. Washington Newspaper Publishers Association, Inc., November 1967.

Sheerin, Chris. "A Distinguished Nevadan: Wells' Jean McElrath." *Nevada State Journal*, July 1, 1965.

Stewart, Patricia. "Postscripts." *Nevada State Journal*, October 10, 1967.

Triplett, Bud. "A Little Baloney." *Wells Progress*, Nov. 6, 1965.

"Wells BPW Publishes Jean McElrath Book." *Wells Progress*, April 3, 1970.

"Wells Noted Author Jean McElrath Dies Today." *Daily Free Press*, October 7, 1967.

LAURA MILLS

Laura Mills Papers. Churchill County Museum, 1968.

EMMA WIXOM NEVADA

Ashbaugh, Don. *Nevada's Turbulent Yesterday.* Los Angeles: Westernlore Press, 1964.

Broili, June. *Easy Cookin' in Nevada and Tales of the Sagebrush State.* Reno, NV: Anthony Press, 1984.

Davis, Sam P., ed. *History of Nevada, Vol. II.* Las Vegas: Nevada Publications, 1984.

Hall, Shawn. *Romancing Nevada's Past.* Reno: University of Nevada Press, 1994.

Lewis, Oscar, and Carroll D. Hall. *Bonanza Inn.* New York: Alfred Knopf, 1967.

Watson, Anita Ernst. *Into Their Own.* Nevada Humanities Committee, 2000.

SARAH THOMPSON OLDS

Olds, Sarah Thompson. *Twenty Miles from a Match: Homesteading in Western Nevada.* Reno: University of Nevada Press, 1978.

MARY LEITCH OXBORROW

Geuder, Dr. Patricia. *Pioneer Women of Nevada.* Carson City: AAUW-DKG Publications, 1976.

Read, E.O. *White Pine Lang Syne.* Denver: Big Mountain Press, 1965.

MARY BELLE PARK

Chapter P, PEO Sisterhood. Official minutes and scrapbooks.

Jones, Florence Lee. "Mrs. William Park, LV Resident Since 1909, Dies at 86 in Idaho." *Las Vegas Review-Journal*, September 12, 1965.

Roske, Ralph J. *Las Vegas: A Desert Paradise.* Tulsa, OK: Continental Heritage Press, 1986.

MARIA GARIFALOU PAVLAKIS

Interview with George Pavlakis, May 3, 2002.

Picker, Marc. "Ely's 'Mama' Pavlakis Called Spirit of Community." *Ely Daily Times*, July 27, 1982.

JOSIE REED PEARL

Earl, Phillip. "Woman Prospector Settled Down in Black Rock Desert." *Reno Gazette-Journal*, November 22, 1993.

Murbarger, Nell. "Queen of the Black Rock Country," in *Sovereigns of the Sage.* Tucson, AZ: Treasure Chest, 1958.

Zanjani, Sally. *A Mine of Her Own: Women Prospectors in the American West, 1850-1950.* Lincoln: University of Nebraska Press, 1997.

ALICE PEARSON

Oral interview, 2002.

MARJORY GUSEWELLE PHILLIPS

Ainsworth, Diane. "Board Members Advocate Change." *Las Vegas Review-Journal*, February 29, 1976

"Centennial Group Meet at Sahara." *Las Vegas Sun*, May 1, 1963.

Deskin, Ruth. "Where I Stand." *Las Vegas Sun*, January 19, 1978.

"Governor Picks Appointees to State Board." *Las Vegas Sun*, June 14, 1961.

Little, Lynnette. "Family Portrait: The Gusewelles." *Las Vegas Sun Magazine*, May 25, 1980.

"Marjory G. Phillips Will Be Remembered." *Las Vegas Review-Journal*, January 13, 1978.

Phillips Family Scrapbook, courtesy George William Phillips Jr. and Lynne Ladwig, children of Marjory Phillips.

Phillips, Marjory Gusewelle. Oral interview by Jodi Tenuta, May 11, 1976, University of Las Vegas, Special Collections.

"Propose Sweeping Juvenile Changes." *Las Vegas Review-Journal*, August 24, 1960.
"Service League Benefit Party Will Speed Construction of New Building." *Las Vegas Sun*, June 12, 1952.
"Sun Youth Forum." *Las Vegas Sun*, November 16, 1977.
Wedding Announcements. *Reno Evening Gazette*, March 9, 1944.

BERTHA RAFFETTO

Elko Daily Free Press, February 6, 1985.
Obituary. *Nevada State Journal*, October 27, 1952.
Vogel, Ed. "Reno Contralto Composes Song for Nevada." *Nevada Appeal*, February 16, 1986.

ANNA FRANCES ELLESER RECHEL

Zanjani, Sally. *A Mine of Her Own: Women Prospectors in the American West, 1850-1950*. Lincoln: University of Nebraska Press, 1997.

OLGA A. REIFSCHNEIDER

Olga Reifschneider papers. Special Collections, University of Nevada, Reno, 1988.

JENNIE O'HARE RIORDAN

Gottschalk, Gertrude R. Genealogical research papers, unpublished, in Special Collections, Getchell Library, University of Nevada, Reno.
Harris, Judge. "Another Soldier Gone." Obituary written to eulogize Michael O'Hare, December 19, 1886, Carson City, NV.
Oldfield, Lyda, "The O'Hare Women." AAUW- IKG, 1976.
Riordan, Jennie O'Hare. *Capsules of the Past*. Unpublished personal memoirs, early 1940s., Special Collections, Getchell Library, University of Nevada, Reno.
Riordan, Jennie O'Hare. "Meet Your Neighbor: Jennie O'Hare Riordan." *Carson City Appeal*, 1964.
Tuttle, Gene. "First White Pine Child, James Riordan, and Wife, Carson Native, Wed 59 Years." *Las Vegas Review-Journal*, April 22, 1956.

AGNES LOUISE ELFORD ROCHE

Audiotape recording of Agnes E. Roche conducted by Barbara A. Roche, 1993.
Diary of Agnes Elford, 1927–1928.
"Ruth Community Church: A Protestant Presence," by Agnes E. Roche, 2000.

BERTHA B. RONZONE

American Mother's Committee. *Mothers of Achievement in American History, 1776–1976*. Rutland, VT: Tuttle Co., 1976.
Cronan, John. *Nevada Men and Women of Achievement*. Las Vegas: Author, 1966.
Las Vegas Review-Journal, April 11, 1948.
Las Vegas Review-Journal, October 1, 1967.
Las Vegas Sun, November 11, 1969
Walton, Clifford. *Who's Who in Nevada*. Portland: OR: Capital Publishing, 1949.

MARY G. ROSE

Binheim, Max, & Charles A. Elvin, eds. *Women of the West: A Series of Biographical Sketches of Living Eminent Women in the Eleven Western States of the USA*. Los Angeles: Publishers Press, 1928.
Humboldt County Voters Registry, No. 2189.
Journal of the Assembly, 1925.
Ellen O'Donnell Obituary. *The Humboldt Star*, February 21, 1925.
David Rose Obituary. *Reno Evening Gazette*, July 23, 1933.
Helen Rose Obituary. *The Humboldt Star*, March 4, 1921, and March 11,1921.
Mary Rose Obituary. *The Humboldt Star*, June 15, 1935.
Winnada, 1921 edition, Winnemucca High School publication.

FERMINIA SARRAS

Zanjani, Sally. *A Mine of Her Own: Women Prospectors in the American West, 1850-1950*. Lincoln: University of Nebraska Press, 1997.

Zanjani, Sally. "The Copper Queen." *Nevada Magazine*, November/December, 1995.

HELEN RULISON SHIPLEY
Source material collected from the Washoe County Historical Society.

MAY BRADFORD SHOCKLEY
Doughty, Nanalia S. Obituary. *Las Vegas Review-Journal*, November 30, 1969.

BLANCHE SPRAGUE
Dutton, Alfred. *Notable Nevadan Caricatures*. n.p., 1915
Goldfield Tribune, various issues, 1906–1920.
Goldfield Women's Club Minutes.
Goldfield Remembers. Reno, NV: Great Basin Press, n.d.
Lillard, Richard G. *Desert Challenges*. Ames, IA: Iowa University Press, 1949.
Shamberger, Hugh. *Goldfield*. Carson City, NV: Nevada Historical Press, 1982.
The Woman Citizen. Nevada Edition 1912.

DELPHINE ANDERSON SQUIRES
Evans, K.J. "C.P. Squires, the Father of Las Vegas," in *The First 100 Persons Who Shaped Southern Nevada*. Las Vegas, NV: Donrey Media Group, 1999.
UNLV Nevada Women's Archives Call Number MS 09 (2003). Squires, C.P., and Delphine: Correspondence, scripts, drafts, history research & articles, photo albums, 1887–1964. Special Collections, University of Nevada, Las Vegas.

MARY BERNICE STANFORD
"Longtime LV teacher dies at 86." *Las Vegas Review-Journal*, January 14, 1994.
PEO Record, June 19, 1989.
Stanford, Mary. "Life is What You Make It." *Stanford Elementary School News*, December 8, 1987.

HELEN J. STEWART
Source material primarily taken from the numerous personal papers of Helen J. Stewart that reside in the Nevada Historical Society in Las Vegas and Special Collections Department of Lied Library at UNLV.
Las Vegas Review-Journal, September 5, 2004.
Townley, Carrie Miller. "Helen J. Stewart: First Lady of Las Vegas." *Nevada Historical Society Quarterly*, Volume XVI, No. 4, Winter, 1973, and Volume XVII, No. 1, Spring, 1974.

IDAH MEACHAM STROBRIDGE
Zanjani, Sally. *A Mine of Her Own: Women Prospectors in the American West, 1850-1950*. Lincoln: University of Nebraska Press, 1997.

LAURA MAY TILDEN
Connolly, Elaine, & Dian Self. *Capital Women: An Interpretive History of Women in Sacramento, 1850–1920*. Sacramento, CA: Capital Women's History Project, 1995.
Erickson, Mary. *Women Lawyers' Male Connectedness*. Palo Alto, CA: Stanford University Press, 1988.
Evening Chronicle, Virginia City, NV, July 24, 1893.
Noneman, Kathleen F. Unpublished Research.
Rocha, Guy. "Stepping Up To The Bar: Female Attorneys in Nevada." Nevada State Archives, Historical Myth a Month, Myth #72, modified, 3/11/2004, http://dmla.clan.lib.nv.us/docs/nsla/archives/myth/myth72.htm
Territorial Enterprise, Virginia City, NV, February 1, 1894.
United States Federal Censuses: 1850, 1860, 1870, 1880.
Van Tilburg Clark , Walter, ed. *The Journals of Alfred Doten, 1849–1903*. Reno, NV: University of Nevada Press, 1973.

KATHRYN L. MARBAKER TUBB
Bishop Inyo Register. Various articles. September 5, 1907; February 18, 1909; November 3, 1910; December 14, 1916.
"Death Valley Saloon Closes." *Bishop Owens Valley Herald*, October 15, 1909.

Gale, Hoyt C. *The Lila C Borax Mine at Ryan, Cal.: Mineral Resources of the United States... 1911.* Washington DC: Government Printing Office, 1912.

Gerstley, James M. *Borax Years: Some Recollections 1933–1961.* Los Angeles: U. S. Borax & Chemical Corp., 1979.

Glasscock, Carl B. *Here's Death Valley.* New York: Bobbs-Merrill, 1940.

Gower, Harry P. *Fifty Years in Death Valley: Memoirs of a Borax Man.* San Bernardino, CA: Inland Printing, 1970.

Kilgore, Kittie L Marbaker. Social Security application, #530-09-7967, June 3, 1937.

Lewis, Georgia. "Death Valley Junction." *The Nevadan,* June 25, 1972.

Lewis, Georgia. "Real Shotgun Kitty Bigger Than Life." *Pahrump Valley Times,* April 1973.

Lewis, Georgia. "Sad Times at Amargosa." *The Nevadan,* January 16, 1972.

"Robert Tubb Visits Independence." *Inyo Independent,* June 4, 1909.

Rhyolite Herald. Various articles. November 15, 1907; September 2, 1911.

Vincent, Bill. "Ash Meadows Yesterday and Today." *The Nevadan,* September 28, 1969.

Woodman, Ruth. *History of Pacific Coast Borax Company.* Unpublished paper. Ruth C. Woodman Papers, Special Collections Library, University of Oregon.

GUE GIM WAH

Melton, Rollan. "Meet Mrs. Wah." *Reno Evening Gazette,* October 29, 1980.

"Nevada's Queen—Our Missy Wah." *The Lincoln County Record,* vol. 109, no. 22, November 6, 1980.

Rubinsteen, Jason. "Taste of China." *Nevada: The Magazine of the Real West,* May/June 1980.

ANNA B. MUDD WARREN

Curran, Evalin, comp. *History of the Order of the Eastern Star.* State of Nevada. 1949.

Mack, Sarah Emmeline. Papers. Nevada Historical Society, Reno.

Noneman, Kathy. Unpublished research files.

Warren, Anna, & Sadie Hurst. *Summary of Laws Concerning Women & Children.* Nevada League of Women Voters, 1923.

HANNAH REESE WELDE

2000 Ely Renaissance Society. *Mining Our Richest Veins.* D-Books Publishing, 2000.

Elliott, Russell R. *Nevada's Twentieth-Century Mining Boom: Tonopah, Goldfield, Ely.* Reno & Las Vegas: University of Nevada Press, 1966.

Interviews with John Carlson and Ann Schroeder, 2002.

Notes taken by Elizabeth Stark, June 2, 1965.

MARGARET M. WHEAT

Interviews: Ruth Coleman 2/11/92; Anne Berlin 2/16/92; Sylvia Jesch 2/17/92; Maya Miller 2/18/92; Linda Nelson 2/20/92.

Nevada State Journal, April 25, 1969.

Reno Gazette Journal, August 30, 1988, and February 23, 1992.

Kosso, Lenora, & Susan Searcy. *A Guide to the Margaret Wheat Collection.* Special Collections, University of Nevada, Reno.

Mackedon, Michon. Keep the Recorder Turned On: The Papers of Margaret M. Wheat. *In Focus, The Annual Journal of the Churchill County Museum Association,* Fallon, Nevada, Vol. 5, 1991–92.

Wheat, Margaret M. *Survival of the Arts of the Primitive Paiutes.* Reno: University of Nevada Press, 1967.

JEANNE ELIZABETH WIER

Cerveri, Doris. *Nevada, A Colorful Past, Vol. II.* Elko, NV: Nostalgia Press, 1990.

Gueder, Patricia A. *Pioneer Women of Nevada.* Carson City, NV, n.p., 1976.

Mackenzie. Resolutions and Memorials Assembly Concurrent Resolutions No. 2.

Reno Evening Gazette, April 14, 1950.

State of Nevada 15th Biennial Report of Nevada State Historical Society. Nevada Historical Society. Reno, Nevada. July, 1918–June 30, 1940, inclusive.

Works Progress Administration, Nevada Writers Project. *Nevada: A Guide to the Silver State.* Portland, OR: Binfords and Mort, 1940.

SOPHIE ERNST WILLIAMS
Ashbaugh , Don. *Nevada's Turbulent Yesterday*. Los Angeles: Westernlore Press, 1963.

Doten, Samuel Bradford. *An Illustrated History of the University of Nevada*. University of Nevada, 1924.

Hall, Shawn. *Preserving the Glory Days' Ghost Towns and Mining Camps of Nye County, Nevada*. Reno: University of Nevada Press, 1891

Lincoln, Francis Church. *Mining Districts and Mineral Resources of Nevada*. Las Vegas: Nevada Publications, 1982.

Williams Family Primary Source: The bulk of this biography is taken directly from a manuscript submitted to NWHP by the family of Sophie Ernst Williams.

FRANCES WILLIAMSON
Anthony, Susan B., & Ida Husted Harper. *The History of Woman Suffrage, Vol. IV*. New York: Arno Press, 1969.

Cerveri, Doris. *Nevada Historical Miscellany*. Sparks, NV: Nevada Press Women, Western Printing and Publishing Co., 1976.

Earl, Phillip "The story of the Woman Suffrage Movement in Northeastern Nevada, 1869–1914." *Northeastern Nevada Historical Society Quarterly*, Vol. 6, #4, 1976.

Mack, S.E. *History of the Suffrage Movement in Nevada*. Special Collections, University of Nevada, Reno.

BIRD MAY WILSON
Earl, Phillip I. *Bird M. Wilson*. Nevada Historical Society, n.d.

Erickson, Mary. *Women Lawyers' Male Connectedness*. Palo Alto, CA: Stanford University Press, 1988.

Ford, Jean. Bird Wilson, The Saga of Nevada Women's Suffrage. Dramatic Script.

Howard, Ann Bail. *The Long Campaign: A Biography of Anne Martin*. Reno: University of Nevada Press, 1985.

Rocha, Guy. *Stepping Up To The Bar: Female Attorneys in Nevada*. Nevada Library and Archives Myth 72. Accessed 2/12/2005, http://dmla.clan.lib.nv.us/docs/nsla/archives/myth/myth72.htm.

Wilson, B.M., *Women Under Nevada Laws*. Reno, NV: Nevada Equal Franchise Society, 1912–1913.

Newspaper Articles

"Girl Lawyer in Federal Courts." *Chicago Legal News*, June 6, 1903.

"Young Truckee Woman Wins a High Honor." *Nevada State Journal*, June 10, 1905.

"A Lady Lawyer at Manhattan." *Tonopah Bonanza*, May 19, 1906.

"Lady Broker in Town." *Tonopah Bonanza*, August 18, 1906.

"A Woman Lawyer Wins Her Case." *Tonopah Bonanza*, October 15, 1907.

"Recognition for Nevada." *Reno Evening Gazette*, December 23, 1912.

"World Famous Suffragists Aid in Fight." *Nevada State Journal*, February 2, 1913.

"In the Realm of Society." *Nevada State Journal*, November 2, 1913

"Convention is Ended Today." *Reno Evening Gazette*, February 25, 1914.

"Miss Martin to Work in East." *Nevada State Journal*, June 19, 1915.

"Pumping Irrigation a Success in South." *Nevada State Journal*, June 23, 1915.

MARGARET CHRISTINA ARNOLDUS WINDOUS
Gueder, Patricia A., ed. *Pioneer Women of Nevada*. Carson City, NV: The Alpha Society and AAUW, 1976.

Oxborrow, Margaret Reid et al., eds. *White River Valley Then and Now 1898–1980*. Provo, UT: Melayne Printing, 1980.

Reade, Effie O. *White Pine Lang Syne*. Denver: Big Mountain Press, 1965

HAZEL BELL WINES
Paher, Stanley W. *The Nevada Official Bicentennial Book*. Las Vegas: Nevada Publications, 1976.

Family records and writings of Gene Wines Segerblom.

SARAH WINNEMUCCA
Hopkins, Sarah Winnemucca. *Life Among the Piutes: Their Wrongs and Claims*. Reno: University of Nevada Press, (reprint), 1994.

James, Ed T. *Notable American Women of 1607–1950*. Washington, DC: Howard University Press, 1971.

Luchetti, Cathy, & Carol Olwell. *Women of the West*. Berkeley, CA: Antelope Island Press, 1982.

Moynihan, Ruth B., Susan Armitage and Christiane Fischer Dichamp, eds. *So Much to Be Done: Women on the*

Mining and Ranching Frontier. Lincoln: University of Nebraska Press, 1982.

Seagraves, Anne. High Spirited Women of the West. Lakeport, CA: Wesanne Publications, 1992.

Stewart, Patricia. "Sarah Winnemucca." *Nevada Historical Society Quarterly*, XIV, 4, Winter Edition, 1971.

Zanjani, Sally. *Sarah Winnemucca.* Lincoln: University of Nebraska Press, 2001.

JOSIE ALMA WOODS

ACR 30, Nevada Legislature, May 28, 1997.

Glass, Mary Ellen. "The Lady Lawmakers." Nevada Public Affairs Report, University of Nevada, Reno, October, 1975.

Knudtsen, Molly Flagg. *Here Is Our Valley.* Reno: UNR College of Agriculture, 1975.

Walton, Clifford. *Who's Who in Nevada 1949–50.* Portland, OR: Capital Publishing, 1949.

Photography Sources

Eva Adams, courtesy of Nevada State Museum and Historical Society

Mary Jane Oxborrow Ashworth, courtesy of NWHP, photo by J.J. Booth, photographer

Ruth Ball, courtesy of NWHP, source unknown

Clara Isabelle Smith Beatty, courtesy of *Las Vegas Review-Journal*

Clara Bow Bell, courtesy of NWHP, source unknown

Minnie Nichols Blair, courtesy of Churchill County Museum & Archives

Kittie Bonner, courtesy of University of Nevada, Las Vegas, Special Collections

Mildred Bray, courtesy of NWHP, source unknown

Julia Bulette, courtesy of *Las Vegas Review-Journal*

Florence Lee Jones Cahlan, courtesy of *Las Vegas Review-Journal*

Eliza Cook, courtesy of NWHP, source unknown

Beda Brennecke Cornwall, courtesy of *Las Vegas Review-Journal*

Hilda M. Covey, courtesy of NWHP, source unknown

Martha Cragun Cox, courtesy of NWHP, source unknown

Clara Dunham Crowell, courtesy of Nevada Historical Society

Dat-So-La-Lee, courtesy of University of Nevada, Las Vegas, Special Collections

Nellie Mighels Davis, courtesy of Nevada Historical Society, Reno

Clarabelle Hanley Decker, courtesy of Nevada State Museum and Historical Society

Hazel Baker Denton, courtesy of Ralph Denton

Geneva Smith Douglas, courtesy of *Las Vegas Review-Journal*

Anna Neddenriep Dressler, photo by and courtesy of Luetta Bergevin

Edna Crauch Trunnell Eddy, courtesy of NWHP, source unknown

Charlotte Rowberry Ellsworth, courtesy of NWHP, source unknown

Ruth Mary Cooper Ferron, courtesy of Shirley Ferron Swanson

Imogene (Jean) Evelyn Young Ford, courtesy of *Las Vegas Review-Journal*

Katie Christy Frazier, courtesy of NWHP, source unknown

Maude Frazier, courtesy of *Las Vegas Review-Journal*

Dr. Mary Hill Fulstone, courtesy of Nevada Department of Education, Carson City

Laura Kitchen Garvin, courtesy of NWHP, from funeral program, Griffith United Methodist Church

Wuzzie George, courtesy of University of Nevada, Reno, Special Collections

Glenn Edna Park Grier, courtesy of Nevada State Library and Archives

Doris Virginia Hancock, courtesy of University of Nevada, Las Vegas, Special Collections

Grace Hayes, courtesy of University of Nevada, Las Vegas, Special Collections

Sarah Dotson Hurst, courtesy of Nevada State Library and Archives

Thelma Brown Ireland, courtesy of NWHP, source unknown

Lubertha Miller Johnson, courtesy of *Las Vegas Review-Journal*

Laura Belle Kelch, courtesy of *Las Vegas Review-Journal*

Bertha C. Knemeyer, courtesy of North Eastern Nevada Museum, Elko

Molly Flagg Knudtsen, courtesy of *Tonopah Times-Bonanza and Goldfield News*

Moya Olsen Lear, photo by John McDonnell, courtesy of *The Washington Post*, ©1981 *The Washington Post*

Jessie Callahan Mahoney, courtesy of Aileen Schlager.

Lillian Malcom, courtesy of Nevada Historical Society

Anne Henrietta Martin, courtesy of Nevada Historical Society, Reno

Mila Tupper Maynard, courtesy of NWHP, source unknown

Jean Sybil McElrath, courtesy of NWHP, source unknown

Laura Mills, courtesy of Churchill County Museum and Archives

Emma Wixom Nevada, courtesy of Nevada Historical Society

Sarah Thompson Olds, courtesy of NWHP, source unknown

Mary Leitch Oxborrow, courtesy of Jeanette Clark

Mary Belle Park, courtesy of NWHP, source unknown

Maria Garifalou Pavlakis, photo by Richard Menzies, ©Richard Menzies, courtesy of Stephens Press, LLC

Josie Reed Pearl, courtesy of Nevada Historical Society, Reno

Alice Pearson, courtesy of *Las Vegas Review-Journal*

Marjory Gusewelle Phillips, courtesy of Lynne (Phillips) Ladwig

Bertha Raffetto, courtesy of Nevada Historical Society, Reno

Anna Frances Elleser Rechel, courtesy of Sally Zanjani

Olga A. Reifschneider, courtesy of University of Nevada, Reno, Special Collections

Jennie O'Hare Riordan, courtesy of Kay Sanders

Agnes Louise Elford Roche, courtesy of NWHP, source unknown.

Bertha B. Ronzone, courtesy of *Las Vegas Review-Journal*

Mary G. Rose, courtesy of North Central Nevada Historical Society Humboldt Museum

Fermina Sarras, courtesy of Sally Zanjani

Helen Rulison Shipley, courtesy of Nevada State Museum, Carson City

May Bradford Shockley, courtesy of University of Nevada, Las Vegas, Special Collections

Fanny Soss, courtesy of NWHP, source unknown

Delphine Anderson Squires, courtesy of University of Nevada Las Vegas, Special Collections, Squires Collection

Mary Bernice Stanford, courtesy of NWHP, source unknown

Helen J. Stewart, courtesy of Nevada State Museum and Historical Society

Mayme Virginia Clifton Stocker, courtesy of *Las Vegas Review-Journal*

Idah Meacham Strobridge, courtesy of Nevada Historical Society, Reno

Laura May Tilden, courtesy of Nevada Historical Society

Kathryn L. Marbaker Tubb, courtesy of NWHP, source unknown

Gue Gim Wah, courtesy of University of Nevada, Las Vegas, Special Collections, Single Accessions Collection

Anna B. Mudd Warren, courtesy of Nevada Historical Society, Reno

Hannah Reese Welde, courtesy of NWHP, source unknown

Jeanne Elizabeth Wier, courtesy of NWHP, source unknown

Bird May Wilson, courtesy of University of Nevada, Reno, Special Collections

Margaret Arnoldus Windous, courtesy of NWHP, source unknown

Hazel Bell Wines, courtesy of NWHP, photo by O.L. Dowe Artistic Fotographer

Sarah Winnemucca, courtesy of *Las Vegas Review-Journal*

Josie Alma Woods, courtesy of NWHP, source unknown

Index by Occupation